Before Feminism

Books by Miriam Schneir

The history of feminism series:

Feminism: The Essential Historical Writings
NY: Random House/Vintage, 1972, 1992, 1994, 2014

Feminism in Our Time: World War II to the Present
NY: Vintage, 1994

Before Feminism: The History of an Idea Without a Name
NJ: Mews Books, 2021

The Vintage Book of Historical Feminism
London, UK: Vintage, 1996

The Vintage Book of Feminism
London, UK: Vintage, 1995

Also:

"Remember the Ladies": Women in America, 1750-1815
(with coauthors) NY: Viking Press, 1978

"She Merchants" in 17th-Century Holland and New Netherland
Center for the Social Sciences, Columbia University preprint, 1980

Invitation to an Inquest (with Walter Schneir)
NY: Doubleday, 1965; Penguin, 1973; Pantheon, 1983

Final Verdict: What Really Happened in the Rosenberg Case
(with Walter Schneir) NY: Melville House, 2011

Before Feminism

The History of an Idea Without a Name

Miriam Schneir

Copyright © 2021 Miriam Schneir

All rights reserved

No part of this book may be reproduced, or stored in a retrieval system, or transmitted in any form or by any means, electronic, mechanical, photocopying, recording, or otherwise, without express written permission of the author.

ISBN: 978-0-578-85760-2

COVER ART: *Clio, The Muse of History*
                Artemisia Gentileschi, 1632

COVER DESIGN: Rick Celano
                RickmanArt@yahoo.com

Mews Books, Montclair, NJ

To the scholars who have recovered the history of women,

to Walter Schneir,

and to my granddaughters, Isadora and Rosalie,

who make it all worthwhile

CONTENTS

Books by Miriam Schneir
Copyright
Dedication
Epigraph

INTRODUCTION

THE MYSTERY OF SENECA FALLS	1

PART 1   WHAT'S PAST IS PROLOGUE

1	WHEN WOMEN WERE GODS AND PRIESTS	13
2	THE WEAVE OF MYCENAEAN LIFE	21
3	THE GREAT CODE AT GORTYN	29
4	THE HERITAGE OF CELTIC WOMEN	35

PART 2   SEIZING THE MOMENT

5	DECLINE AND FALL OF THE PATERFAMILIAS	45
6	THE MINISTRY OF WOMEN	55
7	ILLUMINATING THE DARK AGES	67
8	PEASANT WOMEN: THE POWER OF THE WEAK	79
9	IN AL-ANDALUS	89
10	WOMEN OF THE NORTHLANDS	99
11	HERETICAL WOMEN	109
12	THE FREEDOM OF THE CITIES	119

PART 3   FORCING THE PACE OF CHANGE

13	CHRISTINE DE PIZAN AND HER READERS	133
14	THE RENAISSANCE FOR WOMEN	143
15	DAUGHTERS OF THE WORLD	157

16 ENTERPRISING WOMEN IN THE DUTCH REPUBLIC	169
17 SHE-MERCHANTS	177
18 DISSENT AND DEFIANCE	187

PART 4 WOMEN MAKING HISTORY

19 REVOLUTIONARY WOMEN IN AMERICA	201
20 CITOYENNES	215
21 FIRESIDE TO FACTORY	229
22 FREE WOMEN	241
CODA	253
Acknowledgments	256
List of Illustrations	257
Notes	258
Index	292

"…it was the women who could or would not conform . . . who would force the pace of change. The happy ones or the ones who saw no alternative to their lot were not to be the history makers."

— Olwen Hufton, *A History of Women in the West,* vol. 3

INTRODUCTION:
THE MYSTERY OF SENECA FALLS

Main Street in the village of Seneca Falls, New York, hummed with anticipation on the morning of July 19, 1848, as some three hundred women and men headed for the town's Wesleyan Chapel, a Methodist church. They were on their way to take part in an extraordinary event: a two-day convention devoted to "the social, civil, and religious condition and rights of woman."[1] The word "feminism" did not yet exist in any European language, but many women were painfully aware of legal and social restrictions that denied them opportunity and bound them to the home.

No one could have predicted that this modest gathering in a small country church heralded the dawn of a new era for womankind, or that the five middle-class white women who had planned it would set in motion a social revolution of vast dimension. But appearances in this case were deceptive, for Seneca Falls was located in a district known for religious and social activism, and the event's principal organizers—Elizabeth Cady Stanton, 32, a resident of the town, and Lucretia Mott, a 55-year-old Quaker minister from Nantucket, Massachusetts—had previously tested the waters of social protest in the anti-slavery movement.[2] In fact, it was at an anti-slavery convention in London that Mott and Stanton first met and agreed to do something to improve the condition of women.

On the opening day of the Seneca Falls convention a Declaration of Sentiments modeled on the Declaration of Independence was read aloud. "The history of mankind," it charged, "is a history of repeated injuries and usurpations on the part of man toward woman, having in direct object the establishment of an absolute tyranny over her." It accused men of denying women equal access to education; depriving them of the rights of citizenship; harming them psychologically by endeavoring to destroy their self-confidence; and enacting unjust marriage, divorce, and property laws.

Also presented to the assembly were a dozen resolutions. One, introduced by Lucretia Mott, demanded "overthrow of the monopoly of the pulpit" and "an equal participation with men in the various trades, professions, and commerce." Another, proposed by Elizabeth Cady Stanton, asserted women's "sacred right" to the vote.[3] The latter, the only resolution that failed to win unanimous approval, passed by a narrow margin only after Stanton and the abolitionist writer and editor Frederick Douglass—a former slave and the sole Black person known to have attended the conference—stoutly defended it from the floor.

Reading the Seneca Falls Declaration today, one cannot but be impressed by its strong, unequivocal language. Nonetheless, one hundred of those present in the chapel that day dared to sign it, two-thirds of them women. Douglass published their names in a "Roll of Honor" in his weekly newspaper, *The North Star*.[4] Still, a certain mystery presents itself: How had they come to believe the audacious affirmation of the third resolution, "woman is man's equal"? What gave them the self-assurance to repudiate the widely held belief that the female of the species is innately inferior to the male—a belief supported by biblical command and enforced by legal statute throughout the Western world?

. . . .

The circle of dedicated activists who set out in 1848 to free women from injustice and oppression had the advantage of more than a decade of experience in the anti-slavery movement. Fifteen years before the Seneca Falls convention two of its chief organizers, Lucretia Mott and Mary Ann McClintock, had founded—along with the free Black women Charlotte Forten and her three daughters, and twelve other women, both Black and white—the nation's first all-female abolitionist group, the interracial Philadelphia Female Anti-Slavery Society. Its members, and the members of similar groups established soon afterward in other cities, learned to face down ridicule, contempt, and even hostile mobs. They found the courage to travel alone to meetings and to collect petition signatures. They had practice preparing agendas, electing officers, and raising money. And they overcame what Mott criticized as "the false notions of delicacy and propriety" that had long prevented women from speaking in public.[5]

Yet the women's-rights pioneers labored under a difficulty that had no counterpart in the anti-slavery movement: the lack of a word comparable to "abolitionism" to define the set of beliefs that underlay and inspired their struggle—and they would not have such a word until the end of the nineteenth century, when "feminism" finally came into general use. How does one talk about, or even think about, an idea so outside common experience that it has never acquired a name? How does one justify laboring on its behalf? It is no exaggeration to say that the absence of a defining label robbed the concept itself of legitimacy.

Nor could the early activists look to the annals of history for validation, guidance, or encouragement since the men who had for centuries been in charge of recording the past had found precious little of what women had ever said or done worthy of transmitting to later generations. Deprived of an historical context, the movement seemed adrift, unmoored in time. Small wonder that Stanton lamented in what she later described as her first public address, "the history of woman is sad and drear and dark, without any alleviating circumstances, nothing from which we can draw consolation."[6]

A fledgling women's movement also emerged in Western Europe in 1848, for the anti-monarchist uprisings that erupted in many parts of the Continent that year had created a favorable climate for reform. But while women's protests were soon silenced in Europe, in the United States the women's movement grew steadily. Over the next decade supporters organized ten "national conventions," delivered scores of speeches, and launched groundbreaking new periodicals.[7]

The Civil War brought a pause to the movement in the United States as women voluntarily suspended work on their own behalf in order to focus on supporting the Union cause. Thus, the ratification in 1868 of the Fourteenth Amendment to the U.S. Constitution—which granted voting rights to African-American men but not to women of either race—shocked the proponents of gender equality. Elizabeth Cady Stanton and her lifelong comrade-in-arms, Susan B. Anthony, angrily denounced the amendment and gave voice to ugly racist and xenophobic rhetoric. As the women's movement foundered on the shoals of racism, its goals narrowed to the single issue of suffrage. Discord arose, and two separate national organizations were created with disparate tactics and policy.

After two decades of disunity, suffragists finally came together and in 1890 founded the National American Woman Suffrage Association (NAWSA). In a cynical bid to gain the backing of the southern states, the leaders of NAWSA made common cause with white supremacists in the South. The extreme expediency—and racism—that prompted NAWSA's bargain with the devil helped to legitimize Jim Crow segregation laws. It dishonored the suffrage organization and betrayed the origins of the women's movement in the anti-slavery struggle. Speaking at a NAWSA meeting in 1904, Mary Church Terrell, an eminent Black educator, appealed to her white "sisters" to "stand up not only for the oppressed sex, but also for the oppressed race." However, the women of NAWSA did not rise to her challenge. Leadership positions were denied to African-American women; the fearless Black anti-lynching crusader Ida B. Wells was instructed to march at the back of the 1913 suffrage parade in Washington D.C. rather than with the Illinois delegation; and Frederick Douglass was asked not to attend a NAWSA convention in Atlanta. African-American suffragists courageously advocated for both gender and racial justice in white groups as well as in separate African-American organizations.[8] But the failure of white, middle-class activists to fully engage with Black, immigrant, and working-class women impeded the progress of women for generations.

. . . .

By the time the first volume of the *History of Woman Suffrage* was published in 1881, a few intrepid scholars in Europe and the United States had already begun to investigate a previously unexplored terrain: the hidden history of women. Thus, the volume's authors—Elizabeth Cady Stanton, Susan B. Anthony, and Matilda Joslyn Gage—were able to dedicate the book to more than a dozen female precursors who were "a constant inspiration to the Editors," and to name dozens more illustrious women of the past in the first chapter. Matilda Gage was no doubt the source for many of these references. Educated at home by a father who believed her capable of studying such "masculine" subjects as Greek and mathematics, Gage labored for decades to overcome the silences of history regarding women. In a chapter of the suffrage history signed by her alone, she wrote: "In many ancient nations woman had secured a good degree of respect and power, as compared even with ... the present era." But another chapter presents an opposite point of view. In language that is recognizably Stanton's, it refers to "the universal degradation of women in all periods and nations."[9]

The American historian Mary Ritter Beard, writing in 1946, challenged head-on the idea that "women had been a subject sex throughout history." This tradition she asserted, "has exercised an almost tyrannical power over thinking about the relations of men and women," tragically undermining women's faith in themselves and impeding their progress. Beard chastised the leaders of the nineteenth-century women's movement for the way they had "represented women as rightless in long history and passive in that condition." That representation, she pointed out, had given birth to a thorny "logical dilemma": How could "a creature who had been nothing or nearly nothing in all history ... suddenly, if ever, become something?"[10]

Beard's question intrigued me for many years. I understood the immediate circumstances that had sparked the nineteenth-century women's movement: the Enlightenment, the political revolutions of the late-eighteenth and nineteenth centuries, the Industrial Revolution, the anti-slavery campaign. Those things had supplied the moment; but what had formed the character of the women who had dared to seize it?

• • • •

As the feminist second wave gathered force in the 1970's, historians of women undertook a monumental endeavor: the recovery of the history of one-half of humanity. They re-examined archives and found hidden within them fragments of information about women's lives that earlier generations of researchers had overlooked; they uncovered the names of the creators of unsigned poetry, memoirs, artwork, and music, revealing that Anonymous was often a woman; and they rescued from oblivion many worthy texts written by women who had been dismissed as bluestockings, interlopers, scribblers, and worse. The sheer magnitude of what was lost is hard to encompass. Even the foundational treatise of feminism, *The Book of the City of Ladies*, written in French by Christine de Pizan in 1401, had no English edition for over four and a half centuries, from 1521 until 1983.

The historians' findings were published in new scholarly journals and in splendid, carefully documented books. Fiction and poetry that explored feminist themes began to appear. Feminist presses, bookstores, and research institutes multiplied. The mass-market feminist magazine *Ms.*, founded in 1972, ran a regular column entitled "Lost Women," in which the stories of long-forgotten women of exceptional talent or influence were resurrected for a new generation. Colleges and universities revised their curricula in response to students' requests for more courses on the history of women. A *New York Times* reporter covering a women's history conference in the fall of 1974 commented exuberantly, "the study of women in history is exploding in the academic skies like a supernova."[11]

Looking back at the anthology I edited in the early 1970's, *Feminism: The Essential Historical Writings*, I saw that Mary Beard's question had interested me even then—overshadowed though it was by the excitement of the early days of second-wave feminism. In the introduction to the collection, for instance, I had referred to "a literature urging wider opportunities for women" in fifteenth- and sixteenth-century Europe, and had quoted a line from the first American poet in English, Anne Bradstreet, who in 1642 contested conventional notions of what was appropriate for women, asking, "Who says my hand a needle better fits?"[12] Later, while serving as research historian for a museum exhibit and catalogue-book on women in the era of the American Revolution, I learned about women who had challenged mainstream gender prescriptions long before Seneca Falls.[13] Finally, a project I conducted under the auspices of Columbia University's Teachers College—a study of the coverage and treatment of women in the twenty-two-volume *World Book Encyclopedia*—convinced me that whenever the door to a new opportunity stood open, some women inevitably dared to cross the threshold. Ambitious, freedom-loving, restless in the domestic spaces to which they were confined, they had seized the chance to live more fully in their time.

In her trailblazing volume *The Second Sex*, which was published in France in 1949, Simone de Beauvoir had declared that women "have no past, no history . . . of their own." Unlike any other oppressed group, she wrote, women accepted their subordinate status; never seriously contesting male sovereignty.[14] But when the distinguished American historian Gerda Lerner came to consider the question of the rise of feminist consciousness in 1986, she had the advantage of a mountain of new information. Although she praised de Beauvoir's "brilliant work," she took issue with her observation that women have no history. Several decades of scholarship, Lerner pointed out, had succeeded in uncovering the history of women, and had proved that "women are and always have been agents and actors in history." On the other hand, Lerner contended, "Women have for millennia participated in the process of their own subordination because they have been psychologically shaped so as to internalize the idea of their own inferiority." A major reason for this long-term inferiority complex, she suggested, was "unawareness of their own history of struggle and achievement."[15]

Yet as I looked across the broad sweep of women's past, I saw that despite the cruel silencing of their voices, women themselves never entirely accepted demeaning stereotypes of their own mothers, daughters, sisters, and themselves. Nor, for that matter, did men fully embrace a view of the other sex as passive and acquiescent. Indeed, women are often portrayed in the popular culture as insolent usurpers of male privileges, and a large vocabulary exists to describe female individuals who fail to conform. In English, we use harridan, shrew, vixen, virago, amazon, fishwife, battle-axe, termagant, harpy, and more. Chaucer's Wife of Bath was far closer to the reality of European womanhood than was Patient Griselda, the long-suffering wife in Boccaccio's *Decameron*.

Pride in womanhood was maintained and reinforced across the generations by a separate women's culture comprised of shared skills, traditions, "old wives' tales," myths, and fragments of history that were transmitted from woman to woman within female spaces to which men had little access: birthing rooms and rooms where the dead were prepared for burial; Greek and Roman gynaecea and medieval textile workshops; cattle milking pens and riverside laundries; convents, heretical sects, and prayer circles; literary societies, charitable organizations, clubs dedicated to moral and social reform; and many other primarily female realms. Within such spaces, women also learned to conform when necessary to the rules of patriarchal society since failure to do so could result in ridicule, physical punishment, ostracism, or even death.

While long-term denigration no doubt injured the self-esteem of many women, to regard that as the only reality would be to distort the totality of women's experience. For the history of women reveals the existence of healthy egos. There have always been some who believed that women are mentally and morally equal to, or even superior to, men and dared to defy, resist, or circumvent male authority. Where Lerner and de Beauvoir had seen passivity and even complicity, I saw accommodation in the face of a social structure maintained by law and custom and upheld by enforced economic dependency and threat of violence. Fierce punishments meted out to ultimate transgressors more than psychological annihilation sustained European patriarchy.

• • • •

The opening chapters of this book profile four ancient cultures in which gender attitudes differed greatly from those of later eras. They form a prologue that challenges us to rethink assumptions about the essential nature of women and their role in Western societies. The subsequent chapters focus on specific moments in time when women took advantage of extraordinary social and economic circumstances to surmount gender restrictions. In selecting moments to investigate, I was encouraged to find an embarrassment of riches: archaeological discoveries, works of art, historical chronicles, religious and biographical writings, codes of law, letters, poetry, and literary texts. Although documents created before the advent of printing were written mainly by men, one can often surmise what women were doing based on what men said they should—or, more often, should not—do. The final section of the book—Part 4, Women Making History—describes the expansion of feminist consciousness and the emergence of leaders dedicated to the emancipation of women.

The study of any oppressed group poses special difficulties. And if one wishes, as I did, to include those doubly or triply oppressed—not only by gender but also by race, class, ethnicity, or sexual orientation—the difficulties are multiplied. Regrettably, my canvas was not large enough to encompass the history of feminist protest in parts of the world where women's struggle for equality differs greatly from that of Europe and North America.

The struggles described in the pages that follow were waged on behalf of an idea that had no name. It was carried forward by women whose voices were ignored, belittled, and silenced. But the history of their striving, as handed down from mother to daughter through many generations, served to keep alive the conviction that "woman is man's equal" and to perpetuate a longing for freedom and opportunity. The small band of activists who came together in the upstate New York chapel was heir to that struggle. It sustained their dreams and helped to nerve them for the trials ahead, and it continues to fortify us today.

PART 1

WHAT'S PAST IS PROLOGUE

1 WHEN WOMEN WERE GODS AND PRIESTS

Europe's first urban civilization arose more than three and a half millennia ago on the island of Crete. So extraordinary were its achievements that hundreds of years after it had disappeared Homer still knew of the "land called Crete, ringed by the wine-dark sea," a kingdom with many cities, the greatest of which was "magnificent Knossos, the site where Minos ruled."[16]

The material remains of Knossos are fragmentary and difficult to interpret, yet they bear mute witness to a complex Bronze Age culture—a culture in which the principal gods and priests were female. In the view of a distinguished Greek archaeologist this long-vanished world "lies at the root of our Western civilization."[17]

The first systematic excavation of Knossos began in 1900 under the direction of British archaeologist Arthur Evans.[18] Almost immediately the remains of a monumental multi-storied structure emerged. Built in about 1700 BCE, it extended over approximately three acres and was equipped with running water and a system of canals for disposal of waste. Evans called his spectacular find the New Palace since it had been raised over the ruins of an earlier "palace." As archaeologists gradually learned, it had functioned for three centuries as the religious, administrative, and economic center of an advanced civilization which Evans named Minoan, after the mythical King Minos.[19]

Smaller Minoan-style settlements have been uncovered at other locations on Crete as well as on several Aegean islands, notably Santorini (or Thera), where a remarkably well-preserved town was found buried in volcanic ash. Contemporaneous Near Eastern civilizations in Egypt and Mesopotamia could boast comparable wonders, but the refinements of Minoan civilization at its height were a world apart from the farming-and-herding settlements that existed in most of Western Europe during the second millennium BCE.

Scholars generally agree that the Minoans were polytheistic, and that their principal deities were female. Goddess-like figures are depicted on Minoan seal-stones in transcendent poses: magically riding above the waves of the sea, for example, or poised on a mountaintop. A wonderful stone found at Knossos shows a bare-breasted woman wearing an ankle-length flounced skirt. She stands on the summit of a mountain flanked by two lions, while a nearby male worshipper presses a clenched fist to his forehead in a stylized attitude of adoration. On another stone a similarly gowned figure is depicted seated under a tree as she receives offerings from devotees.

Although we know the names of goddesses worshipped by the Minoans' trading partners in the ancient Near East—Ishtar in Babylonia, Isis in Egypt, Ashtoreth or Astarte in Phoenicia—the names of Minoan goddesses are uncertain at best. One Minoan deity whose name we *do* know is Eileithyia, a goddess associated in the Homeric epics with the travails of childbirth, the "spear-sharp . . . labor-pangs that pierce a woman." Following clues in Homer, archaeologists located Eileithyia's cave sanctuary on Crete. Offerings found within the cave indicate that women worshipped there long before the Minoan era and continued to seek Eileithyia's protection long afterward.[20]

A few modern writers have questioned the importance of goddesses in Cretan religious practice. "There is no clear evidence . . . of powerful female goddesses," says one book, while another speculates that some of the images traditionally labeled "goddess" actually portray mortal women.[21] It may indeed be true that the best-known Minoan artifact, the iconic figure Evans identified as a "snake goddess," is not the image of a goddess at all, for when it was found, it was broken, with so many pieces missing that the reconstructed figure may differ considerably from the original.[22] On the other hand, it was discovered in a temple repository, as were several other comparatively intact Cretan "snake goddesses." No one knows if these figurines depict goddesses or priestesses, but the idea that they were not religious icons at all but simply "women with snakes" does not seem credible.[23]

In Egypt and other major Bronze Age civilizations, the priesthood was entirely male,[24] but hundreds of Minoan objects show women carrying out

*1. MINOAN "SNAKE GODDESS,"
1600 BCE*

sacerdotal roles. Two especially convincing priestesses are depicted on a stone casket discovered in a tomb at Aghia Triada, a villa located near the Minoan ruins at Phaistos in southern Crete. One side of the casket is decorated with the image of a woman clothed in an animal skin. Her arms are raised, the palms of her hands face downward, and behind her a sacrificial bull lies strapped to a table. On the opposite side of the casket are three figures: a woman with buckets suspended from a shoulder yoke, a male musician playing a lyre, and a woman in an animal skin standing in front of a shrine and pouring a liquid—possibly blood from a sacrificed bull—into a vat.

An ancient tomb discovered in Greece in 2015 contained four beautifully wrought gold rings made on Crete during the Minoan era. Each of the rings is engraved with images of women performing religious rituals. On one, a woman carrying sacramental bull's horns approaches a seated female figure. On another, a woman holding a staff topped with bull's horns stands between two mountain peaks, each of which is capped by a fancifully depicted bird. On the third, five women dance on a seashore near a shrine that is similarly topped by a bird. The most prominent dancer, like the "snake goddess," has bare breasts and wears a long flounced skirt.

Other Minoan artifacts show women presiding over religious observances in palaces, homes, and caves, before seaside shrines and at mountaintop altars. Since religion was at the heart of Minoan life, those who mediated between mortals and the gods—most of whom were also female—must have held positions of high importance. Feminist historian Gerda Lerner has pointed out that idolatry of females may coexist with a low status of actual women, as was the case during the Middle Ages, when Mary was a near deity.[25] However, there is a crucial difference, for while the medieval priesthood was male, religious ceremonies in the Minoan world were led primarily by women.

. . . .

Colorful frescoes adorned the walls of Minoan palaces and villas. As reconstructed (too freely, in some cases), they depict pastoral scenes with flowers, darting birds, and graceful animals; seascapes with dolphins and flying fish; imaginary creatures, like winged griffins; and elaborately gowned women dancing, walking in processions, and attending public ceremonies. Women are readily identifiable because men's skin was painted a reddish-brown, women's white, an artistic convention also followed in ancient Egypt. The famous bull-leaping fresco from the New Palace at Knossos highlights courage, agility, and strength in women. In this extraordinary image, two white-skinned women wearing male attire and a brown-skinned man are engaged in a hazardous sport that appears to have involved somersaulting over the horns of a charging bull into the arms of a waiting teammate. Similar depictions of bull-leaping are also pictured on vases and seal-stones. If these images were realistic representations of an actual Minoan sport, it would seem to have been bloodless—at least so far as the bull was concerned.

In a large Knossos wall-painting of a grand public event, the female spectators wear the typical ankle-length skirt and low-cut bodice. They are bedecked with necklaces and bracelets, their long black curls are festooned with ropes of beads, and they smile and gesture as they converse animatedly. Significantly, they are larger than the male spectators, occupy a more prominent position in the composition, and are depicted in greater detail. The elegance of their dress plus their self-confident bearing indicate that they were members of the palace elite.

The Cretan frescoes, so far as we know, did not portray ordinary people at work or engaged in everyday activities. However, a fresco found in the ruins of a Minoan town on the island of Santorini, seventy-five miles north of Crete, shows several young women out in the countryside gathering saffron-yielding crocuses. In another Santorini painting a group of women and men are on a rooftop gazing out to sea at a fleet of boats. On the street below, women wearing high-necked shifts that fall from the shoulders to below the knee carry jugs on their heads; a woman and man linger beside a stream, evidently conversing. The women's unrestricted use of public space stands in sharp contrast to the situation of well-off Athenian matrons over a thousand years later whose fate it was to be confined much of the time to their homes.

Arthur Evans was so impressed with the role of women in Minoan society that he suggested that Knossos was a matriarchy governed by a queen.[26] The director of the British School at Athens also thought it was "likely enough that customs of the kind described as Matriarchy (Mother Rule) persisted in Crete."[27] And a few modern scholars have embraced the long-cherished theory that women were the dominant sex in prehistory.[28] But although a number of ancient civilizations were indeed ruled by women—the reign of Hatshepsut of Egypt, for example, coexisted with the final decades of Minoan civilization—several contemporary historians have warned against jumping to the conclusion that females wielded more authority than males in Minoan society. Their calls for prudence are well-founded since there is no evidence as to whether men, women, or neither, were dominant in the temporal sphere. Minoan remains, abundant though they are, are silent as to sexual mores, marriage, child-rearing, and inheritance practices. Given our ignorance of Minoan society, classical scholar Sarah Pomeroy has cautioned, it would be "as foolish to postulate masculine dominance in prehistory as to postulate female dominance."[29] Evans himself later changed his mind about a Minoan queen, asserting that only male buttocks could have fitted the narrow seat of a supposed "throne" discovered at Knossos![30]

Some commentators have piled interpretation on supposition to theorize that female dominance in Minoan society encouraged such allegedly feminine attributes as gentleness, respect for life, affinity with the earth, and so forth. Building on these surmises, they have urged a return to a society in which woman-centered values predominate.[31] Indeed, Minoan culture, as viewed from our vast distance in time, does appear wonderfully harmonious and tranquil. Minoan artists depicted the beauty of the natural world, the fruitfulness of the earth, and the bounty of the sea, rather than warriors or military exploits. Minoan Crete apparently had no massive fortresses or monuments dedicated to military heroes. Relatively few examples of Minoan weaponry have been recovered, and most of those were probably hunting implements.[32] Physical prowess and the presumably masculine attribute of aggressiveness would not have counted for much in such a culture, while woman's procreative ability would have occasioned respect—or so the theory goes.

Yet the Minoan world may not have been quite as peaceable as its art would lead one to believe, for ancient defensive structures have been uncovered along one section of the Cretan coastline.[33] Moreover, the Minoans, an island people, may have relied mainly on the surrounding ocean and their seafaring skill for defense. But there is a more fundamental objection to the theory, for it rests on the highly dubious premise that characteristics stereotypically deemed "feminine" or "masculine" today were the same thousands of years ago. In reality, we simply do not know what "woman" denoted then.

To think authentically about women in Minoan society one must cast aside assumptions about the nature and role of the sexes that are so deeply ingrained as to seem natural laws rather than social constructs. Consider this: Minoan New Palace–era artists never depicted human females as mothers. Not one of the surviving artifacts from a period of several hundred years portrays a pregnant woman, mortal or immortal. Nor is there a single work of art that illustrates a woman giving birth or breastfeeding. Minoan artists did show nursing animals, and sometimes older children. A Santorini fresco shows two young boys boxing, for instance, and there is a carved ivory figurine that shows a child alone, but no views of babies and mothers exist. Why the exclusion of a motif frequently seen in Egyptian art of the same period? In explanation, Barbara A. Olsen proposed in the journal *World Archaeology* that Minoans chose to depict women engaged in public activities rather than in activities related to maternity. In the Minoan view of womankind, "emphasis is on the social rather than the biological, the public rather than the domestic," she wrote.[34]

Our knowledge of Minoan society is frustratingly incomplete. However, surviving artifacts indicate that women were free to navigate public spaces independently; goddesses were more numerous and powerful than gods; elite women participated in the life of the palaces; and in a society where religion played a central role, some women served as priests. To be a woman in the Minoan world did not close off opportunity but rather opened a path to spiritual leadership and honor.

2 THE WEAVE OF MYCENAEAN LIFE

While exploring ancient ruins at Mycenae, an archaeological site on Greece's Peloponnese peninsula, the nineteenth-century scholar Heinrich Schliemann unearthed a princely treasure of artifacts wrought in gold, silver, ivory, amber, alabaster, and amethyst. His fabulous discovery led others to explore the scores of culturally similar settlements that flourished on the Greek mainland during the late Bronze Age, between about 1600 and 1200 BCE. This post-Minoan civilization was dubbed Mycenaean, after Schliemann's original site.[35]

Mycenaean digs yielded an abundance of spears, swords, helmets, shields, and other military paraphernalia, evidence of a bellicose, warrior-based civilization. But when a baffling archaeological puzzle was finally solved in the 1950's, an additional facet of Mycenaean society came to light—one in which women played a central role. The initial clue consisted of thousands of bits and pieces of ancient clay tablets unearthed near the Minoan palace at Knossos. The fragments were inscribed with symbols and pictograms, some of which, remarkably enough, were still legible. But although archaeologists soon determined that the inscriptions were written in two related but different languages (which they labeled Linear A and Linear B), no one was able to read either one.

A second large cache of broken clay tablets was discovered at Pylos, a major Mycenaean settlement on the southern shore of the Peloponnese. But unlike the tablets found on Crete, the Pylos tablets were inscribed only with Linear B. When additional tablets with only Linear B turned up at several other mainland sites, investigators speculated that Linear B represented the Mycenaean language, while Linear A was an earlier written language developed by the Minoans. But if that was true, they wondered, why were both scripts used on Crete? Ultimately, the theory that best fit all the available evidence was that the Mycenaeans had invaded the island and ruled there for some three hundred years.

Linear B remained undecipherable until the early 1950's, when a young English architect and amateur cryptanalyst, Michael Ventis, unlocked its secret. His achievement was facilitated by the meticulous groundwork done by an American classics professor, Alice Kober, who according to a recent study had built the "foundation on which Ventris's decipherment was erected."[36] Amazed scholars eventually confirmed the Ventris hypothesis: Long before the Greek golden age, the Mycenaeans spoke and wrote an archaic form of what was essentially the language of Socrates and Euripides. We now have more than five thousand Linear B inscriptions from at least seven different sites. Although we are still unable to make sense of Linear A, Linear B is largely comprehensible.

If Linear B ever was used for correspondence, for literature, or to chronicle historical events, no trace of it has been found. In the view of an early proponent of Ventris's theory, philologist John Chadwick, the tablets are "deplorably dull," simply "the account books of anonymous clerks." Their primary virtue, wrote Chadwick, is their "utter authenticity."[37] The apparent purpose of the tablets was to keep track of land ownership, supplies of grain and livestock, allocation of food rations, and other matters of importance to the Mycenaean aristocracy. Yet embedded in these dry factual jottings is information about the work of non-elite women.

The Linear B tablets found on Crete describe a network of woolen-textile workshops in which more than a thousand women were engaged in producing fabric for the Mycenaean overlords. The tablets record the workers' gender—indicated by stick figures scratched into the clay—as well as the specific job each woman performed, the location of the workshop in which she was employed, and occasionally an ethnic or geographic label. In all, twenty-two different women's occupations are itemized, most of which were connected to cloth-making.[38]

The tablets found at Pylos show that it, too, was a major textile-producing center where approximately 750 women were employed in workshops that ranged in size from fewer than ten to fifty or more. About half of the workshops were located within the Pylos palace complex, the remainder in outlying areas. Young children and grown daughters evidently stayed with their mothers, but when sons reached maturity, they were placed with groups of male workers.[39]

Some scholars believe that the female cloth-makers employed by the Mycenaeans, like the thousands of women who worked in similar state-run textile centers in the early Mesopotamian cities, were slaves, and that the geographic labels on the tablets refer to foreign slave markets or possibly to wars in which the women were taken captive.[40] Indeed, it was customary in the ancient world for victorious armies to abduct women and use them as Agamemnon planned to use the woman he claimed as a war prize in *The Iliad*: "at the loom, forced to share my bed."[41] However, some historians argue that the evidence of slavery in the Mycenaean world is too slight to draw any conclusion.[42]

The tablets also identify a number of other jobs women performed for the palace elite, most importantly, grinding wheat and barley into flour. The Homeric epics, which are set in the Mycenaean era but were written down hundreds of years afterward, also describe the production of textiles and the preparation of food as women's work. In *The Odyssey*, for example, the hero encounters at the mythical island of Phaeacia "fifty serving women" who are grinding "the apple-yellow grain," weaving, and spinning.[43]

Yet the mere fact of a division of labor by gender need not mean that the contributions of one sex were seen as less important or prestigious than the other's, and the duties of Mycenaean women and men appear to have been complementary: Men harvested the wheat, women ground the grain into flour; men shepherded the sheep that grazed the hillsides, women spun the fleece into wool. Their separate tasks were of roughly equal value to the economy since textiles were a principal Mycenaean export items. (The other leading export, metalwork, was produced mainly by men.)

Since the Greeks did not begin to use money until about 500 BCE, we cannot assess the value assigned to men's and women's occupations by comparing wages. However, Mycenaean workers were supplied with food, and when scholars analyzed food-distribution data on the tablets, they found that ordinary workers, irrespective of gender, received two measures of wheat or four of barley per month for each adult individual, plus equal allotments of figs. Women may have had to share a portion of their rations with their children, but it is noteworthy that the men's diet was not superior to the women's. Two historians writing in the journal *Women's Studies* point out by way of comparison that in the coexistent civilization of Babylon men were allocated three times as much food as women, which, they speculate, may reflect the "importance of women in the Mycenaean labor force and perhaps in the society in general."[44] In short, what we know about Mycenaean society suggests no reason why women workers should have viewed themselves or have been viewed by others as any less competent or socially valuable than male workers.

About two hundred of the Pylos tablets refer to children who lived at the palace with the women.[45] A unique tablet found at Mycenae apparently described sleeping arrangements, for it has the word "bedding" in its title and lists pairs of females. In two instances, it identifies the second person as a daughter.[46] The relationships among the women and children is not documented, but it is pleasant to speculate that something of its nature is revealed by an exquisitely carved mid-fourteenth-century BCE ivory figurine from Mycenae. In this freestanding sculpture of two seated or kneeling women, the arm of one encircles the shoulders of the other, their hands touch, and a shawl enfolds both. A young child leans across their laps. Their closeness to one another and to the child is manifest.

Little can be gleaned from the tablets about Mycenaean family life since the activities of people who did not serve the palace were not normally recorded. Among the thousands of tablets that have been found, only a dozen or so allude to households made up of a man, a woman, and their children,[47] but family units of this type may well have been more common than the paucity of texts implies.

The Linear B tablets do however tell us something about political and religious beliefs and practices. They indicate, firstly, that Mycenaean society was ruled by kings and dominated by a warrior elite. They also suggest that the predominance of goddesses in the Minoan era had given way to an approximately equal number of male and female deities.[48] One deity whom we know made the transition from the Minoan to the Mycenaean world was Eileithyia, goddess of childbirth, for her name appears on a Linear B fragment from Crete. Also found on Mycenaean tablets are the names of a number of goddesses who subsequently survived the passage of centuries to reappear in classical-era Athens, including

Hera, Atana (Athena), and the huntress Artemis. However, a number of the immortals mentioned on the tablets did not make it to Mount Olympus, including "Diwia," apparently a female equivalent of the chief Olympian god Zeus, and "Posidaeia," a female counterpart of Poseidon.

The name Potnia, which means "the powerful one," appears a number of times on tablets, sometimes with an epithet, as in *Labyrinthos Potnia* (Lady of the Labyrinth) or *Sitos Potnia* (Lady of the Grain). Also mentioned are the Divine Mother, and the Two Queens. The latter were possibly predecessors of the classical era's Demeter and Persephone.

Priesthood and secular status may sometimes have been interconnected. Thus, among the individuals cited on tablets by name or title—a sign of exceptional importance[49]—were two priestesses affiliated with a shrine near Pylos. Both were property-owners who were accused of failing to fulfill the obligations of their position. The priestess Eritha, a devotee of the goddess Potnia, possessed a sizable tract of land which she held "for the deity."[50] She was involved in a dispute with local authorities over whether her property was subject to taxation (the outcome of the case is unknown). Some of Eritha's female subordinates also had property; indeed, one of her assistants owned nearly as much land as she did.[51] The second priestess, Karpathia, is described as a "Keybearer," a mysterious title which possibly referred to a cult and may have conferred high political as well as religious rank. Even her assistant was important enough to have her name, Huamia, recorded on a tablet. Like Eritha, Karpathia was embroiled in a controversy involving land ownership. According to the scribe who made the record, Karpathia held two tracts of land that she was required to cultivate, but she had failed to do so.[52]

Little is known about the lives of secular elite women. A few scattered inscriptions show that they could own property: Perieia, for instance, was the proprietor of an orchard in the vicinity of Knossos, and Kessandra was a landlord at Pylos.[53] And some Mycenaean women were buried with quantities of jewelry and other valuable personal items.

The frescoes that decorated the walls of Mycenaean palaces include many formulaic pieces imitative of Minoan themes, while others focus on animal hunts and battles, scenes that generally do not involve women. However, one extant work of art, a fresco from the Mycenaean settlement at Tiryns, is more revealing. It shows two female figures standing upright in a brightly painted two-wheeled "chariot." One of the women holds the reins to a pair of horses. Dressed in simple unbelted shifts that fall from their shoulders, they are traveling alone, perhaps setting out on an excursion to the countryside, perhaps on their way to watch the boar hunt depicted on an adjoining wall.

By 1100 BCE the great Mycenaean civilization, which had prospered for five hundred years, had all but disappeared. Its principal settlements, ravaged by fire, were never rebuilt. In the end, the cyclopean stone walls surrounding the palaces at Mycenae and Tiryns, the remains of which are still awe-inspiring, were not invulnerable. Tribal peoples commonly known as Dorians migrated into the region and drove out, assimilated, or enslaved the local population.

But amid the devastation, buried deep underground, bits of fragile clay tablets that were never intended to be permanent survived. They speak of a time and place when the wealth and well-being of society was based in substantial part on the productive activities of women, and of a civilization in which some women held positions of wealth and prominence.

2. TIRYNS FRESCO, 1200 BCE

3 THE GREAT CODE AT GORTYN

Ancient Athens is often called the cradle of democracy, yet female citizens, like slaves of either sex, could not vote, appear in court, serve on a jury, sign any official document, or hold any civic office. Citizenship for the Athenian woman meant essentially that her sons could be citizens. Her father chose her marriage partner, and her husband controlled her person and any property she might nominally possess. The Greek "golden age"—between about 500 and 300 BCE—was not a golden age for Athenian women.

In a Platonic dialogue written in 402 BCE, a wealthy young man from northern Greece tells Socrates that to be deemed virtuous a woman need only "manage the house well, and keep the stores all safe, and obey her husband." Some sixty years later the Athenian orator Demosthenes defined the duties of a wife similarly: "the procreation of legitimate children and to be faithful guardians of the household."[54] Wives and daughters in well-off Athenian families spent most of their time in the gynaeceum, a separate part of the home where their days were devoted mainly to spinning and weaving.

Still, seclusion in the home was not a practicable lifestyle for the great majority of Athenian women. Foreign-born and poor women as well as female slaves must have been a common sight on the streets of Athens as they shopped in the marketplace, drew water from public fountains, and went about their work as laundresses, midwives, and vendors.[55] In the countryside, women worked outdoors at a wide variety of farming tasks. Even upper-class wives and daughters were able to leave their homes on occasion to visit female friends, attend funerals and weddings, assist at lying-ins, and celebrate religious festivals.

Although female deities were less central to Athenian religion than they had been to Minoan or Mycenaean worship hundreds of years earlier, there

*3. WEAVING AT AN UPRIGHT LOOM,
ATHENS, 550-530 BCE*

were still many powerful goddesses. And according to one historian's estimate, as many as forty Athenian cults were led by priestesses.[56] Indeed, if certain important festivals were to be celebrated to the satisfaction of the gods, the participation of women was essential. Both the Panathenaea festival honoring Athena and the Eleusinian mysteries dedicated to

Demeter required female participants, while the three-day rites of the Thesmophoria were performed exclusively by women.

• • • •

So brightly did Athens shine that it eclipsed all other Greek city-states. But a discovery made by Italian archaeologist Federico Halbherr in 1884 in the city of Gortyn on the island of Crete adds a fascinating new chapter to the history of women in ancient Greece. Intrigued by the inscriptions on a pair of ancient stones found at Gortyn, Halbherr decided to go there to study them firsthand. The timing of his visit was fortuitous, for the waters of a millstream had been temporarily diverted, exposing the top of a stone wall that was ordinarily submerged. When a trench was dug alongside the wall, four massive limestone columns incised with Greek lettering were revealed. Eight more similarly incised columns were soon afterward located in a nearby field. Now reassembled, they form a curved wall over 26 feet long with about six hundred lines of text in an archaic dialect of Greek. The inscription dates from about 450 BCE—within the era of Athens' commercial, artistic, and intellectual preeminence. Although the text is incomplete and damaged in places, it is still legible. What it comprises is the most extensive European code of law we have from that early a date.[57]

The Great Code of Gortyn begins with an invocation to the gods, an appropriate opening for a message of such high importance: the precepts by which the people of the city were expected to conduct their lives. Law was a sacred matter embodying oral traditions and customs. Carved in stone and displayed in a place accessible to all, the code was intended to provide an enduring foundation for an orderly society. Although laws are often flawed indicators of how people actually behave, they do accurately reflect how their society *wished* them to behave. And what it describes is a society that supported the independence of women.

Most significant for female citizens of Gortyn was what the code did not say. The surviving text contains no hint of the restrictions imposed on wives and daughters in Athens, less than 250 miles away. Nor does it suggest that women were, or ought to be, secluded. Instead, it grants free Gortynian women the right to own and manage property, to inherit, and to bequeath. Husbands were not permitted to spend their wives' money or mortgage their land.[58] In Gortyn, wrote anthropologist Claudine Leduc, "the husband had no power over his wife's belongings or person, and the wife had none over her husband's." Therefore, Leduc asserted, "dependency and subordination were excluded."[59]

Divorce in Gortyn, as in Athens, could be initiated by wives as well as husbands, but the Gortyn Code also recognized the woman's contributions to the household. "If a husband and wife should be divorced," it instructed, "she is to have her own property which she came with to her husband," as well as half of any profit gained from her property during the marriage and "half of whatever she has woven within." A childless widow was entitled to a similar settlement; but if there were children, the widow received only her original property, everything else going to her offspring.

Yet the Gortyn Code was not evenhanded toward women. Its most grievous injustice was that it gave fathers absolute authority over children, including the decision of whether or not to do away with newborns by exposing them to the elements. And it divided parental estates inequitably, declaring that "the sons, no matter how many, shall each receive two parts, while the daughters, no matter how many, shall each receive one part."[60] Still, Gortynian daughters had an advantage over their contemporaries in Athens since the dowry an Athenian bride received from her family (usually her total inheritance) consisted on average of about a tenth of her father's estate, whereas female offspring in Gortyn were awarded a third.[61]

In both Athens and Gortyn a girl who had no brothers and was therefore her father's sole inheritor (an *epikleros* in Greek) was required by law to marry his eldest next-of-kin, that is, a paternal uncle or perhaps cousin. As Simone de Beauvoir wryly summed up her situation, she "was not a female heir but only a machine to procreate a male heir."[62] However, Gortynian law offered the *epikleros* a loophole: If she relinquished part of her inheritance to the legally designated bridegroom, and satisfied several other requirements, she was free to wed someone else.

Gortynian society was highly stratified. At the top were the elite, who were citizens; at the bottom were slaves. Ranking somewhat higher than the slaves was a class of people whom historians refer to as serfs, for want of a better term. Serfs and slaves had a higher status than did their counterparts in Athens.[63] Although they were not citizens and owned no land, they had the right to marry and divorce and to inherit parental bequests in the same proportion as citizens. When they married, they lived under the husband's master, but if the marriage terminated, the woman returned to her original master, taking with her whatever property she had brought to the joint household. When a female citizen wed a male serf, their children would acquire the status of the parent in whose home the family lived. So exceptional for the time were these provisions that it has been suggested that Gortynian serfs were the descendants of the old Minoan-Mycenaean population of Crete, and that the rights apportioned to them reflected thousand-year-old traditions.[64]

The surviving portions of the code do not specify a penalty for an adulterous wife. However, a man who committed adultery or rape was fined according to the perceived severity of the violation, which depended upon the social class of the victim and of the perpetrator. Thus, a married male citizen who committed adultery with an unfree woman went unpunished, while rape of a female citizen penalized sexual transgression. If a Gortynian widow was accused of appropriating assets that should have gone to the children or other heirs, that became "a matter for trial." And if a divorced woman was accused of taking more goods from her former home than she was entitled to, she could appear in court to contest the charge. The code instructed judges to order her to "take an oath of denial by Artemis, before the statue of the Archeress in the ... temple."

To study the Gortyn Code is to recognize that coexistent civilizations, even those as close geographically as Athens and Gortyn, may have differed greatly in their attitudes toward and treatment of women. In fact, Gortynian female citizens had more in common with their counterparts in Sparta, who had unique personal and sexual liberties and extensive property rights.

In her book *The Lady*, Emily James Putnam, the first dean of New York City's Barnard College, observed that while Athenian drama and mythology had many powerful female figures, real-life Athenian women were condemned to dependency and incapacity. How could one account for this startling discrepancy between life and art? Perhaps, she speculated, a dim awareness of an earlier social order had survived the passage of millennia. Perhaps the fictional women of classical Athens represented a "shadowy vision" of a vanished time when the "gods were apt to be female and their rites to be conducted by women." The memory of that time, she suggested, may have lingered outside the realm of conscious thought, giving rise to Medea and Clytemnestra, to legends of fierce Amazon warriors, and to the goddess Artemis, "strong, fearless, unconquerable, with a strain of antique cruelty pointing plainly enough to her primitive origin."[65]

Athens bequeathed the West artistic riches and an inspiring political ideal, but tragically for European womanhood, it was not Sparta or Gortyn but Athens that shaped gender relations in Europe far into the future.

4 THE HERITAGE OF CELTIC WOMEN

Beyond the limits of the Greek world lay a vast expanse of land blanketed by deep forests and peopled by hundreds of tribes whom the Greeks called *keltoi* and whom we know collectively as Celts. Beginning about 900 BCE, Celtic women, men, and children embarked on a historic migration. Setting out from their homeland in Eastern Europe, they walked across the Continent, establishing settlements along the way.[66] The geographic range of their travels was so great that by 200 BCE one could have journeyed from Portugal in the West to Turkey in the East without leaving Celtic territory.

The Celtic tribes differed in many respects, but their language, religion, and art were similar, and—in the view of contemporaries at least—they shared an inordinate fondness for fighting. Fierce Celtic warriors sacked Rome in 390 BCE, looted the Greek treasuries at Delphi a century later, and served as mercenaries in the armies of several Mediterranean powers. One might assume that women would have little status in such a bellicose world, but that was not the case. As the authors of the masterly study *The Celtic Realms* wrote, "It is indeed impossible to have any true understanding of either Celtic history or literature without realizing the high status of Celtic women, and something of the nature of their place in society."[67]

Yet an understanding of women's place in Celtic society is not easy to come by since the tribes' rich store of literature and learning—codes of law, sagas, histories, poetry, genealogies, and collections of wise sayings ("wisdom texts")—was communicated by word of mouth. Thus, until relatively recently our main information on Celtic women came from two unreliable sources: Greek and Roman historians, who considered the Celts barbarians, and medieval Irish monks, who were hostile to the pagan faith of their ancestors. In the mid-twentieth century, however, archaeologists began to apply new scientific methods to a source of information whose impartiality is indisputable: Iron Age graves in France, Germany, and England.

....

In 1953 in the Burgundy village of Vix, archaeologists uncovered a 9-foot-square burial site from about 500 BCE. This extraordinary tomb contained the remains of a 30-year-old woman known today as the "princess of Vix." Her body had been laid out on the platform of a four-wheeled wagon, a mode of interment normally reserved for tribal chiefs and others of high rank. Around her neck was a heavy golden torque, further evidence that she was a person of consequence.

Buried along with the "princess" was a huge wine-mixing bowl from Greece. This exquisitely wrought bronze vessel stands about five feet tall, weighs 350 pounds, and has a capacity of 1,250 quarts. To have buried an object of such great value—one that must have required enormous effort to transport from Greece to France—is another indication of the prominence of the woman with whom it was entombed. Nor was the Vix princess unique. Another opulently furnished female grave from the same time period was found at neighboring Sainte-Colombe, near the modern town of Chatillon-sur-Seine. It too held a wagon, gold jewelry, and other valuable artifacts.[68]

Richly appointed Iron Age tombs with female remains were also found in Germany. Workmen repairing a granary in a village near Stuttgart, for example, came upon a woman's grave that yielded rings and pins of gold, bronze, and coral; a bronze anklet; and gold bracelets, some with serpent-head decoration.[69] Referring to a group of gravesites located between the Rhine and Moselle rivers, an archaeologist noted, "Some women were buried in graves fitted out with burial goods which were equally sumptuous, and in some instances even more magnificent than those of the majority of their contemporary warrior chiefs." Such burials, the writer added, "most certainly confirm that some Celtic women played an exceptional role in their society."[70]

In the Champagne region of France thousands of fifth-century BCE Celtic graves were haphazardly ploughed under by farmers and plundered by grave robbers and amateur collectors. But when researchers revisited the area, they were surprised to find that female graves were more numerous than male and sometimes just as splendid. "One cannot fail to note the undeniable predominance of lavish female graves," commented one investigator.[71] But whether the women so amply outfitted in death were queens, noblewomen, poets, priests, prophets, or warriors is unknown.

Thousands of Iron Age graves were also discovered in Yorkshire, England. Most contained no goods at all, while a minority held only a few simple objects. The presence of cooking pots and spindle weights invariably indicated that the remains were female.[72]

· · · ·

In 50 BCE a Roman army led by Julius Caesar vanquished the Celts of Gaul, a region that encompassed present-day France plus parts of Belgium, Switzerland, the Netherlands, and Germany. The conquered peoples gradually adopted the language and customs of the victors. However, the people of the British Isles remained unaffected by Roman mores until 43 CE (Common Era)—almost a hundred years after the conquest of Gaul—when the Roman behemoth turned its attention westward to launch a full-scale invasion of England. We are fortunate to have accounts of the Roman campaign from the pen of the historian Tacitus, whose narrative gains credibility from the role of his father-in-law, Gnaeus Julius Agricola, who led a Roman legion in England and served as governor of the province.

Writing just decades after the events, Tacitus claimed that the "Britons" made "no distinction of sex in their leaders."[73] He recounted the story of one such leader, Cartimandua, queen of the Brigantes, a tribal confederation in the north. When a dispute broke out between the queen and her husband, she repudiated him, took his armor-bearer as her new partner, and rallied an army to fight for control of the kingdom. Despite assistance from the Romans, she was defeated and barely escaped with her life.[74] Afterward, she disappeared from history, yet as one modern historian pointed out, her story shows that "among the Brigantes a woman could be a ruler, hold property, divorce her husband, [and] lead armies."[75]

The most famous and best attested warrior woman in England was Boudicca (sometimes called Boadicea), the wife of a king of the Iceni tribe in what is now East Anglia, on England's southeast coast. The Iceni were among those Britons who voluntarily allied themselves with the Romans. But when Boudicca's husband died in the year 60 CE, the Romans, apparently assuming that there was now a power vacuum, went on a rampage. They plundered property, enslaved some of the king's relatives, publicly flogged Queen Boudicca, and raped her two young daughters before her eyes. Enraged, Boudicca fomented an insurrection boldly aimed at ousting the Roman legions.[76] The Roman historian Dio Cassius, writing more than a century after the events, claimed that the queen directed the entire war. He sketched this striking word-portrait of her, based partly on legend, partly on reports from the time:

> In stature she was very tall, in appearance most terrifying, in the glance of her eye most fierce, and her voice was harsh; a great mass of the tawniest hair fell to her hips; around her neck was a large golden necklace [a torque]; and she wore a tunic of divers colours over which a thick mantle was fastened with a brooch.[77]

Boudicca's forces won some early victories. They captured and burned Camulodunum (Colchester), the administrative capital of Roman Britain, and invaded Verulamium (near the present St. Albans) and the Roman commercial center at Londinium (London). Finally, they advanced northwest to what would prove a decisive battle. Many women evidently marched with the army, for Tacitus says that the Roman general disparaged Boudicca's force, claiming that it consisted of "more women than fighting men." Boudicca arrived at the battleground in a two-wheeled horse-drawn "chariot." (Similar two-wheeled carts have been found in Celtic female graves that date from hundreds of years before the Roman invasion of Britain.[78]) Boudicca then rallied her forces with these words, as reported by Tacitus:

> We British are used to woman commanders in war. . . . I am descended from mighty men! But I am not fighting for my kingdom and wealth now. I am fighting as an ordinary person for my lost freedom, my bruised body, and my outraged daughters

And she challenged her soldiers to fight to the death, declaring, "That is what I, a woman, plan to do!—let the men live in slavery if they will." The Romans, though greatly outnumbered, were victorious, and Boudicca took her own life in fulfillment of her vow not to live as a slave.[79]

Legends of warrior women were passed down orally for generations in Scotland, Ireland, and remote areas of Wales until they were finally recorded by medieval Christian scribes. Just why those pious Christians chose to preserve the ancient tales with all their heathen magic, gore, and sex is unclear. Perhaps ethnic pride played a part, maybe it was sheer love of language and a good story. The Irish epic *The Cattle-Raid of Cooley* (*Táin Bo Coalinga*), for example, features a powerful Irish queen named Maeve (or Medb), a haughty woman who insists on sexual freedom after marriage and boasts of her skill in "battle and warlike combat." When she orders her army to invade Ulster to capture a marvelous bull she covets, she herself directs the bloody fight and occasionally joins in. Her opponent, Cuchulain of Ulster, is able to defeat her only because he has supernatural powers.

Among other women who are credited with military expertise in Irish legend are Aife, a woman warrior; Scáthach, her rival, who presided over a celebrated school for warriors in Scotland (the Isle of Skye is named is named for her); and nine prophetic women clad in armor who instruct the hero of the Welsh legend of Peredur in the use of weapons.[80]

. . . .

Our understanding of the religious practices of Europeans during the Iron Age is shadowy, but archaeological digs in Europe and the British Isles have revealed that the tribes worshipped a multitude of local gods, both female and male. One especially widely dispersed deity was the goddess Epona, who was often depicted riding a horse.

Also ubiquitous were images of mother goddesses, who were often shown in triplicate holding babies, baskets of fruit, and other symbols of fertility.[81] The goddess Brigit, for example, an important deity in pre-Christian Britain and Ireland as well as on the Continent, was often portrayed in triplicate, signifying her tripartite nature: poet, metalworker, and healer.[82] (During the early Middle Ages Brigit acquired a namesake,

4. ROMANO-BRITISH MOTHER GODDESSES, 100-300 BCE

a Christian saint, Brigit of Kildare, who was considered a patron of the creative arts, blacksmithery, and maternity.)

Shrines dedicated to goddesses of healing were often located near rivers, wells, and natural springs. A sanctuary at the source of the river Marne, for example, was devoted to a tripartite mother goddess, while the goddess Coventina was worshipped alongside a spring of water in Northumberland. Offerings to the goddess Sulis have been fished from the hot springs in the English city of Bath, where Iron Age Britons had deposited them long before the Romans erected a temple over the site. And at a spring situated at the source of the river Seine, not far from the modern city of Dijon, supplicants in Gaul addressed their prayers to a goddess with curative powers named Sequana. Sequana's devotees threw replicas of afflicted body parts into the spring—legs, eyes, breasts, genitals, feet, and so forth—hundreds of which have since been recovered. Coins found in the vicinity show that pilgrims continued to wend their way to Sequana's spring until at least the year 388 CE, well into the Christian era.[83]

At the apex of Celtic religion and society were the Druids, revered spiritual leaders and judges who were entrusted with the sacred duty of committing to memory the laws, poetry, myths, and history of their people. Julius Caesar described the long and arduous training the Druids underwent but made no reference to women among them.[84] And although Tacitus penned a dramatic account of a Roman invasion of a Druid sanctuary where the soldiers encountered a crowd of "frenzied women," he did not identify the women as Druids.[85]

Less ambiguous are the Roman historians' reports of the special spiritual gifts attributed to women by the German tribes. Caesar reported that captured soldiers from Germania told him that their military leaders sought the counsel of women prior to launching an offensive.[86] And Tacitus wrote that the Germans "believe that there resides in women an element of holiness and a gift of prophecy; so they do not scorn to ask their advice, or lightly disregard their replies."

Tacitus also described a woman named Veleda who had long been "honored by many Germans as a divinity." Emissaries who came seeking Veleda's advice, he wrote, were not permitted to approach her. "She dwelt in a lofty tower, and one of her relatives, chosen for the purpose, conveyed, like the messenger of a divinity, the questions and answers." After she correctly predicted her tribe's victory in a battle against the Romans, she was showered with gifts, among which were a captured Roman ship and a Roman general who had the misfortune to be taken prisoner. Tacitus also mentioned a woman named Aurinia and several other women whom the Germans credited with oracular powers.[87]

....

Celtic culture—or, more accurately, a highly romanticized version of it—has had several revivals. In the late eighteenth century, a group calling itself the Ancient Order of the Druids was founded in London. The visionary writer and artist William Blake, a member of the Ancient Order, wrote of "high-rear'd Druid temples" that once stood on "Albions rocks."[88] Some members of the group mistakenly identified Stonehenge and other ancient stone circles in Britain as druidic temples. Later, a group of Irish poets and playwrights, including John Millington Synge, William Butler Yeats, and Lady Augustus Gregory inspired another Celtic resurgence. Yeats, who published a collection of stories titled *Celtic Twilight* and wrote admiringly of Queen Maeve, lamented the disappearance from Ireland of "all the wild witches, those most noble ladies."[89]

A third Celtic revival took place in the latter decades of the twentieth century. Enthralled by tales of strong, sexually uninhibited females with remarkable spiritual powers, groups of women came together to celebrate Celtic holidays and enact supposed druidic ceremonies. Much of what they admired was a fantasy that strayed far from the rude realities of Celtic life, but they were right that in the Celtic world female strength and courage were valued, female gods worshipped, and female seers honored, while some women, like the princess of Vix, commanded extraordinary respect, wealth, and prestige. Because the Iron Age tribes shared the stage of history with the surpassingly brilliant Greek and Roman civilizations, their influence is frequently underestimated; but their social and cultural mores are part of the mix that shaped the consciousness of Western women.

PART 2

SEIZING THE MOMENT

5 DECLINE AND FALL OF THE PATERFAMILIAS

At the time of its founding—in 509 BCE according to time-honored myth—the Roman Republic was a minor agricultural state sandwiched between sophisticated Etruscan cities to the north and prosperous Greek colonies to the south. Although the young republic traded actively with its neighbors, its economy was undeveloped and no national coinage yet existed. Family life was dominated by the household's eldest male, the paterfamilias, who wielded authority over his wife, children, grandchildren, daughters-in-law, and slaves. All of these individuals, male and female, free and unfree, youngsters and adults, were subject to *patria potestas*, the power of the father.

The destiny of male and female children differed fundamentally, for sons over the age of 14 became independent upon the death of the paterfamilias, while daughters remained dependent all their lives. An unmarried girl whose father died was assigned a new guardian, most often an older brother or a paternal uncle.[90] If she married according to the usual form of matrimony in the early republic, *cum manu* (literally, with hand), her father-in-law became her guardian or, if he was deceased, her husband. A female slave who was released from bondage was assigned a male guardian, usually her former master.[91]

The rationale for the lifelong supervision of women was spelled out in the Roman Republic's earliest written law code, the XII Tables. While the XII Tables and the Gortyn Code date from roughly the same period, about 450 BCE, they differ significantly in their treatment of women, for while Gortynian law supported women's independence, the XII Tables decreed: "Women, even though they are of full age, because of their levity of mind (*levitas animi*) shall be under guardianship."[92]

The paterfamilias in an upper-class Roman household had the right, indeed the duty, to select a marital partner for his daughter and provide her with a dowry. Divorce was relatively common and easily accomplished, and widowhood was frequent since girls were often matched with much older men. Although a widow could inherit from her husband, she and her children (along with her inheritance) normally remained under the supervision of her deceased spouse's family. If she remarried, she could be deprived of her children.[93]

A prime responsibility of the paterfamilias was to preserve or enlarge the wealth of his household. He alone controlled the dwellings, land, slaves, animals, inheritances, dowries, income, and even personal possessions of all of his dependents. Thus, they could not buy, sell, or bequeath anything without his approval. Only a foolish person would have dared to defy his orders, because he had the authority to impose punishments as severe as exile or sale into slavery. It was he who decided whether a baby born to a member of his household would be allowed to live or would be exposed to the elements—a fate more likely to be suffered by a female infant.[94] So awful was his authority that if he discovered his wife or daughter in an act of adultery, he had the right to kill her and her lover.[95] Still, such murders were apparently rare—if not on account of parental affection, perhaps because of the shame that would rebound to the adulterer's family.[96]

• • • •

With the defeat in 201 BCE of the Carthaginian general Hannibal in the Second Punic War, the Roman Republic became the dominant power in the Mediterranean region. However, the victory cost the Roman people dearly in treasure and men. One consequence of the enormous loss of life was the creation of a great many heiresses. In the ancient world as in the modern, wealth often conferred autonomy; thus, well-to-do women were soon able to buy and sell property independently and write wills. The Roman Senate, unhappy about this turn of events, passed a law that set limits on the size of female inheritances. But as the authoritative *Cambridge Ancient History* commented, "Legal fictions were of course soon invented which made the law practically void."[97]

Since the assets of an heiress who contracted a traditional *cum manu* marriage would go to her spouse's family, a different form of matrimony—marriage *sine manu* (without hand)—became increasingly popular. This change had far-reaching consequences for women, for in a *sine manu* union, the bride's father continued to be her guardian, while she herself lived with her husband's family. Although this arrangement preserved her father's control of her assets, it made it difficult, if not impossible, for him to maintain day-to-day supervision of the woman herself. Moreover, when the father of a woman who was wed *sine manu* died, she was often declared *sui juris*, that is, independent.

Although documents from the past usually center on the deeds of men, women insistently elbowed their way onto the pages of both literature and history. In the comedies of the Roman dramatist Plautus, for example, we encounter wives who are imperious, disobedient, and—not incidentally—rich.[98] And Livy's *History of Rome* describes an invasion of the Roman Senate staged by wives and widows from Rome's old patrician families and new moneyed class.

What provoked the invasion according to Livy's account (which was written long after the fact) was a proposal to repeal the Oppian law, an austerity measure that had been enacted during the anxious years of the Second Punic War. It had been six years since the defeat of Hannibal, yet wartime restrictions on luxury expenditures by women were still in place, though limitations on men had been rescinded. Livy reported that when a motion to do away with these restrictions came up for debate, women "could not be kept indoors either by the authority of the magistrates or the orders of their husbands or their own sense of propriety." Filling the streets and blocking approaches to the Forum, they implored the senators to "allow women to resume their former adornments now that the commonwealth was flourishing and private fortunes increasing." According to Livy, the crowd around the Forum grew daily as women flocked to Rome from outlying towns and villages.

The Roman statesman Marcus Porcius Cato—a narrow conservative on social issues—opposed repeal of the Oppian law. In his argument to the Senate as recounted by Livy, Cato complained that he had been forced to make his way to the Forum "through a regular army of women." Warning that grave dangers to male authority were apt to arise from female "intrigues, plots, secret cabals," Cato reminded fellow legislators, "Our ancestors would have no woman transact even private business except through her guardian." Cato viewed the "female insurrection" then in progress as an opening wedge for more substantive demands in the future. What women really want, he cautioned, "is unrestricted freedom." He likened women's unruliness to that of wild beasts chafed by long confinement and then released. The day after the debate, wrote Livy, "the women poured out into the streets in much greater force" and besieged unfriendly legislators. In the end, they won their way, and in 195 BCE the Oppian law was repealed.[99]

The Roman matron was clearly a person to be reckoned with, a companion and advisor to her husband, a guide and teacher to her children, and the supervisor of the home. Although she could not vote or hold public office, she was not subject to the social prohibitions imposed upon upper-class women in Athens. As the Roman biographer Cornelius Nepos later observed, "No Roman would hesitate to take his wife to a dinner party, or to allow the mother of his family to occupy the first rooms in his house and to walk about in public."[100]

. . . .

The first century BCE was a time of multiple crises in Rome: slave revolts, political conspiracy, the assassination of Julius Caesar, civil wars, and more. Men from some of Rome's most prominent families were pronounced outlaws, stripped of property, and forced into exile or executed. Some women risked their lives to hide male relatives or help them escape. The extraordinary deeds of one wife are recounted in a long funeral inscription commissioned by her grieving husband. He praised her for acting courageously to save him when his life was threatened by political foes and for successfully pursuing a lawsuit on behalf of herself and her sister while he was away in Macedonia and her sister's husband was in Africa. "Even if we had been present," he acknowledged, "we could not have done anything more." During their harmonious forty-year marriage, he recalled, he and his wife had shared the management of their finances "in such a way that I stood as protector of your fortune, while you kept a watch over mine."[101]

In the year 42 BCE, fourteen hundred female relations of men who had been banished from Rome marched into the Forum *en masse* to protest an exceptional financial assessment. Unwilling to comply, the women had appointed Hortensia, the daughter of a famous orator and the sister of a proscribed man, to speak on their behalf to the triumvirate, the three-man government that then ruled Rome. In her speech—which we know only from Appian's history of Rome, written about a century after the event—Hortensia is said to have argued that taxing the women was unjust because they were not responsible for the deeds of their male kin. Basing her argument on the fact that women were excluded from any voice in affairs of state, she reportedly asked, "Why should we pay taxes when we have no part in the honors, the commands, the statecraft, for which you contend against each other with such harmful results?" The triumvirs ordered the women expelled from the Forum, but the public sided with them. The following day more than two-thirds of the protesters were excused from the tax.[102]

Hortensia, like many other upper-class Roman girls, had received some education, for by one means or another—perhaps alongside a brother who was tutored at home by a Greek slave, perhaps at one of the recently opened primary schools for girls[103]—elite Roman women were often not only literate but knowledgeable about a wide range of subjects. The essayist Plutarch noted that Cornelia, the last of Pompey's wives, "was highly educated, played well upon the lute, and understood geometry." She also attended public lectures on philosophy, he added, which she listened to with understanding.[104]

Sempronia, according to the Roman historian Sallust, was well-read in Greek and Latin literature, a skilled poet, a talented dancer, and a conversationalist of wit and charm.[105] And Pliny the Younger praised the writing style of a friend's wife, which, he said, was so admirable he found it hard to believe it was the work of a woman.[106]

We know of a number of women who composed poetry in Latin during the last century BCE, but their verse has mostly disappeared. Among the survivals are six love poems by Sulpicia that were preserved only because they were included in a collection of work by male members of a literary circle to which she belonged. Women's participation in Roman literary salons was characterized by historian Sarah Pomeroy as "one of the most important developments in women's intellectual history."[107]

Rome evidently did not lack for women who were proud of their intellectual attainments, and the satirist Juvenal took delight in ridiculing them. Some women, he later wrote, run about town "attending men's

5. ISIS WITH HER SON, HORUS, 664-332 BCE

meetings"; others, in an apparent breach of good breeding, know "what is going on all over the world," from China to Thrace. "But most intolerable of all," in his opinion, was the woman who at dinner parties discoursed volubly on poetry, comparing Virgil with Homer. As for the woman who "observes all the rules and laws of language" and "quotes verses that I never heard of," she should correct her girlfriends' grammar and leave her husband alone.[108] Still, Juvenal's acid pen unintentionally documented the wide range of women's intellectual interests and the enthusiasm with which they pursued them.

....

A Roman army led by Octavian, Julius Caesar's adopted son, vanquished the Egyptian queen, Cleopatra, and her lover, Mark Antony, in 31 BCE. Four years later the Roman Senate gave Octavian the honorary title Augustus. For the next four decades, until his death in the year 14 of the new millennium, Augustus ruled over the Roman colossus. So many people from every corner of the vast empire settled in Rome that by the beginning of the second century CE the population had swollen to roughly a million, about a third of whom were slaves.[109]

Nearly as diverse as the people of the vast empire were the deities they worshipped. Many Roman goddesses were adopted from the Greek pantheon, including Ceres (Demeter in Greece), Juno (the Greek Hera), Diana (Artemis), and Minerva (Athena). Others came from Asia Minor, such as Cybele, who was celebrated in the East at orgiastic rites led by priestesses and castrated priests dressed in female garments.[110] Rome domesticated Cybele, however. Labeled Magna Mater (the Great Mother), she was worshipped at dignified rites conducted by august state priests. Her cult, minus its exotic features, spread across Europe. Today, statues honoring Cybele may be seen in Madrid, Lyon, Munich, and other cities. Also imported from the East was the Egyptian deity Isis, who—unlike Rome's unsympathetic, sometimes vindictive gods—was warm, approachable, and compassionate. A loving wife and mother, Isis was a protector of women in pregnancy and childbirth and a bestower of fertility. She was revered by Romans from every walk of life, from patricians to slaves, and was particularly beloved by women.[111]

Romans also sought advice and comfort from female fortunetellers, sorcerers, and vendors of magic amulets and potions, many of whom were foreign-born, Jewish, or otherwise socially marginal. Widely suspected (no doubt justly in some cases) of secretly dispensing contraceptives, abortifacients, and even poisons, they practiced what was essentially an underground religion in competition with official state cults. Juvenal mocked his countrywomen for consulting "a palsied Jewess" who claimed to be able to interpret dreams, or an Armenian or Syrian soothsayer, a Chaldean astrologer, or a Phrygian or Indian oracle. And Juvenal's contemporary, the essayist Plutarch, earnestly advised a young woman of his acquaintance to "shut her door to all magic ceremonies and foreign superstitions. For no god can be pleased by stealthy and surreptitious rites performed by a woman."[112] But Romans of all classes and both genders continued to seek the aid of untraditional religious practitioners. Augustus tried to rekindle devotion to the official state religion by expanding the number of priests, enlarging their allowances and privileges, and restoring several archaic temples that had fallen into disrepair, but his efforts bore little fruit. Faced with a decline in the birthrate, the emperor tried to promote childbearing through legislation. His most dramatic legislative gambit was the *lex Julia* of 18 BCE, which formally granted emancipation from guardianship to female citizens who had three offspring and freedwomen who had four.[113] The *lex Julia*'s promise of freedom as a reward for fecundity was a tacit acknowledgment that women were eager to rid themselves of male supervision. But it failed to bring about the hoped-for boost in population. Explained Tacitus: "Marriages and the rearing of children did not become more attractive, so powerful were the attractions of a childless state."[114]

Some women had evidently begun to defy the sexual double standard. Greek Stoic philosopher Epictetus claimed that Roman women ostentatiously carried copies of Plato's *Republic* in the mistaken belief that the text endorsed sexual freedom.[115] The poet Sulpicia, rejoicing in an illicit love affair, defiantly announced in a poem, "I'm glad I've erred," and added, "falsely posing disgusts me."[116] The satirist Juvenal commented tartly that a particular woman would sooner be satisfied with one eye than with one man. He claimed that while poor women had to endure the trials of childbirth, the wealthy could obtain drugs to bring about sterility or abortion.[117]

Women who wished to prevent pregnancy could avail themselves of a number of birth-control and abortion techniques. Some of the methods described in about 100 CE by the physician Soranus in his book *Gynecology* were somewhat effective: blocking the entrance to the uterus with a wad of soft wool or with olive oil, honey, sap from evergreen trees, or the pulp of figs or pomegranates, for instance; or inserting vaginal suppositories made from caustic substances that would inflame the cervix, like pine bark, ginger, or the ground-up peel of pomegranates. Of lesser or no value were his recommendations that women wash themselves, jump about, or squat immediately following intercourse; or that men apply certain salves or ointments to the penis before penetration. Soranus disparaged the efficacy of amulets, which "according to the outcome, reveal themselves as falsehoods." To cause abortion he suggested strenuous activity, diuretics, enemas, hot baths, potions, and bleedings; but he warned against inserting a sharp implement into the vagina.[118]

Things had gone so far, in the overblown estimation of a Roman general, that women were now "loosed from every bond" and had begun to "rule our houses, tribunals, even armies."[119] Hoping to reinforce traditional gender roles, Augustus commanded the women of the imperial family to spend their days spinning and weaving,[120] and he enacted a series of laws whose fundamental purpose was to replace the shrunken authority of the paterfamilias with the authority of the state. One of the new laws made premarital sex (on the part of a free woman) and adultery (by either gender) criminal offenses that could be penalized severely. Still, some women took the risk, apparently including Augustus's own daughter who, in spite of her compulsory work at the loom, found time to engage in love affairs. Her father sent her into exile.

. . . .

In the mid first century CE, Emperor Claudius placed daughters on a nearly equal footing with sons by ruling that when a father died or voluntarily relinquished guardianship, his adult daughters automatically became emancipated. To the second-century jurist Gaius, the laws that had formerly bound the female sex seemed inexplicable, like quaint relics from a bygone day. Observing that "Women of full age deal with their own affairs for themselves," he saw "no very worthwhile reason why women who have reached the age of maturity should be in guardianship." As to the claim engraved in the XII Tables some six hundred years earlier—that women needed guardians because of their "levity of mind"—he characterized it as "specious rather than true."[121] Finally, in about the year three hundred, Emperor Diocletian abolished female guardianship as a legal institution, thereby codifying what already existed in fact.

Simone de Beauvoir commented dryly that the Roman woman enjoyed many liberties, but since she was denied meaningful employment, she was "'free' for nothing."[122] This dismal appraisal, while not untrue, discounts women's gains. For as the power of the father eroded, upper-class women transacted business, wrote wills, staged protests, acquired knowledge, wrote poetry, joined literary salons, and took lovers. And although no woman ever officially held the reins of government, a number of later empresses wielded political influence and, in a few instances, real power.[123]

When there was an opportunity for greater autonomy, Roman women seized the moment. Resolute, self-confident, and shrewd, they succeeded in reshaping and expanding the parameters of their world.

6 THE MINISTRY OF WOMEN

In the Roman province of Judea, between the years 6 and 4 BCE, a Jewish woman gave birth to a son, Yeshua, or Jesus. By the age of 30 Jesus had attracted a band of devoted female and male disciples who accompanied him as he traveled through Palestine.[124] For a woman to leave her home and take up an itinerant life was a bold act, but the Jesus movement was an alternative community with unconventional ideas in which all believers found acceptance and, what was rare for women, a sense of high purpose.

Jesus is portrayed in the Gospels of the New Testament as a reformer who challenged the fundamental social arrangements of the Jewish community. He ridiculed rank, declaring, "Whoever would be great among you must be your servant, and whoever would be first among you must be slave of all"; and he disdained wealth, warning, "It is easier for a camel to go through the eye of a needle than for a rich man to enter the kingdom of God."[125] He listened to women's concerns and based parables on domestic activities like sweeping the floor, mending a torn garment, baking bread, and spinning. And he likened the sorrow his followers would feel at his departure and their joy at his return to a mother's delight in her child after the pain of childbirth.[126]

The Gospels say that when Jesus was arrested by Roman soldiers, his male disciples fled in fear for their lives, but the women accompanied him on his final journey from Galilee to the site of the crucifixion. The Gospels of Mark and Matthew report that among the women present at the crucifixion were Mary Magdalene, Mary the mother of James and Joseph, and Salome; according to John, Mary Magdalene stood at the foot of the cross with Jesus's mother and her sister. Women accompanied Jesus's body to the tomb, and Mary Magdalene, possibly in the company of other women, returned a few days later to anoint the body. It was women who discovered that the tomb was empty and women to whom the resurrected Jesus first showed himself.[127]

Jesus's reputation for holiness grew after his death and spread rapidly. Within thirty years of the crucifixion, a congregation that revered him as a messiah, or Christ, was established in Rome, and a century later Christian assemblies existed in all the principal cities of the Roman Empire. The New Testament's Acts of the Apostles, which recounts the missionary labors of the Apostle Paul, indicates that women played a vital role in the Church's growth. Indeed, female believers may well have been more numerous than male in some of the earliest Christian congregations.[128]

Several of the new faith's precepts—especially its disapproval of forced marriage, concubinage, and adultery—tended to enhance the dignity of women and elevate the status of wives. However, Saint Paul's letters suggest an ambivalent attitude toward women. He sent a stirring declaration of Christian egalitarianism to Galatia (in the present Turkey), writing, "There is neither Jew nor Greek, there is neither slave nor free; there is neither male nor female; for you are all one in Christ Jesus."[129] But he counseled the Christian assembly at Corinth that man "is the image and glory of God; but woman is the glory of man. For man was not made from woman, but woman from man. Neither was man created for woman, but woman for man." And he admonished the women of the Corinthian congregation to "keep silence in the churches. For they are not permitted to speak. . . . If there is anything they desire to know, let them ask their husbands at home."[130]

Still, the apostolic Church needed all the support it could get, so it did not reject women's help as teachers, missionaries, and leaders of congregations, nor did it spurn monetary gifts donated by Roman heiresses. But centuries were to pass before the true magnitude of women's contributions could be appreciated, because editors and translators of the New Testament neglected, diminished, and even distorted their role in the early Church.

For example, translators routinely referred to Paul's co-workers in Rome as "brethren." Yet Helmut Koester of Harvard Divinity School has pointed out that the Greek word used by Paul in his letter to the Christian congregation at Rome, *adelphoi*, can encompass both genders. Koester suggested that since six of Paul's forty co-workers at Rome were female, "brothers and sisters" is a more accurate rendition.[131] Several Bibles published since the advent of the modern women's movement correct this mistranslation,[132] while Today's New International Version, published in 2002, goes further, replacing "sons of God" with "children of God," and "man" with "person."[133]

Another instance of editors obscuring the contributions of women occurred with Paul's identification of "our sister Phoebe" as a *diakonos* in a Christian congregation near Corinth. The Greek word *diakonos* is normally translated "minister," but English-language editions of the New Testament have traditionally called Phoebe a deaconess (or in European editions, *diaconesse, diaconisa, diaconessa,* or *Dienerin*) [134]—despite the fact that the office of deaconess did not exist in western churches in her day.[135] Phoebe was accorded her rightful title in the 1989 Revised English Bible, and while the New Revised Standard Version (NRSV) published that same year calls her "deacon," there is a footnote suggesting "minister" as an alternative.

Paul had never visited Rome at the time he wrote to the Christian congregation there, but he was already able to greet by name half a dozen women: "the beloved Persis," Mary, Julia, Tryphaena, Tryphosa, and Junia. Junia must have been particularly outstanding because Paul referred to her as an apostle. But later translators apparently found the idea of a female apostle unacceptable, and Junia underwent a change of gender. Sometime in the late thirteenth century, "Junia" became "Junias," the masculine form of the name in Greek. As late as 1946, the Revised Standard Version (RSV) of the Bible unambiguously refers to Andronicus and Junias as "men of note among the apostles."[136] Finally, in 1989, the NRSV restored the feminine form, describing "Junia" as "prominent among the apostles."

Paul also referred in his Roman epistle to the Christian missionaries Priscilla (or Prisca) and her husband Aquila. According to Acts of the Apostles, Priscilla and Aquila were forced to leave Rome when Emperor Claudius issued an edict expelling Jews from the city. After resettling in Corinth, they converted to Christianity and established a Christian congregation in their home. Paul met them during his first visit to Corinth in the year 51 CE and lodged with them for some eighteen months. Afterward, the couple labored for the Church in Ephesus, where they distinguished themselves as teachers of religious doctrine. In Ephesus they again made their home a center of Christian worship.[137]

It was customary for early Christians to assemble for prayer and a communal meal in private residences, and women and men who had commodious homes often made them available for this purpose.[138] The home church had several advantages. It could be set up and maintained with minimal expense, and believers could come and go without attracting attention. Discretion was necessary since Christians were persecuted throughout the Roman Empire. In one horrendous episode in Lyons in the year 177, forty-seven young Christians, half of them women, were put to death in the city's amphitheater. According to a Christian chronicle, one of the women, the slave Blandina, endured unspeakable tortures with a fortitude that astonished observers. Finally, when the wild animals to whom she was exposed failed to attack her, her persecutors ended her suffering with a dagger.[139]

The best-known female martyr is Vibia Perpetua, a 22-year-old aristocratic Christian woman from Roman-occupied Carthage. Her story—much of it told in the simple but poignant words she herself set down in a prison diary—was preserved by a sympathetic contemporary. Imprisoned in about the year 200 with her infant son and her maid-servant Felicitas (who gave birth while incarcerated), Perpetua described her suffering, her fears for her baby, and the visions that sustained her. She showed no pain while being mauled by a wild animal, and she guided the hand of the Roman gladiator whose sword ended her life.[140] Female martyrs helped immeasurably to advance the religion since their unshakable belief in the Christian promise of eternal life inspired others. "The oftener we are mown down by you, the more we grow in number; the blood of martyrs is the seed of the Church," wrote the second-century Christian theologian Tertullian.[141]

Christianity implicitly gave women permission to follow an unconventional and potentially liberating lifestyle. For hadn't Jesus instructed Martha that it was better to attend to his teachings than to be distracted by serving at table? And hadn't Paul praised Priscilla and Phoebe, both of whom chose travel and public activities over settled domesticity?[142] Women who rejected traditional gender roles are presented in a favorable light in several apocryphal Christian texts. In the second-century tale of Thecla of Iconium (modern-day Konya in Turkey), for instance, the 18-year-old Thecla hears Saint Paul preach and resolves to consecrate her life to Christ. To avoid marrying the man to whom she is promised, she runs away to find Paul. While searching for him, she survives attempted rapes, a plan to burn her at the stake, and attacks by wild beasts. When she finally makes contact with Paul, he authorizes her to "Go, and teach the word of God!"[143]

As the membership and prestige of the Church expanded, the role of women contracted. One important change was the replacement of home-based congregations with dedicated church buildings in which women were consigned to a back seat, literally as well as figuratively, for female worshippers were seated apart from male.[144] More detrimental to women in the long run, however, was the unification of all Christian communities under a centralized hierarchy from which women were excluded.

Women did not retreat without a struggle. Complained the fourth-century Church Father, John Chrysostom: "The divine law has excluded women from the ministry, but they endeavor to thrust themselves into it."[145] Especially troublesome were widows, who were warned that they were not permitted to teach or to perform baptisms, and deaconesses, who were firmly advised that the Church had not established their office "for the practice of priesthood or any liturgical function, but for the sake of female modesty at . . . the time of baptism."[146] Yet even after the Church had declared widowhood "a religious state devoid of clerical status" and had eliminated the office of deaconess,[147] women persisted—sometimes with the complicity of male clergy.

In 494, Pope Gelasius I criticized bishops in southern Italy and Sicily for encouraging women "to officiate at the sacred altars, and to take part in all matters imparted to the offices of the male sex."[148] And in 515, bishops from dioceses in northern Gaul rebuked two erring Breton clerics for allowing women to assist in the celebration of the Mass, "so that while you are distributing the Eucharist, they hold the chalice and presume to administer the blood of Christ to the people of God." Correct all such "depraved practices" at once, they implored.[149]

When a tenth-century Italian bishop was queried by a colleague as to "how we should understand the terms female priest or female deacon," he responded sensibly that "since in the primitive Church, according to the Lord's word, many were the crops and few the laborers," women had to be admitted to the ministry.[150] The Catholic priesthood has been an entirely male preserve since at least since the sixth century. But those who contend that women served at the altar in the early Church have solid historical grounds for their claim.

. . . .

While orthodox Christianity was sidelining women, dissident Christian sects that admitted women to priestly duties developed. As early as the second century, Tertullian objected: "The very women of these heretics, how wanton they are! For they are bold enough to teach, to dispute, to enact exorcisms, to undertake cures—it may be even to baptize."[151] But women continued to join religious groups that offered them respect and opportunities for spiritual leadership.

One early sect, Montanism (also known as the New Prophesy), arose in the latter half of the second century in the part of western Turkey known as Phrygia and spread into Rome and around the Mediterranean basin. It was based on the ecstatic visions of its founder, a priest named Montanus, and two women, Prisca and Maximilla. The latter claimed that Christ spoke through her, while Prisca (or perhaps a later Montanist prophet, Quintilla) announced that Jesus had appeared to her as a woman.[152]

We have the fourth-century Cypriot bishop Epiphanius to thank for preserving the Montanists' remarkable pro-woman reinterpretation of several biblical texts. In his voluminous catalogue of eighty "heresies" (one of them is Judaism), Epiphanius explained that the Montanists praise Eve "because she was the first to eat from the tree of wisdom," and to justify their ordination of female clergy, they say that Moses' sister was a prophetess."[153]

Another unorthodox group accused of improperly elevating women was the Gnostics. Irenaeus, the second-century bishop of Lyons, claimed that female Gnostics were offering the Eucharist and baptizing. He further charged that a local Gnostic leader had "seduced" many women by postulating a feminine aspect of God and even encouraging female prophesy.[154]

When Christianity became Rome's official state religion in the late fourth century, "heretical" documents were confiscated and burned, and many priceless writings were lost forever. However, in December 1945, near Nag Hammadi, Egypt, Arab peasants found large clay jars containing papyrus codices bound in gazelle leather. Unaware of the documents' importance, they allowed some of the pages to be destroyed, but fortunately many escaped. The surviving texts are Coptic translations from the Greek of religious tracts written by Gnostics and other early Christians. Although placed in their desert hiding-place sometime between about 350 and 400 CE, they were composed several centuries earlier.[155] Thus, they are authentic expressions of Christian beliefs in the era of the apostolic Church.

The Nag Hammadi archive consists of a complex and often contradictory mix of poetry, sermon, dramatic narrative, and obscure mystical thought. To add to its difficulties, some of the texts are partially illegible or incomplete. Since the 1970's, when all the documents were finally published, scholars have been at work interpreting them, a project that will likely continue for generations. It is our great good fortune that after having been lost for some fifteen-hundred years, they came to light at a moment in time when a body of experts existed who were disposed to study them from a woman-centered perspective. They already have yielded startling new insights.

Several of the texts refer to Christian groups that prayed to God the Mother as well as to God the Father. Some favor the first version of Genesis—in which God fashions human beings "in his own image . . . male and female he created them"—over the second version, in which Eve is made from Adam's rib.[156] A document entitled On the Origin of the World turns Genesis on its head, for it recounts a scene in which Adam credits Eve with giving him life (a situation more consistent with human reality, it might be remarked). In another text, The Secret Book of John, Eve brings Adam spiritual understanding.[157] And in The Testimony of Truth, the serpent persuades Eve to eat from the tree of knowledge so that "the eyes of her mind will be opened." The serpent explains that God has forbidden Adam and Eve to eat because he is a "malicious envier" who wishes to keep wisdom for himself.[158]

One of the major surprises of the Nag Hammadi texts is the inclusion of women among Jesus's first apostles. In The Sophia of Jesus Christ, twelve men and seven women gather to hear the resurrected Jesus speak. At the end of his sermon, Jesus announces that he has given these chosen individuals "authority over all things" so that they can preach. The Savior's emissaries then set off to spread the Word.[159] The most prominent of the women and the only one of the seven identified by name is Mary Magdalene. In fact, as portrayed in several Nag Hammadi texts, Magdalene is every bit as deserving of the title apostle as the twelve recognized males.

Mary Magdalene is of course an important figure in the canonical Gospels of the New Testament. She is the only woman aside from Jesus's mother who is mentioned by name in all four Gospels. She was a member of the Jesus circle, a witness to the crucifixion, and the first person to whom the resurrected Christ showed himself.[160] In the newly discovered Dialogue of the Savior, Magdalene is also one of three disciples (the others are Thomas and Matthew) to whom Jesus has granted the privilege of special instruction; moreover, he commends her as "a woman who knew the All."[161] Says the non-canonical Gospel of Philip, "There were three who always walked with the Lord: Mary his mother, and her sister, and Magdalene, the one who was called his companion." A tantalizing fragment of text—from which key words are missing—reads: "the companion of the [...] Mary Magdalene. [...] loved her more than all the disciples, and used to kiss her often on her mouth."[162] A kiss may not imply a sexual relationship, however, for as Elaine Pagels has pointed out, it served "for some gnostic Christians, to symbolize the intimate communion between the believer and Christ."[163]

Mary Magdalene is the primary figure in the Gospel of Mary, a non-canonical text that may have circulated widely. In addition to the copy found at Nag Hammadi, we have several others: a Coptic version from the mid-second century that came to light in Cairo in 1896 and two partial texts in Greek discovered later. One of the latter, evidently a treasured possession of its third-century owner, was found wrapped in a protective covering of feathers and tucked into a cranny of the wall of an ancient cemetery in Egypt.[164] The Gospel of Mary recounts a gathering of the apostles shortly after the crucifixion. They are grief-stricken and frightened for their own safety, and Mary Magdalene attempts to comfort and reassure them. She tells them that though Jesus is gone, his grace is with them still and will protect them. Peter remarks, "Sister, we know that the Savior loved you more than the rest of women," and he asks her to relate any teachings Jesus imparted to her. She then delivers the shocking news that Jesus appeared to her in a vision that very day and spoke to her. Andrew and Peter challenge her veracity. Asks Peter: "Did he [Jesus] really speak privately with a woman? . . . Are we to turn about and all listen to her? Did he prefer her to us?" Magdalene, weeping, responds: "My brother Peter, what do you think? Do you think that I thought this up myself in my heart, or that I am lying about the Savior?" Levi (Matthew) says that Peter is "hot tempered" and adds, "If the Savior made her worthy, who are you indeed to reject her? Surely the Savior knows her very well. That is why he loved her more than us."[165]

Conflict between Peter and Mary Magdalene also appears in the document Faith Wisdom (*Pistis Sophia*), where Peter appeals to Jesus to silence Magdalene, exclaiming, "We cannot abide this woman [Magdalene] who does not allow us to speak, but speaks often [herself]." Magdalene confesses to Jesus, "Peter makes me hesitate; I am afraid of him, because he hates the female race." But Jesus reassures her that any divinely inspired person may speak.[166] Peter again lashes out at Magdalene in the Gospel of Thomas, demanding, "Mary should leave us, for females are not worthy of life." Jesus's response is enigmatic: "Look, I shall guide her to make her male. . . . For every female who makes herself male will enter heaven's kingdom." This statement is sometimes interpreted as an indication that the Gnostics believed that females were excluded from entering the celestial realm. However, in the same document Jesus seems to describe an androgynous Paradise: "When you make the two into one . . . and when you make male and female into a single one, so that the male will not be male nor the female be female . . . then you will enter [the kingdom of heaven]."[167]

The canonical Gospel of Luke says that Jesus rid Magdalene of "seven demons.,"[168] and Pope Gregory I in 591 merged Magdalene's identity with that of the unnamed female "sinner" who anointed Christ's feet.[169] Scripture offers no basis for regarding either her "demons" or her sins as sexual, but Magdalene nevertheless has come to be regarded as a penitent prostitute. In Victorian England charitable institutions for "fallen women"

6. SEQUANA, ROMANO-GAUL, c. 100 CE

were called Magdalenes. And in Ireland up until 1996 girls accused of sexual wrongdoing were virtually imprisoned in church-affiliated "Magdalenes," where they were forced to work without pay.

• • • •

It is not surprising that Christianity, striving to supplant thousands of years of goddess worship with a single male god, found it necessary to respond to deep-seated human deference and love for a mother. Thus, resourceful Church leaders might merge the identity of a cherished pagan goddess and a Christian saint, as happened when the Celtic deity Brigit was associated with a possibly legendary, possibly real, Irish abbess also named Brigit. Cementing the link between the two Brigits was the designation of February 1—the date of the festival *Imbolc* honoring the pagan goddess—as the feast day of the Christian nun.[170] Or, a pre-Christian goddess site might be converted to a Christian holy place. One such transformation took place at the temple complex devoted to the Celtic goddess of healing Sequana. After a Church council held at Auxerre in 585 banned worship at sacred lakes, springs, and rivers,[171] Sequana's devotees were offered a substitute deity named Sequanus who was not only Christian but male. Sequanus became the patron saint of a new Christian sanctuary about six miles from Sequana's healing waters. Today, one can visit the abbey and stroll in the garden, which is noted for its collection of medicinal herbs.

But Christianity's most profound answer to peoples' desire for a female deity was the elevation of the mother of Jesus. The Virgin Mary is not a primary character in the New Testament. Only the infancy narratives of Luke and Matthew give her any real prominence, while Paul refers to her in a single epistle, and then not by name. In the fourth century the Church Father Jerome composed a thesis entitled *On the Perpetual Virginity of the Blessed Mary* which underscored her supranatural character by asserting that she was not only a virgin but that her virginity was absolute, unaffected even by giving birth.[172] And Augustine of Hippo soon afterward pronounced Mary "a Virgin conceiving, a Virgin bearing, a Virgin pregnant, a Virgin bringing forth, a Virgin perpetual."[173] Thus, Mary became a being unlike any flesh-and-blood woman. Indeed, her uniqueness implied that the physical nature of ordinary women was innately defective, if not corrupt.

Devout women had helped to build Christianity. They had dedicated their labor and wealth to the young movement, had taken the risks and suffered the martyrdoms. The immensity of women's contribution was acknowledged by Augustine in a letter that chastised men for avoiding the moral responsibility conferred by baptism. "You are easily beaten by your women," he wrote. "Chaste and devoted to the faith, it is their presence in great numbers that causes the church to grow."[174] Yet as Christianity became the dominant religion of the West, women encountered a church hierarchy that deemed them unfit for spiritual leadership.

7   ILLUMINATING THE DARK AGES

Christianity had been at war with human sexuality ever since the Apostle Paul instructed the Corinthians, "It is well for a man not to touch a woman."[175] And although Christianity's anti-pleasure principle was not initially directed against women, it quickly acquired a decidedly misogynist cast. Before the end of the second century the theologian Tertullian had labeled women "the Devil's gateway." Blaming womankind for the primal sin in the Garden of Eden, he demanded, "Do you not know that you are an Eve?"[176] Observed the twentieth-century historian Eileen Power, "The view of woman as an instrument of the Devil, a thing at once inferior and evil, found expression very early in the history of the Church, and it was the creation of the Church."[177]

The conflict between spirit and (female) flesh deepened as the fourth-century Church fathers Jerome and Augustine of Hippo promoted the idea that sexual thoughts, feelings, and acts are wicked. Emphasizing sexual abstinence as the cornerstone of a virtuous life and the key to salvation, they recounted how they themselves had wrestled with sexual desire and exhorted others to do the same. Both contended that celibacy is a supreme good; and while Augustine permitted marital sex for the purpose of procreation, Jerome thought that to be certain of a welcome at Saint Peter's gate, married couples ought to agree to give up sexual relations entirely and live together as brother and sister.[178]

Saint Jerome's writings make clear his strong aversion to the female body. He asserted that for nine months Jesus had endured "revolting conditions" in the womb; that "women big with child are a revolting spectacle"; that a virgin ought to "blush at the thought of seeing herself naked"; and that not even the blood of martyrdom could wash away the defilement of the marriage bed.[179]

Devout Christian women searched for a way to overcome the stigma of femaleness. Some emulated the male hermits who went into the Egyptian desert to purify their minds and bodies through physical suffering. Others followed a less extreme course. Vowing perpetual virginity and donning veils, they dedicated their lives to contemplation, prayer, charity, and self-denial.[180] Ultimately, they created a new role in the Church hierarchy: the holy woman, or nun. Paradoxically, it was an identity that evolved as a by-product of the Church's teaching that women's bodies are corrupt and sexual relations, sinful.

The "virginity movement," as historian Jo Ann McNamara termed it, grew rapidly.[181] By the fourth century, maidens and widows who had renounced sex could be found in all the major cities of Roman Europe. While most continued to live in their family homes, small clusters of women pledged to celibacy gradually came together to share a common life. Ambrose, the bishop of Milan during the fourth century, described a group of twenty virgins in Bologna who dwelt under one roof and devoted themselves to menial labor, charity, and prayer.[182]

In Rome, Jerome became acquainted with a group of women who followed a severely ascetic lifestyle amid the luxury and decadence of the late imperial city. Although born to great wealth and high station, the women disdained the trappings of money, avoided social events, prayed assiduously, and gave liberally of their treasure to the poor. In addition, they inflicted various forms of physical discomfort on themselves, including heroic fasts and strict celibacy. In response to their entreaties, Jerome agreed to be their teacher and advisor. He subsequently formed spiritual and intellectual relationships with the widows Marcella and Paula and Paula's daughter Eustochium.

Jerome came to respect his Roman women friends for their learning and intelligence nearly as much as for their piety. He commended their penetrating questions and corresponded with them on complex points of Christian doctrine. Paula and Eustochium, who already knew Greek, studied Hebrew in order to better assist Jerome in his greatest labor, a Latin translation of the Bible. Unfortunately, the women's letters to Jerome were not preserved, only his part of the correspondence.[183]

Jerome's love for Paula and Marcella made him loath to thrust them into the same pit as the baser daughters of Eve. He asserted in a written tribute to Marcella that he judged virtue "not by the sex but by the mind."[184] Theorizing that a female who abstained from sexual intercourse became a virtual male, he advised a husband who had agreed with his wife to remain celibate that the wife was "once a woman but now a man; once an inferior but now an equal." Reiterating this notion in another context, Jerome wrote that a woman who "wishes to serve Christ more than the world . . . will cease to be a woman and will be called man."[185]

For hundreds of years afterward the biographies (or vitas) of saintly virgins praised their masculine strength of character. The vita of the seventh-century Abbess Austreberta, for instance, asserted that in avoiding a marriage bed the young girl had shown that "the heart in her breast was in no way feminine but virile." Similarly, the Abbess Burgundofara was said to have turned aside a suitor "not in a feminine manner but with a virile response," while the behavior of Abbess Rictrude had been "not womanlike but manly."[186]

To put the best face on it, this peculiar conceit may have stemmed from the stirring affirmation of the equality of the sexes expressed by Paul: "there is neither . . . male nor female; for you are all one in Christ Jesus." However, for medieval clerics that "one" was clearly a male. No woman, no matter how pious, could entirely cast off her female identity; indeed, professed virgins were commonly referred to as "brides of Christ," a designation which affirmed that they still occupied, if only symbolically, a subordinate, female status. Still, women who renounced sexual relations were automatically exempted from the supposed moral and intellectual feebleness of womankind. As honorary males, they enjoyed respect and even a quasi-clerical standing.

We cannot know what impelled individual Christian women to renounce sex, but piety may not always have been the sole motivation. Speaking with unusual candor, Bishop Ambrose of Milan pointed out that celibacy had practical advantages for women since it offered freedom from childbearing and from the "galling burden" of wifely subjection. Jerome, too, cited "the drawbacks of marriage, such as pregnancy, the crying of infants, the torture caused by a rival for her husband's love, the cares of household management."[187]

Professed virgins were not expected to observe strict seclusion. Those who took the veil at that early point in time could, and did, entertain guests of both genders, visit public baths, engage in business dealings, and go on pilgrimages. (A portion of a Latin narrative written by Egeria, a fourth-century virgin who toured holy sites in the East, has survived.) Regarded by ordinary mortals with deference, if not awe, the virgins had seats of honor in church, received Holy Communion before the rest of the congregation, and led religious processions on holy days.[188]

Several Churchmen felt it necessary to warn virgins against excessive pride.[189] And since they were not answerable to any man, they inevitably became the targets of salacious gossip. Jerome claimed that some alleged virgins were "nothing but tavern women" and that "even adulteresses may be found among them." Some, he said, "change their garb and assume the mien of men." They "cut off their hair and are not ashamed to look like eunuchs."[190] Concern for authentic celibacy sometimes became so overwrought that virgins suspected of violating their vow were examined by midwives to assure that their hymens were intact.[191]

• • • •

As the Roman Empire disintegrated, Germanic tribes invaded and took possession of the former Roman provinces. Ordinary life became increasingly difficult and dangerous, and a few monasteries in Gaul opened their doors to consecrated virgins to protect them from the ongoing violence. In the sixth century, Clotilde—the Christian wife of Clovis I, the king of the Franks—used her personal resources to fund the establishment of a female religious community at Andelys, near Rouen, and perhaps another at Chelles, near Paris. Later Clotilde's daughter-in-law Radegund donated a portion of the wedding gift she had received from her royal spouse to a similar retreat at Poitiers. Describing her motive, Radegund expressed a wish to "forward the cause of other women" and to "be of advantage to my sisters." Clotilde and Radegund both ended their days as widows in the religious houses (later called convents or nunneries) they had founded. When Radegund died, there were already some two hundred women in her Poitiers community.[192]

A convent founded by Bishop Caesarius of Arles for his sister Caesaria in 512 illustrates the speed with which monasticism took hold among Frankish women. Initially, the convent housed only Caesaria and two or three companions, but soon afterward, according to Caesarius's medieval biographers, "great numbers of virgins arrived there in throngs," and within about a dozen years, the abbess was "mother of over two hundred girls."[193] The majority were from wealthy families, but some women of lesser means also became brides of Christ in those early years since no entry fee (known as a dowry) was required of novitiates until the late 700's.[194]

A set of rules devised by Bishop Caesarius for his sister and her flock at Arles enjoined the "holy virgins" to relinquish all worldly possessions and live together as equals, regardless of their former rank. They were further instructed to eat a vegetarian diet, engage in frequent fasts, wear plain clothing that they manufactured themselves, and obey the abbess. Above all, they were to shun the gaze of men and never, under any circumstances, venture beyond the convent walls. Such rigorous enclosure was not a feature of any of the rules for monastic men, but it effectively silenced the rumors of immoral behavior that had plagued earlier, self-regulated virgins. Despite its severity, Caesarius's Rule for Virgins was adopted by other nunneries in the Frankish kingdom, including Radegund's convent at Poitiers.

Among several features of the Caesarius Rule that had a lasting effect on female monasticism was its emphasis on literacy. The sisters were required to "devote themselves to reading for two hours" each day and take turns reading aloud from edifying texts during mealtimes. Girls were not to be admitted to the nunnery until age 6 or 7, when they would be old enough to learn to read and write. And one of the sisters was to be appointed the community librarian.[195] Before long, nuns were better educated than nearly every other Western woman of the time and most secular men as well.

The Caesarius Rule was displaced after the mid-500's by the Benedictine Rule, a more lenient set of regulations that was designed to require "nothing harsh, nothing burdensome." Promulgated by an Italian monk, Benedict of Nursia, it was originally intended for monks but was quickly adopted by nuns as well. A Benedictine nun who felt a sincere religious calling—and was prepared to renounce the pleasures of the body, marriage, and children—could look forward to a satisfying life serving God and the Church, with the prospect of an eternity in Paradise. She would be provided with food, clothing, and a comparatively safe refuge from the ongoing civil disorder. She would never have to endure a loveless arranged marriage or the perils of repeated childbirths. Finally, she would be able to obtain an education; to devote time to reading and contemplation; to become acquainted with the finest art, music, and literature of the day; to develop her own talents; to exercise her leadership and administrative abilities; and to form friendships and love relationships with other women. It was a way of life with more abundant opportunities for self-realization than any that would be open to European women for generations, and many entered upon it eagerly.

On the other hand, not every woman who dwelt behind the walls of a convent had chosen to be there. Some women were enrolled as children before they were old enough to reason for themselves, and then, not knowing any other life and having no other options, stayed on; some became nuns to avoid a forced betrothal; some were unwed mothers, or widows without adequate support, or abandoned or abused wives. Nunneries also served as convenient dumping grounds for girls whose marital prospects were dim, and as virtual prisons for those who obstructed their families' financial, dynastic, or marital ambitions, or were accused of sexual transgressions.

A new form of monastic life in which nuns and monks lived under one roof was brought to the Continent by Irish missionaries in the early seventh century. In these communities, known as double monasteries, the monks performed much of the heavy labor and helped to guard against attack, while the nuns took over domestic duties, provided medical care, and tended vegetable and herb gardens. With their dormitories, infirmaries, chapels, cooking and dining facilities, workshops, gardens, orchards, and burial grounds, the double monasteries resembled small walled towns—towns that were usually governed by a woman, the abbess. Several of the Frankish kingdom's earliest nunneries were re-established as dual institutions, among them Chelles and Poitiers.[196] New double monasteries were frequently situated in the countryside so that local peasants who still clung to pagan ways might more easily be persuaded to convert.

The English did not fully embrace Christianity and begin to establish monastic dwellings until the early 600's. Since they were familiar with the renowned Benedictine double foundations in Gaul—some aristocratic Englishwomen had already crossed the Channel to study in them— many of the new English communities adopted the double model and the

Benedictine Rule. The abbesses who presided over them were invariably noblewomen and often members of royalty.[197] They exercised all the rights of landlords over their communities' properties, and some assumed broad ecclesiastic powers, including hearing confessions and assisting at the altar. Abbesses often traveled outside the walls, even making pilgrimages to holy sites in Rome.[198]

The medieval chronicler the Venerable Bede reported that Hilda, the seventh-century abbess of a double monastery at Whitby, hosted a historic synod attended by the king and chief noblemen of the region as well as by bishops and abbots.[199] Mildred, abbess of a double monastery on an island off the east coast of England near Dover, and four other English abbesses took part in a Church council held in the kingdom of Kent in about 700. The signatures of all five abbesses appear on a charter granting privileges to monasteries and churches.[200]

• • • •

Christian convents and monasteries were Western Europe's primary centers of learning. Nuns ran schools for local children, established libraries, and dispersed knowledge by interchanging manuscripts. An English bishop compared the nuns at Barking, a double monastery in east London, to busy bees, "roaming widely through the flowering fields of Scripture . . . scrutinizing with careful application the hidden mysteries of the ancient laws . . . exploring wisely the fourfold text [the Gospels] . . . rummaging through the old stories of the historians and the entries of chroniclers . . . sagaciously inquiring into the rules of the grammarians and . . . [of poetic] metrics."[201]

When the eighth-century missionary priest Boniface asked for nuns to assist him in his work on the Continent, thirty English sisters answered his call. It must have been a lonely and dangerous existence for these upper-class Englishwomen living in the midst of an alien and sometimes hostile populace in southern Germany. But even after Boniface and scores of his associates were murdered by pagans in Frisia, in the northern Netherlands, the women did not abandon their mission.

Medieval nuns also worked as scribes in workspaces known as scriptoria. Writing with split-reed pens (or later, feather quills) on bound sheets of specially prepared animal hide, they spent months or years copying a single manuscript. Often they worked long hours in bone-chilling cold with inadequate light. Although evidence attesting to the nuns' work was present all along, it is only relatively recently that historians have acknowledged that nuns as well as monks were scribes. A biography of Caesarius of Arles mentions that at his sisters' community "the virgins of Christ beautifully copy out the holy books, with their mother [the abbess] herself as teacher." A medieval biography of two Belgian sisters, Herlinda and Renilda of Maaseyck (now Maaseik), reports that their education in an eighth-century convent included "copying and illuminating."[202] And a letter from the missionary priest Boniface asks an English abbess to "copy out in letters of gold the epistles of my lord, St. Peter."[203]

Female scribes even signed their work on occasion. An eighth-century collection of Isidore of Seville's writings, for example, bears an unambiguous message: "I, Dulcia, wrote and signed (*scripsi et susscripsi*) this book." Such evidence would seem clear-cut, but as medievalist Suzanne Wemple explained, some historians simply dismissed female signatures "as attempts on the part of women readers to immortalize themselves, or alternatively, as garbled versions of masculine names."[204] As late as 1987, the respected multi-volume *History of Private Life* asserted, "Scribes were monks," and "It took a man a year to copy a Bible."[205]

Skepticism about the existence of female scribes was finally laid to rest by twentieth-century historians of women whose scholarly detective work succeeded in uncovering the lost history of female copyists. Historian Rosalind McKettrick, for instance, examined a group of manuscripts with female signatures from about the year 800. Realizing that the distinctive style of the lettering on the manuscripts indicated that they were the product of the same workshop, she compared them with other documents from the same period. After further study, she was able to pinpoint their source as a nuns' scriptorium in the double monastery of Chelles.[206] It is now clear that the labor of early monastic women helped to advance what was arguably the greatest achievement of the Middle Ages: the preservation of the cultural heritage of Western civilization. Those who signed their work were proud of it and hoped it would survive. Against all odds, some of it did.

Regrettably, that was not true of textiles, for the altar cloths, priests' robes, and other objects embroidered by medieval nuns seldom survived the passage of time. More durable, however, were book illuminations painted on vellum. The earliest known illuminations attributed to a woman are a series of brilliantly colored miniatures in a volume called the Gerona Beatus. Dated to about 975 and preserved in the treasury of Gerona Cathedral in Spain, these paintings have been called "one of the great achievements of mediaeval art." The nun who was their principal creator affixed a signature: "Ende painter and servant of God" ("*Ende pintrix et Dei a[d]iutrix*").[207] A twelfth-century German nun who created a self-portrait within an illuminated letter also signed her name: "Guda, a sinful woman, wrote and painted this book" ("*Guda peccatrix mulier scripsit et pinxit hunc librum*").

Several early literary works are now attributed to women. One of the earliest, a narrative written in English in 778, was considered anonymous until a historian deciphered a cryptogram which showed that the author was an Anglo-Saxon missionary nun named Huneberc (or Hugeberc) who resided at Heidenheim, a double monastery in Bavaria.[208] In a preface to her book, which recounts a monk's journey to Palestine, Huneberc took care not to be thought guilty of the sin of pride. She conceded that the reader might judge her presumptuous for undertaking to write a book when there were so many men who were "more outstanding, not only in being of the male sex, but also in their dignity of divine ministry," while she herself was "unworthy," "a little ignorant creature," "puny," and "corruptible through the womanly frail foolishness of my sex."[209]

Similar protestations are also found in the writings of Hroswitha (or Hrotsvit), a tenth-century poet and dramatist who lived in Gandersheim, a female religious retreat in eastern Germany. Hroswitha's literary work was admired and encouraged by the emperor Otto I and by his niece Gerberga, the abbess of Gandersheim.[210] Yet the writer repeatedly berated herself for lack of intellect and talent—deficiencies she attributed largely to gender. She complained that a certain poetic meter was "difficult and arduous for women, frail as we are"; she begged the reader not to scorn the "woman of no importance who played these melodies on a frail reed pipe"; and she expressed amazement at the idea that her noble patrons

7. GUDA SELF-PORTRAIT, TWELFTH CENTURY

thought the work of "a worthless little woman" deserving of their attention.[211]

This extravagant display of humility was a common medieval literary convention that men made use of too—although perhaps less effusively than women. Even Einhard, a leading scholar and the author of a widely admired biography of Charlemagne, described his literary powers as "feeble, scanty, next to nothing" and referred to his "little talents for composition."[212]

Peter Dronke, the foremost authority on women writers of the Middle Ages found the tone of the nun Huneberc's preface ambivalent, characterizing it as "half-fearful, half-defiant," a "mixture of confidence and diffidence."[213] As for Hroswitha, Dronke and others have commented that her apparent humility has an air of insincerity. There is an element of "deliberate over-acting," wrote Dronke, which can be interpreted as "ironic glances at the double standards... of the powerful male-dominated world."[214] Hroswitha's six plays—in which the female characters regularly outwit the male through courage and moral fortitude—support this assessment.

. . . .

In the early Middle Ages, when violence and disorder were endemic, the Roman Church stood strong, a pillar of stability in a turbulent world. By any reckoning, it was the most powerful institution in the West. Although respected Church spokesmen repeatedly denigrated womankind as morally weak and untrustworthy, nuns and abbesses discovered that by withdrawing from the world they had an opportunity pursue satisfying careers in the world. Some abbesses were renowned for virtue and learning not only during their lifetimes but even beyond. Remembered long after their deaths, they were elevated by common acclaim to the Christian sainthood. Newborns were named for them,[215] and their tombs became centers of cultic worship.

Literally, as scribes and illustrators, and figuratively—as philanthropists, educators, missionaries, and writers—holy women illuminated the Dark Ages. They comprised a small minority of women, most of them from the upper strata of society, but those willing to make the enormous sacrifices monasticism demanded could fashion productive, meaningful lives.

8 PEASANT WOMEN: THE POWER OF THE WEAK

In the medieval villages of Western Europe people who considered themselves Christians often continued to observe the customs of their pagan ancestors. Even as they went to church and recited the Lord's Prayer, they worshipped sacred trees, springs of water, and stones, and welcomed the new year by donning animal masks, cross-dressing (men as women), drinking, singing, and doing lewd dances.

These vestiges of paganism were anathema to the Church, but country folk were not easily persuaded to give them up, nor were they willing to forswear the use of amulets, charms, and magic potions. Even more distressing, they persisted in seeking advice from supposed "wise women." Two sixth-century Church councils denounced freelance female prophets as "pythonesses," a word that harked back to the Greek priestess of Apollo at Delphi, known as the Pythoness.[216] Caesarius, a sixth-century bishop of Arles whose sermons circulated throughout Christendom, warned: "When a woman recites an incantation, a serpent recites it."

Bishop Caesarius also criticized the mothers of sick children who, he said, were "wont to persuade each other that . . . they should consult that soothsayer or divine, that fortuneteller, that woman with a knowledge of plants." He imagined the mothers whispering to one another: "Let us sacrifice the clothing of the sick boy, his belt should be examined and measured; let us offer some magical spells, let us attach some charms to his neck." Mothers would do better, he said, to "ask the priest to anoint the child with blessed oil."[217] And he chastised women for attempting to control their reproductive lives. "Women do wrong," he said, "when they seek to have children by means of evil drugs," or "kill the children who are already conceived or born," or take "impious drugs to prevent conception." Although he was not without compassion for the poor, and he sympathized with mothers who feared they would be unable to feed another child, he urged women to have faith that God, who gave children to them, would provide for them.

Tales of miraculous cures brought about by prayer were common. A medieval biography of Bishop Caesarius, for example, claimed that while he was touring rural parishes, a girl complained to him that she was being beaten at night by a female demon called Diana. (It would not have escaped contemporaries that the demon bore the name of a pagan goddess.) Caesarius blessed the girl and gave her consecrated oil with which to anoint herself, and Diana soon was driven away.[218] A seventh-century saint's vita described a woman from Rouen who was relieved of pain in her feet and legs by praying to the Virgin. But when she accepted an herb from a "certain little woman" and tied it to her legs, her pain instantly returned.[219]

Still, it was obvious to everyone that women's herbal preparations sometimes worked, while the remedies offered by priests—basically, prayer and a few drops of holy oil—were not noticeably helpful, at least not in this life.[220] And at a time when forceps did not exist, when cesarean section could not be performed on a living woman, and when accurate information about reproduction was lacking, many women sought the aid of experienced midwives and herbalists, whose knowledge and skills had been passed down from mothers to daughters through the generations.[221]

To counter this reality, officials of the Church warned that female prophets were assisted by Satan, who was ever eager to ensnare the souls of wayward Christians. Bishop Caesarius explained that God sometimes permitted Satan to triumph as a test, to see if people who had resorted to unholy measures "afterwards more readily believe in the Devil." The sixth-century Bishop Gregory of Tours thought that spirits associated with the Devil had a certain "mystic potency" which enabled them to manipulate events. Satan, he cautioned, was "deceitful and malignant in purpose." Therefore, "women, cringing creatures, must always fear him."[222]

Yet despite the warnings, women continued to intrude upon territory clerics regarded as their exclusive domain. The missionary priest Boniface reported in the mid-700's that women had been seen "wearing pagan amulets and bracelets on their arms and legs and offering them for sale"—in the very shadow of Saint Peter's in Rome.[223] And as late as the ninth century, a Church council charged that "certain people, chiefly women," gathered on Christian holy days "to dance [and] to sing shameful words." Such women, the council added, were "behaving just like pagans."[224]

. . . .

One of the Church's most effective weapons in its struggle against the old religion was confession. Although penance was not officially adopted as a sacrament until the thirteenth century, the custom of seeking pardon for one's transgressions from a holy person began as early as the sixth century in Irish monastic communities and gradually spread through Christendom.[225] In the early years abbesses occasionally heard confessions, but later, only ordained priests were deemed qualified to impose penalties and grant absolution. The fact that priests alone were considered divinely empowered to save erring Christians from the torments of eternal hellfire enormously enhanced their authority.

To help simple clerics in country parishes assign appropriate penance, high-ranking Churchmen produced manuals known as penitentials between the sixth and twelfth centuries.[226] With the aid of these handbooks, forty-six examples of which are extant, we can virtually listen-in-on the questions medieval priests put to confessants.[227] The most influential penitential was that compiled by Burchard, a distinguished bishop in the city of Worms, south of Frankfurt. Volume nineteen of Burchard's twenty-volume work was titled the *Corrector* (or, as it sometimes appears, the *Physician*), "since it contains ample corrections for bodies and medicines for souls and teaches every priest, even the uneducated, how . . . to bring help to each person." Although produced between 1007 and 1012, the *Corrector* incorporates edicts from early Church councils as well as material from previous penitentials; thus, it is a selective compilation of the Church's teachings on sin as refined over half a millennium.[228]

The *Corrector* presents nearly two hundred queries a priest could recite word for word to confessants. Most were intended for both men and women, but forty-one of the questions were particularly for women—the first time a penitential had brought together transgressions considered specific to females.[229] In addition, some of the queries intended for either gender actually deal with offenses that were presumed to be chiefly, or even solely, committed by women. Thus Burchard's penitential offers rare insight into the milieu in which non-elite Christian women spun out their days.

Even a brief perusal of the *Corrector* shows that the Church viewed women as especially likely to perpetuate pre-Christian practices. Burchard instructed priests to ask each female confessant if she had ever participated in, or consented to, impious activities that were contrary to the teachings of the Church. Had she, for example, "done what some women filled with the discipline of Satan are wont to do," that is, removed the turf from people's footprints, hoping thereby "to take away their health or life"? Or had she done what "some women do at the instigation of the devil," that is, placed a stake in the body of a child who had died before being baptized, believing it would prevent the child's spirit from arising from the grave and doing harm? Or had she set the table with three extra knives, with the thought "that if those three sisters whom past generations and old-time foolishness called the Fates should come, they might take refreshment there" and in appreciation, bestow a favorable destiny on her family?

The form of penance most often doled out by Burchard was a severely restricted diet "on the appointed days" (usually comprising the month-long periods of Lent and Advent). He proposed five years' penance for a woman who had stolen people's footprints with the intention of harming them; two years for believing that the devil could take control of the body of an unbaptized child; and for a woman who had invited the Fates to dine at her table, one year. Among other penalties suggested in the *Corrector* are reciting the Psalms while maintaining an uncomfortable position, performing acts of charity, the payment of fines, and submitting to "palm thumpings."

Bishop Burchard inadvertently provided glimpses of the separate women's culture that existed in peasant villages. He described one pre-Christian female ceremony—performed when there was need of rain—in such striking detail that one suspects he had observed it himself. First, some of the older women in the community would assemble a group of girls. After selecting a "little maiden" as leader, they would undress her and tie a sprig of the herb henbane to the little toe of her right foot. With each of the other girls holding a sprig of henbane, the group would proceed to a nearby river. Using the sprigs, they would sprinkle the naked girl with water before leading her back to the village.[230]

Burchard also described offenses committed by women who wove and spun communally in textile workshops. Men's mistrust of the all-female world of the gynaeceum had existed for centuries. Hundreds of years before Burchard, the sixth-century bishop of Arles, Caesarius, had charged that some women "refuse to spin or weave on Thursday in honor of Jove [the pagan god Jupiter]." And his contemporary, Bishop Martin of Bracara Augusta (now Braga, Portugal), had condemned "women at their looms [who] call upon [the Roman goddess] Minerva."[231] Burchard's *Corrector* chastised women for reciting "counter-incantations of the devil" while weaving, in the belief that these unholy prayers would prevent the threads from becoming tangled. It further alleged that on January first, some women "at the prompting of the devil" hastened to "wind magic skeins, spin, [and] sew," in the belief that work begun on that supposedly lucky day would prosper.[232]

Several medieval penitentials described strange rites women allegedly carried out to ward off or cure illness. A penitential compiled in a monastery located in the northern tier of the Iberian Peninsula in about the year 800 directed, "If for the health of the living, a woman burns grains where a man has died, she shall do penance for one year." The English "Confessional of Egbert," compiled between 950 and 1000, assigned punishment to any woman who "places her daughter on the housetop or in the oven, wishing to cure her of a fever sickness." And Burchard prescribed appropriate penance for anyone who "collected medicinal herbs with evil incantations" as well as for any "foolish women" who may have poured water under the bier of a dead person "as a kind of means of healing."[233]

The celibate authors of the penitentials believed that women had voracious sexual appetites which they could not or would not govern. Saint, Jerome, whose writings were influential through the Middle Ages, declared, "Woman's love in general is accused of ever being insatiable.... put it out, it bursts into flame; give it plenty, it is again in need."[234] Saint Isidore of Seville argued incorrectly in the seventh century that the Latin word for woman, *femina*, was derived from the Greek *fos* (burning force), on account of the intensity of women's sex drive. "Females are more lustful than males," he wrote.[235]

Some clerics, tormented by their own sexual desires, accused women of using magical means to arouse men. A sixth-century Irish monk alluded to women who dispense a brew intended to encourage "wanton love," and a seventh-century penitential claimed that wives sometimes mixed semen into their husbands' food "for the increase of love."[236] A modern-day scholar who searched the extant penitential literature found twenty-six references to love potions allegedly brewed by women.[237] Burchard's *Corrector* advised priests to ask each female confessant if she had ever baked bread from dough kneaded on her bare buttocks with the intent of exciting a man's passion? Or had she perhaps stirred into her husband's dinner some little fish she had seasoned for a while near her genitals, or a few drops of her menstrual blood, or a bit of ash from a roasted testicle.[238] (Three hundred years after Burchard, a suspected heretic from a tiny village in the Pyrenees told a court of the inquisition that she had saved her daughter's first menstrual blood to use as a love potion to enchant a future son-in-law.[239])

The downside of according women the power to stimulate desire was that they might be equally adept at suppressing it. Thus, Burchard urged priests to ask women if they had ever used spells and incantations to "turn about the minds of men, either from hatred to love or from love to hatred." He warned that an adulteress who found out that her lover intended to wed someone else might use secret means to punish him by extinguishing his passion "by some trick of magic" that made him impotent.[240]

Nothing was too intimate for the probing queries of priests intent on rooting out sin. Burchard's questions for women included, "Have you fornicated with your little boy, I mean to say, have you placed him on your sex and in this way imitated fornication?" "Have you given yourself to an animal?" The *Corrector* encouraged priests to inquire particularly about women's sexual behavior when no men were present. What did they do "to assuage the desire that torments them" when they were alone with other women? Had they ever "made what some women are in the habit of making," that is, a device "of the right size for you," and "bound it to the site of your sex or that of a woman friend'"? Had they ever made use of an object of this sort on themselves?[241]

The medieval Church's catalogue of sexual sin was so all-encompassing that adults must have felt themselves to be under a cloud of iniquity much of the time. For example, husbands, who were theoretically in charge of when marital sex would occur, were directed to refrain from intercourse with their wives for three periods of forty days each—before Easter, Christmas, and Holy Cross Day (in September)—as well as on the nights preceding every Sunday, Wednesday, and Friday. That left roughly 140 "legal" days per year, not counting sundry holy days, days when wives had their periods, and the three months before and forty days after the birth of a child.[242]

Interestingly, Burchard adjudged the sexual practices of men and women differently. He assigned less severe penalties to women who sought pleasure with another woman than to men who engaged in homosexual activities. However, when it came to masturbation, he prescribed a year's penance to a woman who "practices solitary vice," a mere ten days to a man who "defiles himself." The seventh-century "Penitential of Theodore" also treated female masturbation much more severely than male. And like Burchard, Theodore punished male homosexuality more harshly than female.[243]

Even more worrisome than women who were temptresses or who made men impotent were those who employed *maleficium*, that is, malevolent magic. Especially at risk from female *maleficium* were husbands, for some Churchmen assumed that wives wanted nothing more than to overthrow the men who were their rightful sovereigns. This idea can be traced back to the early Church and Saint Jerome, who had warned that a wife who was thwarted in her wish to dominate was likely to "turn to strife and hatred, and unless you quickly take care, she will have the poison ready."[244]

Since a woman might be persuaded to reveal any hostile intentions she harbored toward her spouse in the confessional, Bishop Burchard directed priests to ask female confessants: "Have you concocted a deadly poison and killed a man" with it, or "wished to do so?" Have you done what "some women are wont to do," that is,

> . . . anoint their whole naked body with honey, and laying down their honey-smeared body upon wheat on some linen on the earth, roll to and fro often, then carefully gather all the grains of wheat which stick to the moist body, place it in a mill . . . and so grind it to flour; and then make bread from that flour and then give it to their husbands to eat, that on eating the bread they may become feeble and pine away.[245]

A tenth-century penitential compiled by the abbot Regino of Prüm, in Germany, described a particularly bizarre fantasy:

> Some wicked women perverted by the devil, seduced by illusions and phantasms of demons, believe and profess themselves, in the hours of the night to ride upon certain beasts with Diana, the goddess of the pagans, and [with many other women] . . . to traverse great spaces of earth, and to obey her [Diana's] commands. . . . An innumerable multitude, deceived by this false opinion, believe this to be true and, so believing, wander from the right faith and relapse into the error of the pagans.[246]

Burchard later included a version of this document in the *Corrector*, but with one significant change: the night-riding women now had murderous intent. Priests were to ask female confessants, Do you imagine you can "travel the earthly spaces" with a horde of equally deluded women,

> . . . and kill without visible weapons men baptized and redeemed with the blood of Christ, then together eat their cooked flesh, put in place of their heart some straw or wood or other material, and, having eaten them, make them live again, granting them as it were a truce?[247]

Burchard and Regino believed that women's fantasies of flying with Diana or doing harm to their husbands were a matter of delusion rather than malfeasance. That remained the Church's fundamental attitude toward *maleficium* until about the thirteenth century, when some ecclesiastics began to suggest that certain individuals were capable, with Satan's help, of doing *real* injury to others. It was this altered doctrine coupled with anxiety about religious heresies that ultimately resulted in the execution of tens of thousands of European women as witches.

But before that fatal turn occurred, pre-Christian beliefs and customs gave medieval peasant women an antidote to the misogyny of the Church. At a time when the Church demeaned and even demonized them, women found comfort and a measure of authority in the old religion. Even today it is possible to find women who lay claim to supernatural powers. The female psychics who profess an uncanny ability to solve crimes, the carnival fortunetellers and palm-readers who will predict a client's destiny for a fee, and the mediums who say they are able to contact the dead are debased incarnations of the trusted wise women of the Middle Ages.

9   IN AL-ANDALUS

In the year 711 a raiding party crossed the narrow channel that separates North Africa from the Iberian Peninsula and quickly overcame the Visigoth Christians who dominated the area. For two centuries the peninsula was riven with conflict as Arab and Berber chieftains battled one another for supremacy. Finally, the ruler of the kingdom of Córdoba, Abd al-Rahman III—a descendant of the powerful Umayyad Arab dynasty centered in Damascus—won control of all but the mountainous northern tier of the war-torn land. Acting boldly and decisively, the young monarch established a tenuous peace. In 929 he anointed himself caliph of the first independent Islamic state on the European continent, al-Andalus.

The founding of the caliphate marks the beginning of an era in which gender customs and laws of the Islamic world took root in Iberia, for although the population of al-Andalus consisted of more Christians than Muslims (with smaller numbers of Jews and indigenous peoples), many Christians converted to Islam, and Arabic became the official language of the cities. As the architecture, music, and food of al-Andalus grew to look, sound, and taste like that of Baghdad or Damascus, women adopted Middle Eastern dress, including face veils. Family life, too, came to reflect Middle Eastern tradition.

A study of women in Muslim Spain by historian María Viguera notes that the region's medieval literature rarely deals *directly* with women's lives and experiences, and what little information exists is concerned "almost entirely with Arabo-Muslim women of the upper class, or with those connected with them in some way." Yet by patiently culling literary, legal, and other materials that refer to women *indirectly*, historians have managed to compile an interesting, if incomplete, picture of the lives of women.[248]

The sources indicate, for example, that upper-class women were typically secluded behind the walls of the home, shut away from the sight of all men other than close relatives. On the rare occasions when they were permitted to venture out-of-doors—to attend weddings and funerals, or perhaps to go to the baths—they were expected to veil their faces. The primary aim of female enclosure, whether by walls or veils, was to control female sexual activity in order to ensure the paternity of offspring for inheritance purposes. Since this was of concern only to families with wealth, enclosure of women came to be seen as evidence of a family's high status as well as proof of the irreproachable respectability of its female members.[249]

A woman who dared to violate gender norms shamed not only herself but her entire kin group. Thus, daughters, wives, and sisters, although lacking agency themselves, were responsible for upholding the reputations of fathers, husbands, and brothers. Ironically, this anomalous situation gave women a certain perverse power over men. As a character in the drama *The Trickster of Seville* (*El Burlador de Sevilla*) points out to the legendary seducer Don Juan, fate had seen fit to place men's honor, the one thing they value most, in the hands of women, "who are all fickleness and lightness."[250]

The restrictions imposed on well-to-do women were somewhat mitigated by an extraordinary provision of the Qur'an that grants women, even wives, the right to inherit and control property.[251] Legal obstacles were placed in the way of women exercising these rights, and some women were doubtless vulnerable to pressure by male relatives, but judicial records indicate that many Andalusian heiresses managed their assets independently.[252] To own property—and to have the right to sell and bequeath it—confers a measure of power. Consequently, even wives who were under virtual house arrest might wield considerable authority within their households.

Although the Qur'an sanctions polygyny, the practice was not widespread in al-Andalus.[253] Concubinage, however, was common among men of high rank, irrespective of religion. For while Christianity forbid sex outside marriage, and concubinage was unusual in Jewish communities in other parts of the world, in al-Andalus, Muslim, Christian, and Jewish men alike had multiple sexual partners, both legal wives and slave-concubines.

Slavery was a fundamental component of the predominantly agricultural economy of al-Andalus, as it had been in the past when Romans and then Visigoths ruled the peninsula. The slave market in Córdoba—where female slaves outnumbered male—was one of the largest in the Muslim world.[254] The prospective purchaser had a wide array of women from whom to choose: perhaps a Christian from the Italian coast, the Frankish kingdom, or northern Spain; or a dark-skinned woman seized in Africa; or a blonde Slavic girl captured in central or eastern Europe and transported across the Continent by an international network of merchants who trafficked in human merchandise. The majority of enslaved women were agricultural or domestic workers about whom we know very little. But we know a bit more about the thousands of others who were specially selected and trained to provide entertainment and sex to men of wealth and power.[255]

Female slaves who served in the royal courts of the caliphate comprised an elite stratum of women in bondage. Called *qiyan*, they were educated from an early age in poetry, music, dance, and calligraphy. Elite men not infrequently had children with their *qiyan*. The offspring of such unions were born free,[256] and were entitled to inherit their father's wealth and social position. Indeed, Abd al-Rahman III himself had a mixed ethnic heritage. On the other hand, *qiyan* had no control over their life. They were dependent on their master's goodwill and were required to be sexually available to him.

A document ascribed to the medieval historian Ibn Hayyam describes the father of the first caliph, as "the most desirous of women and the fondest of sex" of all Andalusian rulers. He allegedly "kept a large number of *qiyan* . . . [who] would perform before audiences of male listeners from behind a curtain." A slave rarely emerges from behind the curtain of anonymity, but one who does is Fadl, described as a woman "of superior beauty, skilled in singing and of perfect qualities." Born and educated in Baghdad, Fadl was sent to Medina for musical training before she was purchased for the emir's harem and dispatched to Iberia. Installed in the palace, she became the ruler's favorite and had a son with him.[257]

The surviving sources do not refer to sex between women, but they openly refer to male homosexuality. For example, Abd al-Rahman III's son and heir to the throne, al-Hakam II, is said to have had a large number of male slaves who were his preferred sexual partners. But after he succeeded his father as caliph, al-Hakam was persuaded to marry so as to produce a successor.[258] The woman he wed, a Christian prisoner-of-war from northern Spain named Subh,[259] played a key role in his administration during his lifetime and after his death served for a time as regent to their young son. However, her former secretary, who was a trusted employee of the court, gradually gathered powerful supporters, and when he was ready, he deposed Subh, took control of the government, and reduced her son, the nominal caliph, to a mere figurehead.

· · · ·

Under the governance of the first caliph, Abd al-Rahman III, and his successors, al-Andalus prospered culturally and economically. The magnificent gardens and great libraries of its capital city, Córdoba, were without equal elsewhere in Europe. So celebrated were its wonders that the tenth-century writer Hroswitha, who lived in a distant convent in eastern Germany, had heard tales of its beauty and sophistication. In her *Book of Legends,* she likened Córdoba to ancient Rome: a "new imperial city, the glittering ornament of the world, shining in the western regions."[260]

According to the scholar and poet ibn Hazm, who lived in Córdoba in the early 1000's, women were an integral part of the city's labor force. He mentioned "the lady doctor . . . the blood-letter, the peddler, the broker, the *coiffeuse* (hairdresser), the professional mourner, the singer, the soothsayer, the schoolmistress, the errand girl, the spinner, the weaver, and the like." Not all these employments were considered respectable for women. Mourners, for example, were looked down on because they appeared in public without veils.[261] But even the meanest jobs gave those who performed them a livelihood as well as the freedom to move about in public spaces.

Ibn Hazm also wrote of an elite class of educated women who taught him the Qur'an, acquainted him with poetry, and trained him in calligraphy.[262] Other sources, especially biographical dictionaries, refer to women who worked as scholars, teachers, and copyists; were active in literary circles; and had knowledge of jurisprudence and medicine.[263] A few women were said to have prestigious positions within the court hierarchy, but their names are uncertain, their very existence shadowy. Historians suggest that Labbana (sometimes referred to as Lubna) may have acted as secretary to one of the caliphs, while Fatima and an associate, Layla, may have been in charge of acquisitions for the royal library.[264]

Who were these female intellectuals? Were they slaves or were some of them free? How were they educated? Were their number so few as to be merely grains of sand in a sea of women who were constrained intellectually and physically? Were some of them, as one writer has hypothesized, the "brotherless only daughters of well-off and cultured fathers who gave them the education that they would have given to male children, if they had had any"?[265] Regrettably, there are no answers to these intriguing questions.

We do know, however, that more than thirty Muslim women in medieval Andalusia wrote poetry, for they are mentioned by name in biographical histories and literary anthologies, and a small sampling of their work has survived.[266] Writing and sharing poetry was not just a pleasant pastime in the imperial courts, it was also a form of political and intellectual discourse, and mastery of its highly stylized conventions conferred respect and status on the authors. In addition, poetry written by women offers clues to the inner life of women who gloried in their freedom, disdained matrimony, and wrote openly about the pleasures and problems of love and love-making.

Al-Andalus's best-known female poet, Wallada bint al-Mustakfi, was born in Córdoba in the eleventh century. The only heir of one of the last caliphs, she inherited a fortune. Her rebelliousness was legendary. She refused to veil her face, wore immodest diaphanous robes, never married, and like the *salonistes* of sixteenth– and seventeenth-century France, hosted both men and women at intellectual gatherings held in her palace. Wallada's nine surviving poems include amorous lyrics addressed to her lover, also a poet, as well as blistering attacks on his virility written after she learned that he had been unfaithful to her.[267]

The poet Hafsa bint al-Hajj Arrakuniyya was a member of a twelfth-century noble family in Granada. In one poem, she promised that if her lover, the poet Abu Jafar, came to visit her, he would suffer neither thirst nor heat: "you'll find my mouth a bubbling spring and my hair a refugeshade," she coaxed. Their love affair ended tragically when the powerful governor of Granada became enamored of Hafsa and ordered the execution of his rival. Hafsa poured out her grief and rage in her last known composition, a poem that mourned Abu Jafar.[268] She later moved to Marrakesh, where she became a tutor in the families of Moroccan sultans.

Hafsa's contemporary in Granada, Nazhun al-Garnatiya bint al-Quali'iya, may have been a *qiyan*. Her verbal jousting with a well-known male poet was famous. When he taunted her in verse—"Nazhun's face has a slight touch of beauty, but under her clothes is disgrace"—she shot back: "Although I am a woman by nature, my poetry is masculine."[269]

In the era's brilliant flowering of Hebrew poetry, the work of just two Jewish women is known. A tenth-century poet known only as "the wife of Dunash Ben Labrat," wrote in Hebrew. Her only surviving poem is a tender farewell to her husband, who was involuntarily departing from Spain (perhaps banished), leaving behind her and their child. The second Jewish poet, Qasmuna bint Isma'il ibn Bagdalah, was the daughter of a poet. Her poems, three of which are extant, are written in Arabic.[270]

• • • •

So long as al-Andalus was a unified state, the cherished dream of reclaiming the entire peninsula for Christendom remained only that: a dream. But in the early eleventh century, al-Andalus gradually broke apart into dozens of contending city-states, and the impossible suddenly became possible. Toledo fell to Christian forces in 1085; Lisbon, in 1147; and in the first half of the thirteenth century, Córdoba and Seville succumbed.

The centuries-long wars of reconquest, known as the Reconquista, were especially perilous for women who lived along the shifting Muslim-Christian frontier since both sides viewed females as legitimate spoils of war, fair game to be raped, captured, and held for ransom, or if no ransom was forthcoming, sold into slavery. Yet despite the risks, women were among the earliest settlers in the new Christian towns established in the strife-torn, largely depopulated borderlands. Among those braving danger in order to start life afresh must have been wives fleeing abusive husbands, rural women escaping economic and sexual exploitation, female servants and slaves longing to be free, daughters rebelling against parental controls, poor women hoping to contract advantageous marriages, and destitute widows.

The fledgling Christian communities welcomed female settlers who, it was hoped, would help to repopulate the land and persuade fly-by-night male soldiers and fortune-seekers to settle down. The charters of some of the new towns granted women such valuable economic privileges that they became what one historian characterized as "a formidable presence in the property structure of the towns."[271]

In the turbulent world of the Reconquista, Muslims and Jews who lived in cities that were now under Christian governance suffered social and legal discrimination. A set of laws compiled during the 1200's under the direction of Alfonso X, the Christian ruler of Castile and Leon, authorized especially severe punishments for any Christian woman who had sexual relations with a non-Christian man. Thus, an unmarried Christian woman who had a Jewish or Muslim lover was liable to confiscation of her property, scourging, or death. A married Christian woman who committed adultery with a Jew could be publicly whipped and shut up in a convent for the rest of her life; but if her lover was a Muslim, she was to be "placed in the hands of her husband, who may burn her to death."[272]

Throughout the centuries when Christian forces were advancing across the Iberian peninsula, much of Andalusia continued under Muslim rule. The illustrious twelfth-century Muslim philosopher Ibn Rushd (Latinized as Averroes) pointed out that the sequestration of women—still widely practiced in the city of his birth, Córdoba—was harmful not only to women but to the entire community, especially because so many Muslim men had been lost to the Reconquista. In his *Commentaries on Plato's Republic*, he wrote:

> Our society allows no scope for the development of women's talents. They seem to be destined exclusively to childbirth and the care of children, and this state of servility has destroyed their capacity for larger matters. It is thus that we see no women endowed with moral virtues; they live their lives like vegetables, devoting themselves to their husbands. From this stems the misery that pervades our

cities, for women outnumber men by more than double and cannot procure the necessities of life by their own labors.[273]

Córdoba fell to Christian forces in 1236, not long after ibn Rushd wrote those words, but Granada remained a Muslim stronghold for another two hundred and fifty years. Not until 1492 did it finally surrender to the Catholic monarchs Ferdinand and Isabella, the last Muslim province to become part of Spain. Afterward, forced conversions, mass expulsions, autos-da-fé, and massacres reduced the population of non-Catholics in Spain and Portugal. Yet Muslim cultural traditions, especially those deep-seated customs relating to women and family life, persisted.

A case in point: the veiling of women's faces. In 1586, the Council of Castile, the chief body of advisers to the Crown, recommended outlawing the practice because—in addition to a general antagonism toward all things Muslim—it gave women the freedom to appear in public "as and when they please," while obscuring class distinctions.

The council explained:

> The custom of women to go veiled has become so excessive that it is now prejudicial to the best interest of the State, for, because of this fashion a father no longer recognizes his daughter, nor a husband his wife, nor a brother his sister. Women use the veil as and when they please and it gives men the chance to accost the wives or daughters of gentlefolk, as if they were people of low and vile character.

The king issued an edict in 1590 forbidding veils and imposing a fine on violators, but women continued to cover their faces. The law was renewed several times and the fine raised, to little avail.[274]

Another case in point: female seclusion. In *Don Quixote*, Miguel de Cervantes' seventeenth-century parody of Spanish society, a young Christian girl—the daughter of "a distinguished gentleman, and very rich"—is apprehended on the street at night dressed in boy's clothing. She explains that since the death of her mother ten years ago, her father has kept her indoors. "In all this time," she says,

> I have not seen more than the sun in the sky during the day, and the moon and stars at night, and I don't know what streets or squares or temples or even men look like, except for my father and a brother of mine. . . . I would like to see the world, or, at least, the village where I was born, and it seemed to me that this desire did not go against the decorum that wellborn maidens ought to observe.

The reality of seclusion was probably rarely that extreme by the time of Cervantes—*Don Quixote* is, after all, a satire. However, the traditional proverbs recited by Don Quixote's sidekick, Sancho Panza, no doubt reflected popular sentiment: "An honorable maiden and a broken leg stay in the house"; "a woman and a hen are soon lost when they wander"; and "a woman who wants to see also wants to be seen."[275]

• • • •

The women of al-Andalus can be glimpsed through the mist of time only dimly. They are half-hidden by veils, enclosed by the walls of a house, concealed behind curtains. They appear on the pages of history indirectly, in terms of their relationship to men rather than as individuals. They are captives being bought and sold in a slave market, for example, or anonymous employees in an urban workforce, or pioneers helping to settle and populate a frontier town. It is only an exceptional few to whom we can attach a name and a miniscule, tentative biography. It is often assumed that the obscurity of women is a consequence of lives lived in the shadows. Yet documents of the time show that some women were able to assert agency, protest, and even rebel against customs and laws that were harshly, sometimes cruelly, enforced.

10 WOMEN OF THE NORTHLANDS

The *Anglo-Saxon Chronicle* tells of a band of "heathen men" from the north who sailed toward the east coast of England in the year 793. Landing at the remote island of Lindisfarne, the site of a major Christian monastery, they wreaked "lamentable havoc in the church of God ... by rapine and slaughter."[276] The Viking Age had begun.

Throughout the next century Norse ships plied the oceans and waterways of Europe in search of treasure and slaves. Striking without warning, the Norsemen abducted, raped, and murdered, plundered castles, ravaged churches, and devastated some of Christendom's most important centers of learning, including the great double monasteries of Whitby in Yorkshire, Barking in London, and Chelles near Paris. In the first of several raids on the Iberian Peninsula, they attacked and looted the cities of Lisbon, Cádiz, and Seville.

Accurate information about women in the pre-Christian world of northern Europe is limited, for the people themselves left no written history. Nor are the ancient tales known as Icelandic Sagas entirely reliable as historical sources since they were transmitted orally for centuries before medieval scribes in the thirteenth and fourteenth centuries wrote them down. Nonetheless, the sagas constitute what one historian has described as "the richest and purest source extant for the ideas and attitude to life of the early Germanic peoples," and another credited with having preserved the "otherwise lost worlds of private life, social values and material culture."[277] Thus, they reveal a great deal about the lives of women.

Especially useful to historians of women are the forty narratives known collectively as the family sagas. It has even been suggested that one of them, *The Saga of the People of Laxardal*, was written by a woman, because of "its focus on women as leaders or instigators, its firm grasp of female psychology, its close attention to the details of women's routine life and its insights into the position, and lot of women—from the highest to the lowest ranks of life."[278]

Among the many memorable women of the *Laxardal Saga* is Unn (also known as Aud) the Deep-minded, a resourceful matriarch who migrated to Scotland from Norway along with her extended family in the late ninth century.[279] No sooner had they arrived in Scotland, however, than Unn's adult son was killed in a fight. Realizing that they were not safe there, she immediately made secret arrangements for a ship to be built, assembled a crew, and set sail for Iceland. "People say it is hard to find another example of a woman managing to escape from such a hostile situation with as much money and so many followers," comments the saga.[280] In Iceland, Unn took possession of a vast territory in the west and was the originator of an important dynasty.

Also found in the pages of *Laxardal Saga* is Melkorka, a proud slave-concubine—one of many female captives who were the mothers of future generations of Icelanders. Melkorka enters the saga when its hero, an Icelander named Hoskuld, visits a market located on an island off the coast of Norway in the mid- 900's. According to the saga, Hoskuld went into the tent of a Russian merchant and asked to buy a woman. The merchant lifted an inner curtain, and Hoskuld saw twelve women sitting behind it. One of the women, though poorly dressed and costing more than any of the others, appealed to him, and he decided to purchase her. The merchant warned him that she had not spoken a single word since her capture, although he had "tried in many ways to get her to speak." But her muteness did not matter to Hoskuld since it was not conversation he was seeking. He took possession of Melkorka and slept with her that very night.

Returning to Iceland, Hoskuld installed Melkorka in his home, where the main living space, as was customary in Icelandic farmhouses, consisted of a single large room shared by husband, wife, children, and domestic servants. Although concubinage was common in Iceland, familiarity evidently did not eliminate jealousy, for when Hoskuld asked his wife, Jorunn, to show Melkorka respect, she answered, "I've no intention of wrangling with some slave-woman you have brought home from Norway who doesn't know how her betters behave, least of all since she is obviously both deaf and dumb." That winter Melkorka gave birth to a son, and Jorunn's antagonism increased.

One day an amazed Hoskuld overheard Melkorka, who had been entirely mute to that point, speaking to their child. When he confronted her, she broke her silence and told him that she was the daughter of an Irish king. After she was kidnapped at the age of 15 and sold into slavery, she told him, she had vowed never to speak to her captors—a vow she had kept until that day. Jorunn was skeptical about her rival's alleged royal birth and continued to treat her with contempt, which was apparently more than Melkorka's pride could tolerate, and the two women came to blows. Hoskuld settled the matter by moving his concubine and their son to a separate farm, where he continued to provide for them.[281]

Marriages in pre-Christian Iceland were negotiated between the prospective groom and his male relatives on one side, and the male relatives of the bride-to-be on the other, with little or no regard to the woman's wishes. Although Christianity disapproved of forced marriage, betrothals in Iceland continued to be arranged by men alone long after Christianity became the official religion. Indeed, the secular laws of Christian Iceland (and Norway, too) imposed penalties on women who dared to wed against the wishes of their kinsmen.[282] Even Jorunn, who is characterized in *Laxardal Saga* as "proud" and "headstrong," bowed to custom when it came to choosing a mate—or so the saga reports. For when she is asked her opinion of Hoskuld, a suitor for her hand, she responds, "my father will have the deciding say, as I will abide by his wishes."[283]

Prenuptial financial settlements often included both a Roman-style dowry that the bride's family gave to the groom and a Germanic-style bridegift that the groom presented to his new wife and her parents. Divorce could be initiated by either spouse and was easy to obtain—even the nebulous charge of incompatibility was sufficient grounds. One historian has counted twenty completed divorces in the saga literature, two-thirds of them initiated by the wife. A divorced woman was entitled to everything she had brought into the marriage as well as part of the assets acquired during the marriage. If she could show that her spouse was to blame for the breakup, she could reclaim her dowry and also a portion of the bridegift.[284]

Widowhood was common since the northern sea, as one saga observes, was a "killer of ships,"[285] and in addition, men often settled disputes with battle-axe and sword. Widows were granted authority in many affairs that were normally the province of men, and unlike first-time brides, they had the right to refuse a proposed remarriage. Easy divorce plus frequent widowhood resulted in a sort of serial monogamy for some women. And given inheritance customs—which passed estates to widows if there were no children, and to daughters if there were no sons—some women were able to accumulate substantial assets.

The sagas reveal that it was customary for farm wives to be entrusted with the management of the household. Thus, the hero of *Njal's Saga* grants his new bride "full authority over matters inside the house." When a man comes to their door seeking work and asks for Njal, he is told, "I am Njal's wife, and I have no less authority in hiring than he does."[286] As in other seafaring societies, women's responsibilities multiplied while the men were away. In *Laxardal Saga*, Jorunn supervised the farm and the children for a year while her husband Hoskuld was gone. Another saga woman, Thorbjorg, is described as a "a person of great magnificence, and tremendously wise," who was "the leading personage of the district and managed everything when Vermund [her husband] was away." In *Egil's Saga*, the hero's wife looks after the farm for two years while her husband is abroad.[287]

The saga women are portrayed as strong individuals with particular personalities, strengths, and weaknesses. Some had special qualities or skills that were recognized in an epithet; thus, we read of Unn the Deep-minded, Thorhild the Poetess, Hildigunn the Healer.[288] Some are praised with words that have a masculine connotation in Icelandic, such as "valiant" (*drengr*) or "forceful" (*skorungr*).[289] Vigdis, in *Laxardal Saga*, is said to be "made of sterner stuff than her husband." When he objects to her decision to shelter a man who is being sought for murder, Vigdis responds, "I have already promised him lodging, and do not intend to go back on my word." When her husband subsequently betrays the whereabouts of his unwelcome houseguest, Vigdis helps the wanted man escape and soon afterward declares that she is divorcing her weak-willed mate.[290]

Women use sex, money, and taunts to bend men to their will. In *Gisli Sursson's Saga*, Thorkell accuses his wife, Asgerd, of infidelity and orders her from his bed. Although Thorkell's accusation may have been deserved, Asgerd responds by threatening, "I am not going to argue with you about whether I may sleep in this bed or not. You have a choice—either you take me in and act as if nothing has happened or I will call witnesses this minute, divorce you and have my father reclaim my brideprice and my dowry. Then you wouldn't have to worry about my taking up room in your bed ever again." Thorkell decides to drop the matter, and "they had not been lying together for too long before they made up as if nothing had happened."[291]

The plot of *Laxardal Saga* pivots on the actions of determined women who ridicule their menfolk's virility and goad them into defending the family's honor. The women are brutal, even bloodthirsty, by modern standards, but in upholding the rigorous Viking code, they are doing exactly what good Viking wives were expected to do. When Gudrun's five brothers balk at her insistence that they must kill a man who humiliated their family, she jeers, "With your temperament, you'd have made some farmer a good group of daughters." And when her husband is loath to join in the plot, Gudrun threatens that if he refuses to participate, "it will be the end of our life together."[292] When the men finally commit the murder, it leads to two more killings, both also instigated by women.

The survival of the Icelandic community depended in large part upon the labor of women. It was they who milked the cows and sheep and prepared the dairy products that were a staple of the diet. They, too, were responsible for the production of textiles—from the shearing of the sheep to the fashioning of warm woolen garments and ships' sails. By the late eleventh century, textiles made in Icelandic farmhouses were the nation's major export. Thus, it was women who provided the trade goods that were exchanged for essential commodities unavailable in Iceland, such as flour and timber.

Before long woolen homespun was recognized as legal tender in Iceland. Rents could be paid and debts acquitted with lengths of cloth. The unit of value was an ell, roughly 18 inches (45.7 centimeters), or about the distance from a man's elbow to the tip of his hand.[293] A cow, for instance, was valued at 72 to 100 ells of homespun.[294] Not since the Greek Mycenaean era was spinning as fundamental to the economy of a community as it was in Iceland during the era when homespun served as a national currency.

....

Long after missionaries brought Christianity to the northlands, ancient myths, beliefs, and practices persisted. Thus, while the sagas mention numerous women who eagerly embraced the new faith, they also tell of women who refused to convert, one of whom was Steinunn, the mother of an Icelandic poet. According to *Njal's Saga*, Steinunn "preached heathenism and lectured at great length" to a Christian missionary who was visiting Iceland. She also recited a poem of her own composition that lauded the power of Thor and mocked Christ because he had failed to prevent the recent destruction of the "sea's horse," the missionary's ship, the *Bison*:

> The slayer of the son of the giantess [that is, Thor]
> smashed *Bison* on the sea-gull's rest [the ocean];
> no help came from Christ
> when the sea's horse was crushed.[295]

The great thirteenth-century Icelandic writer Snorri Sturluson commented that in Asgard, a home of the gods, the female deities were said to be "no less sacred and no less powerful" than the male. Frigg, the wife of Odin, knew "the fates of all men"; Freyja, "the most renowned of the goddesses," went on long journeys "in a chariot drawn by two cats"; Gná sat astride "a horse that runs through the air and over the sea"; the women called Valkyries directed battles and chose which men would die and which would be victorious.[296] In *Njal's Saga*, the Valkyries weave the fate of warriors on a dreadful loom that uses men's intestines for the warp and weft and the severed heads of men as weights.[297]

On remote Greenland, where pagan beliefs persisted longer than in Iceland, many people continued to attribute supernatural abilities to certain mortal women who, they believed, could foretell the future, cast spells, shift shape, and magically affect events. A remarkable passage in *Eirik's Saga* tells of a time of famine in Greenland when a well-to-do farmer invited a woman known as the Little Sybil to his home, hoping to learn from her how long the food shortage would last. The Little Sybil is described as the last of her line, the only survivor of ten sisters, all of whom had been prophets (*völvur*). Thus, she is a representative of a rapidly disappearing pagan world in which some women were thought to have powerful spiritual gifts.

When the prophet arrived at the farm, the assembled guests welcomed her deferentially. The saga provides a vivid picture of her appearance:

> [She] wore a blue mantle fastened with straps and adorned with stones all the way down to the hem. She had a necklace of glass beads. On her head she wore a black lambskin hood lined with white cat's fur. She carried a staff with a brass-bound knob studded with stones. She wore a belt made of touchwood, from which hung a large pouch, and in this she kept the charms she needed for her witchcraft. On her feet were hairy calfskin shoes with long thick laces which had large tin buttons on the end. She wore cat-skin gloves, with the white fur inside.

Seated on a high cushion, "which had to be stuffed with hens' feathers," the Little Sybil was offered a ritual meal consisting of a gruel made from goat's milk and the hearts of various animals. The next day, she asked if any of the women knew the songs necessary for performing her magic. Gudrid Thorbjornsdottir, an Icelandic woman who happened to be in Greenland at the time, had been reared by a pagan foster mother and had learned the songs as a child. Although she was a Christian, she reluctantly agreed to participate in the pre-Christian rite to oblige the people of the district. The prophet seated herself at the center of a circle of women, and Gudrid sang the songs. Afterward, the sybil predicted that the famine would ease in the spring.[298]

On her return to Iceland, Gudrid heard that Leif Eirikson had obtained a rich cargo by sailing west to a previously unknown place called Vinland. She urged her husband, Thorfinn Karlsefni, to try his luck there, and he agreed to go. Thorfinn assembled a company of about a hundred men and five women, including Gudrid and Leif's sister, Freydis. The ships also carried livestock of all kinds since the Icelanders intended to establish a permanent colony.

In Vinland, they constructed shelters and settled in. Gudrid gave birth to a son, Snorri, the first European born in North America. But after trading peacefully with Vinland's native inhabitants for some time, a battle broke out. Karlsefni's men started to retreat, but Freydis, who was pregnant at the time, taunted her compatriots for their cowardice and moved onto the field of battle. As the natives closed on her, she took up a sword and prepared to defend herself. Recounts *Eirik's Saga*:

> She pulled one of her breasts out of her bodice and slapped it with the sword. The [natives] were terrified at the sight of this and fled back to their boats and hastened away. Karlsefni and his men came over to her and praised her courage.

Soon afterward, discouraged by the hostility of the local people, the Karlsefni group abandoned the settlement and returned to Greenland.[299]

A second Vinland expedition, this one organized by Freydis herself, is described in the *Greenlanders Saga*. At Vinland, according to the saga, Freydis and her crew encountered a rival expedition made up of thirty men and five women from Greenland. That night she ordered her men to murder the Greenlanders. They proceeded to carry out her command, but after slaughtering the men, they balked at killing the women, so Freydis took up an axe and dispatched the women herself.[300]

For centuries, the location of Vinland was unknown. Many people considered it a figment of the fertile imagination of the saga writers. But in 1961 a Norwegian explorer, Helge Ingstad, found medieval Norse building-sites in the fishing village of L'Anse aux Meadows, on the coast of Newfoundland, Canada. Archaeologist Anne Stine Ingstad, his wife, oversaw the excavation of eight sod structures that were similar in style to some previously found in Greenland. The settlement was unquestionably an early Norse camp whose date of construction, about five hundred years before Columbus, is consistent with the approximate date of the sagas' Vinland expeditions. Remarkably, the presence of women on the site was established by artifacts recovered there: a whetstone for sharpening needles, a sewing needle fashioned from a bone, and a soapstone spindle weight which resembles weights found in Greenland.[301]

. . . .

The women of the medieval northlands did not occupy public office at any level, could not testify as witnesses in trials, lacked equal inheritance rights, and could be forced to wed a man chosen for them by their fathers. But within their world, wisdom, competence, industry, independence, and determination were as highly esteemed in the female as in the male. And some women were accorded special respect because of their supposed ability to see into the future.

The saga women were physically strong, proud, and courageous, but they could also be murderously vindictive, arrogant, and cruel. Like their Viking ancestors, they were dauntless travelers, and when they journeyed from their homes in Scandinavia to settle in other lands, they brought with them their unique gender heritage.

11   HERETICAL WOMEN

The Catholic Church, grown fat in its immense wealth and power, was riddled with corruption. Clerical posts were sold to the highest bidder (simony), papal pardons (indulgences) could be purchased for a fee, members of the upper clergy ate and drank to excess, and priests and monks lived openly with wives and concubines—a practice forbidden by three twelfth-century Church councils.[302] Many Christians, aspiring a purer, more meaningful spiritual life, joined one of the dissident religious sects that had recently sprung up across Europe.

One such group, the Cathars (or Albigensians), gave women unique opportunities for religious leadership. Catharism was a dualist Christian faith that posited two deities: an evil God (Satan) who created the material world and a righteous God who created the immaterial realm of spirit. Followers of the sect rejected the sacrament of the Eucharist because the wafers and wine consisted of matter and so were not holy. They did not attend church services since church buildings were mere wood and stone and were therefore earthly rather than divine. And they did not feel obliged to pay tithes to the degenerate clergy of a false church.[303]

The first indication that Cathar-like beliefs had spread from Eastern Europe into the West came in a letter sent in 1143 to Bernard of Clairvaux, a noted foe of heresy. The letter-writer, the prior of a German abbey, informed Bernard that a congregation of heretics who rejected the material world had been taken into custody in Cologne. They "have among them women vowed to continence," he wrote, adding caustically, "so they say."[304] Bernard was equally skeptical of the women's chastity. But their sexual practices were not his sole (possibly not even his main) concern, for in his view, heretics threatened the essential building block of society, the family. "Women are leaving their husbands," he warned in a sermon he delivered the next year, "men are putting aside their wives, and they all flock to those heretics!" No doubt he was speaking metaphorically when he counseled that the Church ought to pluck out the eyes, cut off the hands, and cast out all such transgressors.[305] Eight men and three women of the group apprehended in Cologne were burned at the stake. Nonetheless, Catharism continued to grow and attract followers, especially in Languedoc, a semi-independent province in southern France with a distinctive culture and a separate language (the *langue d'oc*).

The magnitude of women's role in Catharism might have become another lost chapter in the history of women, were it not that the proceedings at courts of inquisition held in Languedoc in the early 1200's were recorded and preserved. What this extraordinary archive reveals is that thousands of women risked imprisonment, torture, and death to support and serve the Cathar movement for one hundred and fifty years.

What drew women to Catharism? Undoubtedly they, like men, found in the faith a chance to express their religious beliefs within a church they perceived as morally legitimate. But some historians have also cited motives specifically related to gender. The preeminent authority on medieval Toulouse, the capital of Languedoc, has suggested that women felt themselves oppressed and therefore "sought a faith other than that taught by members of the dominant sex." Possibly, he wrote, "women were more inclined than were men to question the values of the world in which they lived" and as an exploited group were "a naturally rebellious or even revolutionary element in society."[306] In the same vein, the distinguished medievalist Jacques Le Goff wrote, "The part played by women in medieval heretical movements, especially Catharism . . . is a sign of their dissatisfaction with the place which was allotted to them."[307]

The place allotted to the female sex was summed up in about 1140 by Gratian, a Catholic jurist from Bologna whose monumental compilation of Church law, the *Decretum*, was one of the most influential documents of the Middle Ages. "The natural order for mankind," the *Decretum* declares, "is that women should serve men . . . for it is just that the lesser serve the greater." It further asserts, "Woman's authority is nil; let her in all things be subject to the rule of man."[308] Similar views were trumpeted from pulpits all across Christendom. Jacques de Vitry, a Belgian priest who was an outspoken opponent of Catharism, delivered a sermon in which he proclaimed that the female sex was "weak," "not to be trusted," "wanton," "slippery like a snake and as mobile as an eel."[309]

The same message was communicated nonverbally in the stone carvings people saw every Sunday in church. For much as we admire the skill and artistry of Romanesque art, it sometimes conveys a disturbingly malevolent view of womankind. The doorframe of the twelfth-century Benedictine Abbey of Saint-Pierre at Moissac in Languedoc, for example, depicts a naked woman who, having been consigned to hell, is being devoured by snakes and toads. Any medieval person would have recognized that woman as *Luxuria* (Lust), a stock character in the iconography of the time.[310] Another twelfth-century depiction of *Luxuria*, this one from a church in Alsace, shows her with a snake issuing from her vagina, slithering across her abdomen, and suckling at her breast.[311] Women also fare poorly in the rendition of the Last Judgment that soars over an entranceway to Saint Lazare Cathedral at Autun. This magnificent work shows, amid images of frightening demons and terrible tortures, only two women headed for heaven, while four are condemned to hell.[312] For churchgoers of the time, most of whom were illiterate, such carvings were, in effect, sermons wrought in stone.

Cathars, though hardly egalitarian, endorsed the fundamental Christian principle of the spiritual equality of the sexes. As a shepherd from the Pyrenean village of Montaillou told a court of inquisition, "I have heard it said by the heretics that the souls of men and women are the same and there isn't any difference between them. The only difference between men and women is in their flesh, which is the work of Satan."[313] Moreover, unlike the Roman Church, Catharism honored this principle in deed as well as word by giving women the opportunity to become ordained ministers.

Cathar priests were called Good Men and Good Women, but also "perfects," a name that started as a term of derision but lost its negative connotation. The high esteem that the female perfect enjoyed in the Cathar community was such that all believers—male and female, highborn and peasant—were expected to venerate her by genuflecting three times whenever she passed and reciting a prayer that began, "Bless us, good lady."[314]

The Good Women lived communally in houses situated throughout Languedoc, supporting themselves by spinning, weaving, and sewing.[315]

Inquisition witnesses spoke of fifty such dwellings at Mirepoix, as many as a hundred at Villemur, each of which accommodated up to twenty residents. While female perfects were required to observe a severely restricted diet, engage in rigorous fasts, and remain celibate, the ambience of their houses, as described by people who had visited them, was warm and welcoming. The residents were of varying ages and life circumstances, and often included mothers and daughters, pairs of sisters, and widows, as well as children, grandchildren, and temporary guests. Female perfect houses also served as havens for unhappy wives. A noblewoman named Azalaïs testified that when she herself was a child, her mother had fled from their home in Mirepoix to a Good Woman residence in another town. Later her mother secretly retrieved her, and both continued to live with the Good Women until Azalaïs left to get married.[316]

Researchers who analyzed the testimony given at a court of inquisition in one district of Languedoc found that about 45 percent of the Cathar ministers named by witnesses were women. Such a substantial female presence in a religious ministry would itself be impressive, but the researchers added that this estimate might be too low since women noticed other women more frequently than men noticed women, and less than a third of the witnesses deposed were female.[317]

Good Women had the right to administer the consolamentum, the fundamental sacrament of the sect. This all-purpose blessing, which was used to initiate converts, ordain new ministers, and purify the souls of the dying, was performed whenever possible by Cathar bishops, their assistants, or deacons—all of whom, so far as we know, were male. But according to an inquisition witness, the Good Women were fully empowered to bestow the consolamentum, "and men as well as women can receive [it] from them at the moment of death, so long as there are no Good Men present; and those who are received by Good Women are saved just as if they had been received by Good Men."[318] Observed one historian, "To be one of the 'perfect' gave a woman a higher status in the Cathar Church than she could ever attain in its Catholic rival."[319]

By the latter decades of the twelfth century, Catharism had become a full-fledged church with dioceses in four Languedoc cities—Toulouse, Albi, Agen, and Carcasonne—with a bishop in each.[320] Priests affiliated with the Roman Church attempted to coax the lost sheep back to the fold by means of sermons, threats, and public debates, but had little success. The popular mood in Toulouse, the capital city of Languedoc, can be gauged by the hostility that greeted a delegation of high-ranking Catholic officials who toured there in 1178. Reported one of the visiting priests: "As we pursued our proper course through the streets," the local people "railed at us, pointed their fingers at us, shouted at us that we were impostors, hypocrites."[321]

The next year, the Third Lateran Council noted that followers of "the loathsome heresy" of Catharism had grown "so strong that they [the heretics] no longer practice their wickedness in secret, as others do, but proclaim their error publicly and draw the simple and weak to join them."[322] The council placed Cathars and their defenders "under anathema." But Rome's condemnation failed to slow the sect's growth.

The murder of Pope Innocent III's legate to southern France in 1208 provided justification for the pope to launch a military invasion of Languedoc led by barons from northern France. The resulting conflict, known as the Albigensian Crusade, lasted for twenty years. Unlike the Fourth Crusade in the East that the Pope had recently invoked, this was not a holy war against "infidels," nor was it yet another assault on communities of Jews. Rather, it was an attack on Western European Christians. Religious fervor no doubt motivated the rank and file of the army, but its leaders had another object as well, for the king had promised them access to Languedoc's rich farmlands and profitable commerce as war booty.

The soldiers of the Albigensian Crusade slaughtered Cathars and other Christians as mercilessly as earlier crusaders had shed the blood of Muslims and Jews. When the citizens of the town of Béziers refused to turn over local heretics, nearly the entire population was slain. The crusaders forced their way into the fortified city of Carcasonne, where many terrified Cathars had taken refuge, and drove them out. In Lavaur, south of Albi, the invaders allegedly hung or beheaded eighty defenders of the town and burned alive four hundred Good Men and Good Women. At Marmande, a small town near Bordeaux, the populace was decimated.

8. CATHAR EXPULSION FROM CARCASONNE IN 1209

Wrote one chronicler: "They killed all the townsmen with their wives and children, everyone, up to the number of five thousand."[323]

The women of Languedoc joined the struggle to defend their political and religious independence. A chronicler reported that during a nine-month siege of Toulouse, which began in 1217, damage to the city wall was repaired by "ladies and squires, girls and boys, great and small," all of whom "carried up the hewn stones singing ballads and songs." A nineteenth-century fresco in Toulouse's Capitole shows women and men together hurling stones from the building's battlements.[324] According to legend, it was a projectile fired by a woman that caused the death of the commander of the attackers, Simon de Montfort. The slaying of de

Montfort was followed by a six-year interlude of relative peace, after which fighting resumed and continued until the Languedoc forces surrendered. In 1229, a large part of the devastated south was ceded to the king of France. Two years later, Pope Gregory IX authorized a formal inquiry into the "loathsome" sect.

Charged with rooting out heresy, the Dominican friars who were the chief inquisitors interrogated suspects under torture, threatened them with execution, and—a key element—demanded that they name fellow heretics. Those who confessed and repented received comparatively light sentences, but those who denied the charges, or who confessed under torture and later relapsed, could be sentenced to be burned at the stake, a nasty job that was left to civil authorities. Such was the vehemence of the courts that bodies of long-dead heretics were exhumed and the bones burned. The people hated the Dominican inquisitors. In 1235 in Toulouse they were run out of town; a Dominican monastery in Narbonne was sacked the same year; and in 1242 two inquisitors were murdered at Avignonet.[325]

As the inquisition tightened its grip, the Good Women houses were disbanded. Some Good Women relinquished their distinctive dark robes and fled into the forests. Like resistance fighters in an occupied land, they took up a clandestine existence, keeping to the back roads and sheltering here and there with sympathetic villagers while continuing to proselytize. A few evidently dared to speak in public during this perilous period. One confessed to inquisitors that she herself had "preached" twice in the 1240's and had been present when other Good Women had risked their lives by delivering public sermons.[326] Some Cathar supporters fled to Spain or Italy; others sought refuge with sympathetic noble families in Languedoc.

A castle perched atop a steep limestone spur in the township of Montségur was one such refuge. This precipitous eagle's nest—the property of a Cathar Good Woman—became home to some four to five hundred people, among whom were noble families with their attendants, female and male perfects, and a hundred or so soldiers with their wives and children. In 1243, an army of about ten thousand soldiers loyal to France and the Church laid siege to the castle and a year later its defenders, cut off from food and other essential resources, were forced to surrender.

While inquisitors set up an impromptu court in Montségur and began to interrogate the Cathar perfects, French soldiers built a large wooden enclosure and filled it with flammable materials. Threatened with death unless they agreed to disavow their faith, approximately two hundred women and men chose death. Among those whose names we know were seventeen women, including the wife of a soldier, a seamstress, and the owner of the castle with her daughter-in-law and granddaughter.[327]

The fiery end of the defenders of the castle at Montségur marked the end of Cathar resistance. As the ravaged territory of Languedoc was absorbed into the kingdom of France, the Church reasserted its religious authority in the region. A key step was an edict issued by a council of bishops at Albi that ordered priests to provide children with a correct (that is, non-Cathar) understanding of the faith.[328] But perhaps nothing better exemplifies the Church Triumphant than Albi's vast, fortresslike Sainte-Cécile Cathedral. Begun in 1282, it was an awesome symbol of the overwhelming power of Rome.

· · · ·

The Roman Church was confronted with another challenge to its authority in 1173 when Peter Waldo, a wealthy merchant from Lyon, gave away his property and adopted a lifestyle of extreme poverty. Waldo attracted a large number of followers—women and men who, like him, wanted to emulate in their everyday lives the austerity and high moral purpose of the apostolic Church. Next, he took an unprecedented step, one that would have far-reaching consequences: He commissioned translations of portions of the Bible from Latin into the local language, Provençal, and instructed his disciples (most of whom could not read) to memorize passages and recite them in public places. As a result, many common folk had an opportunity to hear for the first time the sacred texts of Christianity in a language they could understand.

To make the Bible accessible to the masses would seem a harmless, even laudable, endeavor, but it provoked the wrath of the Church.[329] Bernard Gui, a Dominican inquisitor in Toulouse, remarked that Waldo had "made men and women his accomplices, and sent them out to preach as his disciples. They, men and women alike, although they were stupid and uneducated, wandered through villages, entered homes, [and] preached in the squares and even churches." Gui further charged that the

Waldensians allowed any follower to perform the sacrament of the Eucharist, "even women."[330] Another Churchman compared female Waldensians to the wanton woman of the Bible, Jezebel, because, like her, they "run through the streets and squares like a prostitute preacher."[331]

By 1215, Rome had labeled the Waldensians heretics and excommunicated them. Threatened by the fierce apparatus of the inquisition, many sought safety in secluded mountain hamlets in France, Italy, and Switzerland. For centuries, the long arm of the Church pursued members of the sect, subjecting them to persecution so devastating that the group was several times nearly annihilated. In 2015 Pope Francis visited a Waldensian church in Turin, Italy, to ask forgiveness for the "non-Christian and even inhuman attitudes and behavior we have showed you."

. . . .

During the thirteenth century a spiritual movement founded and carried out by women arose in the textile-manufacturing and trading centers of northern Europe. It appeared first among upper-class Belgian women who organized all-female communities in which they could pursue a lifestyle of poverty, celibacy, charity, and prayer. Known as Beguines, the women were loyal to the established Church at Rome but did not take formal vows. Similar self-governing communities—called Papalarde in France, Coquenunne in the Rhine valley, Bizoche and Pinzochere in Italy—soon formed.[332]

Unlike nuns, Beguines did not surrender their property to the Church, and they were free to resume secular life if they wished, even to marry. Moreover, they were not cloistered but worked in the outside world nursing the ill, assisting at burials, brewing beer, and teaching in the secular primary schools for girls that had recently opened in a few northern cities.[333] Most important, they were not subject to the authority of a monastic order. As American historian Joan Kelly pointed out, Beguines "escaped two of the major institutions of male power: the family and the Church," which suggests a "will to independence from male authority."[334]

At least a hundred Beguine communities, called beguinages, flourished in the Low Countries. The countesses Jeanne and her sister Marguerite, who ruled the independent principalities of Flanders and Hainaut for a dozen years, made generous financial contributions to several beguinages. A few beguinages were extremely large. Saint Christophe at Liège, for instance, had about a thousand residents, while Saint Elizabeth in Ghent had about seven hundred. The walled and moated precincts of Saint Elizabeth, also known as the Great Beguine of Ghent, contained two churches, more than a hundred individual homes, dormitories, an infirmary, a brewery, and a graveyard.[335] This extraordinary medieval city of women is today crisscrossed by the busy thoroughfares of modern Ghent. The name of one of its streets—*Boulevard du Béguinage*—serves as a reminder of the site's former occupants.

In France, King Louis IX (Saint Louis) endowed many residences for lay females, the largest of which, in Paris, is said to have had some 400 inhabitants.[336] In Germany, households of independent religious women were much smaller, but very numerous: Frankfurt had 57; Strasbourg, 60; Cologne, 169.[337] Finally, Pope John XXII acted to suppress the proliferating groups of unsupervised women. In 1317 he directed bishops and inquisitors to investigate the "abominable sect" of Beguines and subsequently ordered that Beguines "must be perpetually forbidden . . . and completely abolished from God's Church." Although he later modified this ruling, drawing a distinction between those women who lived peacefully in settled religious communities and those who traveled about as itinerant preachers, the persecution of Beguines continued.[338] Beguinages throughout northern Europe either disbanded or became shelters for poor women. A woman who wished to remain part of a religious community had no choice but to surrender her freedom and independence and adopt the life of a cloistered nun in a convent supervised by a male monastic order.

Public discourse in the Middle Ages was dominated by Catholic theologians and priests who, when the subject was women, more often than not declaimed on the sex's gullibility, untrustworthiness, and inherently sinful nature. Anyone who relied on the Church's judgment would reasonably conclude that females were, and by rights ought to be, under the control of men. However, when dissident religious groups arose that offered women greater dignity, as well as opportunities for leadership that were unavailable to them in the established Church, many women risked everything to join.

12 THE FREEDOM OF THE CITIES

Amid the violence and chaos of the early Middle Ages, the cities of the former Roman Empire fell into decay. The economies of once-vibrant centers of commerce withered, and large tracts of land within city walls were given over to agriculture. Structures from the glory days of the ancient world—temples, civic buildings, villas, coliseums, aqueducts—stood abandoned, ghostly reminders of a vanished world.

The eleventh century finally ushered in a time of relative peace and stability. But as agricultural yields improved and populations grew in this less turbulent period, competition for farmland increased. Some peasants left their ancestral villages in search of new fields to cultivate in Europe's undeveloped borderlands, while others made an even sharper break with the past and moved to a city. These urban pioneers constituted the first wave of a momentous demographic shift which saw the revitalization of city life and profoundly influenced the course of Western civilization. In this historic transformation, women played a vital role.

The new townswomen and –men were an energetic, ambitious lot who were determined to uproot the feudal privileges long enjoyed by the nobility and high clergy. With the nation-state still a thing of the future in much of Western Europe, the struggle between the rising burgher class and the old order was waged city by city. Many towns issued charters that conceded unprecedented rights to the newcomers, in some cases granting any woman or man who remained in the city for a year and a day emancipation from all previous feudal obligations—a guarantee that gave rise in Germany to the saying "Town air makes one free" (*Stadtluft macht frei*). In some towns, the conflict turned violent.

The account of an urban uprising in Amiens in 1115 written by a Benedictine monk, Guibert of Nogent, indicates that women joined in the fight. Guibert reported that when townspeople who backed social and economic reforms took control of a strategic tower, knights loyal to the king and the Church placed an "enormous siege machine" directly across from them. Wrote Guibert: "While the men defended their ramparts with a courage worthy of Achilles, the women, not to be outdone, hurled stones from the catapults." The reformers ultimately won the day, although all of the women sustained wounds.[339]

Among the urban pioneers were many unmarried girls. Although they seldom ventured far from their native villages, usually no more than twenty-five miles or so,[340] their journeys took them to a different world, for the medieval towns—with their bustling markets, religious processions, miracle plays, and densely populated residential quarters—offered a lively, comparatively unconstrained social environment that no rural village could match. There must have been other women who took as much pleasure in strolling the city streets and visiting from "hous to hous" as did Chaucer's irrepressible townswoman the Wife of Bath who, while her husband was away in London, "hadde the bettre leyser [leisure] for to pleye . . . to see and eek [also] to be seye [seen]."

> Therfore I made my visitaciouns,
> To vigilies and to processiouns,
> To preechyng eek, and to thise pilgrimages,
> To pleyes of myracles, and mariages.[341]

Girls newly arrived in a city usually found positions as maidservants, sometimes through personal contacts, sometimes with the aid of employment agents (known in France as *recomandresses*) who, for a fee, would recommend young women to families looking for household help. Some towns conducted hiring fairs every fall at which prospective employers and job-seekers were brought together.[342] Girls typically entered service at about age 12 and continued to work for a dozen years or so. The duties of female servants included cooking, housekeeping, laundry, and watching over the children. In artisan or merchant households, they might also be expected to assist in their employers' craft or trade.

Unscrupulous employers cheated inexperienced girls of their pay, exploited them, and subjected them to physical and sexual abuse.[343] But a job nevertheless represented a first step away from the patriarchal family and into the larger society. The young girl who took that step was inevitably exposed to new ideas and for the first time in her life experienced the liberating effect of money of her own. Although female servants were paid less than males who performed equivalent tasks,[344] a girl who saved her wages could put them toward a marital dowry and at the end of her service return to her village to wed. If on the other hand she decided to remain in the city, she could use her savings to buy a cottage or small plot of land, or even to launch a modest commercial endeavor.

An older woman who ventured alone on the life-altering journey from a country village to a city had several options other than domestic service. She might join a Beguine community, for example; or serve the city's multitude of sick and destitute people in a hospital, almshouse, or orphanage; or eke out a livelihood doing laundry, spinning thread and yarn, or performing some other marginal, low-paid labor. Some women drifted into prostitution. A neighborhood with a high concentration of female-headed households in the English city of York was known as Rotten Row, a name that tells its own story. The women who congregated in such quarters may have clustered together, as one scholar suggested, as much for companionship, emotional support, and protection as for financial reasons.[345]

Women who came to a city as members of a family unit tended to be fully occupied at first with traditional domestic tasks. However urban life soon imposed its own imperatives and opportunities, and once a family entered the money economy and began to purchase (rather than produce) its own clothing, women's household responsibilities became lighter.[346] Some women took advantage of the reduced workload to supplement their husband's occupation. For example, the wife of an artisan might market her husband's wares; a brewer's wife might operate an alehouse; and a butcher's wife might fashion candles from leftover tallow. All such work, no matter how petty, developed self-reliance and the ability to handle money.

In some cities, laws were amended to enable married women to conduct commercial ventures on their own. In the north of France a statute that denied wives direct access to the courts was adjusted in 1270 to permit any businesswoman to sue and defend herself in court in matters connected with her trade.[347] In 1276, the city of Augsburg, an important commercial center in southern Germany, gave any woman who had "her own business, run from her own shop or cellar," or who was "involved in trading activity independent of her husband" the liberty to dispose of her assets as she wished.[348] Under English common law, a married woman whose husband gave his formal assent was empowered to operate a commercial enterprise as a *feme sole*, that is, as though she were single. In Ghent, a husband could avoid responsibility for any debts incurred by his wife if he publicly declared in each of the city's five parish churches that she was an independent "merchant woman."[349] Married women who benefited from such laws could enter into contracts, write wills, lend and borrow money, and collect and sue for payment of debts—all without the authorization of their spouses.

Jewish women were notably active in the economies of some medieval cities since it was customary in the Jewish community for married women to engage in commerce. Observed a twelfth-century rabbi from Mainz, Germany, about his female co-religionists, "These days . . . the women are bailiffs and money changers and negotiate and loan and borrow and repay and receive payment and make and take deposits."[350] Jews were expelled from England in 1290, but in Paris, according to the 1292 tax rolls, women formed a larger proportion of taxpayers among Jews than among any other ethnic group, and Jewish women overall had a particularly high tax assessment. Despite their contribution to the economy, Jews were expelled from France *en masse* in 1306 with little more than the clothes on their backs.[351]

The Englishwoman Margery Kempe, who was born in the late 1300's, disclosed in her autobiography that prior to her religious conversion she ran several businesses in the town of Lynn. As the daughter of the town's former mayor and the wife of a prosperous merchant, she had no need to earn her own money. But nevertheless—motivated by what she subsequently described as pure covetousness and a prideful wish to dress lavishly—she operated a brewery for several years, and when that failed, a horse-driven corn mill, which also failed.[352] Although wives whose commercial ventures were more profitable than Margery Kempe's doubtless enjoyed their financial success, it might lead to conflict in the domestic sphere over who would rule the roost.[353] The bawdy *fabliaux* that circulated in France between the late 1100's and the early 1300's, for instance, commonly portrayed wives as domineering and lecherous, and husbands as hapless cuckolds.[354]

Widows were frequently knowledgeable enough about a deceased spouse's work to continue it on their own. In London, the widows of rich merchants were among the major exporters of wool. A document from 1274 refers to "widows of London who make great trade in wool and other things." And records from the 1300's refer to several London widows who owned ships and took part in international trade on such a grand a scale that they dealt with courts, guilds, and in at least one case, the English king.[355] In many cities, laws and practices affecting widows reflected their important economic role. Widows in the thriving Flemish city of Ghent were entitled to inherit whatever they had originally brought into the marriage and half of what had been acquired afterward, plus lifetime use (usufruct) of the other half.[356] The minimum widow's portion in England was established by law at one-third of her husband's estate.[357] A widow who did not remarry often retained independent control of her property—some of which she might in fact hold as a usufruct that was contingent upon her remaining single. It was probably for good reason that the great English legal charter from 1215, the Magna Carta, protected widows from forced remarriage. "No widow shall be compelled to marry," it commands, "so long as she prefers to live without a husband."

At the end of the thirteenth century Paris was by far the largest city in Western Europe, with a population of about 200,000. (In comparison, Venice, Florence, and Genoa each had only about 100,000 people; London, something like 80,000.)[358] In the 1292 Paris tax roll, women made up 15.4 percent of all taxpayers listed and were associated with 172 different occupations. Domestic service was the main female employment, with some 40 percent of female taxpayers identified as chambermaids (*chambrière*). However, women also worked as street peddlers, firewood dealers, candle makers, inn and tavern keepers, dressmakers, milliners, hairdressers, fishmongers, dancers, and jugglers. Twenty-nine Beguines appear in the 1292 tally, and two women are referred to as "priestesses." Some women performed physically demanding labor as masons, blacksmiths, and artisans in wood, metal, and leather, and some were medical practitioners. There were eight doctors, twelve nurses, two midwives, two spice dealers (who also functioned as pharmacists), and thirteen barbers (an occupation that included setting broken bones and bleeding people). A few women—moneychangers, jewelers, mint workers, dealers in textiles—were among Paris's richest taxpayers.[359] Nor was Paris unique in the diversity of women's work; historian Merry E. Wiesner reports that women were similarly engaged in "a huge variety of occupations" in the fast-growing cities of medieval Germany.[360]

The tax collectors of Paris based their assessments on the collective earnings of a household, or "hearth," rather than on the income of each individual. Since the tax list included only the head of the hearth—that is, the person who was the principal earner and therefore responsible for the payment of the tax[361]—many working women must have been subsumed under the names of husbands and fathers. Also not listed but certainly numerous were the female working poor, those whose incomes were too insignificant to require payment of any tax at all.

People of both sexes often failed to realize their dreams of personal betterment in the city, but female heads of households were more likely than male to be poor. Historian David Herlihy concluded on the basis of Paris tax rolls from two years, 1292 and 1313, that the wealth of women consistently averaged only about two-thirds that of men in the same occupations.[362] Thus, counterparts to York's Rotten Row—that is, poverty-stricken districts in which the majority of the residents were female—must have existed in any number of Western European cities. With so much female poverty, one would expect to see an active sex trade, and prostitutes were indeed ubiquitous in medieval cities.

The thirteenth-century Belgian priest Jacques de Vitry reported that prostitutes in Paris boldly importuned passing men, even clerics, calling "Sodomite!" after those who spurned their solicitations.[363] As the site of Europe's largest university, Paris was evidently brimming with young men who had time on their hands and money in their pockets. A 1395 survey of households in another university town, Bologna, indicated that prostitution, rather than domestic service, was the principal remunerative work of the city's female inhabitants. However, many of those counted as prostitutes in the Bolognese survey may have resorted to sex work only at times of dire need. A woman named Agnesina, for instance, who was described as "a prostitute or nearly," did not live in a brothel but with her husband, who was termed "poor and a beggar."[364]

Prostitution was by no means confined to university towns. A researcher who combed German archives from the thirteenth to the fifteenth centuries uncovered references to functioning brothels in seventy-five cities, large and small, in Germany alone.[365] Town ordinances generally did not interfere in the operation of brothels, for the fact was, they were lucrative. Municipally owned or regulated houses of prostitution existed in Florence, Seville, Dijon, and Augsburg.[366] In Toulouse, profits from a brothel were divided between the city and the university.[367] In Seville and other cities, income from brothels found its way into the coffers of religious establishments, even nunneries.[368] Church and state alike viewed prostitution as a necessary evil that was useful because it was thought to deter male homosexuality, provide a sexual outlet for men temporarily sojourning in a city, and protect "good" women from sexual harassment and rape. To clearly differentiate prostitutes from other women, cities often required them to wear distinctive items of dress—such as scarves, ribbons, or caps of a specified color—and restricted them to certain streets.[369]

The disproportionate poverty of women was due largely to lack of a level playing field. One major impediment was limited access to even a rudimentary education. Although wealthy girls could study at convent schools, secular institutions that admitted female students were virtually nonexistent until the beginning of the thirteenth century when publicly funded primary schools for girls as well as boys began to open.[370] In the course of the next two centuries, schools that admitted girls were established in Ghent, Florence, Paris, and several German cities.[371] These were the first non-religious girls' schools to be founded in Roman Europe since the Germanic invasions, about a thousand years earlier, but they accommodated relatively few students. At the dawn of the fifteenth century, the majority of European women were still unable to read.

However, archaeologists working in Novgorod, a city located 117 miles south of the present Saint Petersburg, have discovered that women living there between about the ninth and fifteenth centuries had an exceptionally high rate of literacy. Thousands of letters, including many written by women, have been unearthed in Novgorod since the scientific work began in 1951. These fascinating messages—inscribed on specially prepared strips of birchbark and preserved by chance in the heavy clay soil that underlay the medieval city's wooden sidewalks—also prove that women had the right to bequeath and inherit, to participate in the economy, and to sue in court.[372]

An eleventh-century woman named Gostyata, for example, informed a man who was possibly her brother that her former husband had made off with her inheritance. "What I was given by father and relatives he is keeping," she charged. "And having taken a new wife, he is not providing anything to me. He abandoned me and took another woman. Come and do me good." Anna, a twelfth-century moneylender, notified her brother that she intended to sue a client who had insulted her honor by calling her a cow and her daughter a prostitute. Also in the 1100's a woman recorded a bequest to an heir, and in the next century, Uliana, a peasant woman, left her sons a small piece of property she had received from her father-in-law. A letter to Maria from Potr, probably her husband or brother, instructed her to make a copy of a deed proving their (or her) ownership of a disputed tract of farmland.[373]

The female author of a letter from the late 1000's was described by the director of the Novgorod project as exceptionally literate and well educated. Addressing a lover who had failed to appear at a rendezvous, she reproached him, "I have written to you three times. What do you have against me that you have not visited me? . . . I see that you do not love me. If you loved me, you would have eluded [people's] eyes and come." Less elegantly expressed but no less urgent was the love missive written in the 1200's: "Marry me. I want you and you want me."[374]

Nowhere in medieval Europe, so far as we know, did women have access to higher education. But because medicine was considered an assortment of techniques rather than an intellectual discipline, a medical school established in the ninth century in the Italian city of Salerno admitted women and even had female teachers. Situated at the crossroads of Latin and Arabic scholarship, the Salerno school emphasized the traditional practices that had long been the special province of female healers, herbalists, and midwives.

After the 1200's, the education of physicians was increasingly taken over by the universities, and women rapidly lost status in the profession. In 1322, the (all-male) medical faculty at the University of Paris accused a woman, Jacoba Felicie, of treating patients without a license—a catch-22 accusation since licenses were granted only to individuals with university training. Felicie mounted a strong defense. Seven former patients, both men and women, plus the wife of one former patient, testified that she had cured them of afflictions that male physicians had been unable to treat. Testifying in her own defense, she argued that the licensing requirement was outmoded and in any event did not apply to her because it was intended to restrict ignorant individuals, while she was an expert. However, the judge ruled against her, asserting that "a man approved in the aforesaid art could cure the sick better than any woman."[375] Other unlicensed individuals prohibited from practicing medicine in Paris at this time included Joanna, who belonged to a Christian lay religious order; Belora, who was Jewish; and Margaret of Ypres, identified as a surgeon.[376] Barred from the universities and defamed as charlatans and worse, female healers nevertheless continued to provide medical care, especially to women and the poor. Moreover, in medicine, as in other fields, women constituted a reserve labor force that could be called upon as needed. Thus, when the devastating Black Death struck Florence in the mid-fourteenth century, gender prejudices were quickly set aside and female practitioners were welcomed into the influential Florentine guild of doctors and apothecaries.[377]

Among the various customs and institutions that proved disadvantageous to women none was more injurious than the guilds. These organizations, made up of individuals engaged in the same or similar occupations, existed in nearly every Western European city of any size by the thirteenth century. Their basic purpose was to suppress competition, but their influence extended into many other areas. They established quality standards for goods, regulated prices, provided social-welfare benefits to members, set the terms and conditions of apprenticeships, and often dominated municipal councils. To be excluded from guild membership was a formidable handicap—and regulations excluding women were common.

Still, a closer look reveals that some all-male guilds granted women associate membership status, and some offered a back-door entry to members' wives, daughters, and widows on the assumption that they had acquired on-the-job knowledge of the "mysteries" of a husband's or father's craft. Of the one hundred guilds listed in Paris's Book of Trades (*Livre des métiers*)—a compilation of guild regulations from about 1270—eighty-six mention women. Although women were most numerous in guilds representing textile trades, they also were affiliated with guilds of poultry dealers, needle and pin producers, manufacturers of goldsmiths' tools, singers, and actors.[378] In Ghent, women are referred to frequently in guild records, although rarely as masters (the barbers guild was one exception). Paris had seven guilds made up largely or entirely of women, and Rouen, at least five. However, the governing structure of all but one of them was partly or solely male. The single exception was a Paris guild representing weavers of silk headdresses, which was led entirely by women.[379]

Struggling to earn a living, women circumvented, ignored, and sometimes flagrantly violated discriminatory commercial regulations they had had no voice in formulating. Thus, female weavers in Strasbourg persisted in plying their trade despite repeated protests from the all-male wool-weavers guild. The courts in Exeter, England, fined Joan Shippestere (a dressmaker) several times in the course of a decade for cutting up and retailing cloth without a permit.[380] In Ghent, male blue-dyers were pitted against female blue-dyers, who were not licensed by the blue-dyers guild. The men objected that the women were "diminishing and destroying" their position in the industry, "in that they [the women] want to stand at the vats and work in their place." The men's grievance was upheld by the supervisor of small guilds, who ruled that blue-dyeing "is man's work."[381]

Female merchants of petty goods, most of whom barely scraped together enough to subsist, were widely suspected of engaging in a variety of shady dealings. The mainly female candle makers (chandlers) in two English towns were accused in 1300 of conspiring to fix prices, home spinners were suspected of embezzling bits of wool, and female chandlers in Nottingham were charged with selling candles without wicks.[382] In 1395, seven female poultry vendors in Nottingham—where the old poultry market was known as the "Womanmarket"—were indicted for buying up chickens at the authorized "just price" and then reselling them at a profit. This practice, known as "regrating," was highly unethical to the medieval way of thinking. Market women were so generally assumed to be guilty of regrating and other frowned-upon practices that the author of the fourteenth-century English allegory *Piers Plowman* exploited the stereotype to create his character Rose the Regrater, the wife of Avarice. Rose cheated her customers by diluting her ale, mismeasuring her cloth, and overcharging.[383]

Rose was a parody, but the marginal and changeable nature of her commercial activities resembled that of many real-life workingwomen. For like Rose, women frequently switched from one means of livelihood to another. Now brewing ale (brewsters) or baking bread (baxters), later spinning at home at piecework rates (spinsters) or hawking wares in the street (hucksters), this flexible female labor force was vital to town economies. A decree issued in England in 1363 restricted male workers to a single trade, but specifically exempted women. It read: "Women, that is to say Brewers, Bakers, Carders, Spinners and Workers as well of Wool as of Linen Cloth and of Silk . . . may freely use and work as they have done before this time without any impeachment or being restrained by this Ordinance."[384]

. . . .

Excluded from institutions of higher education, elbowed out of medical practice, discriminated against by the guilds, paid less than men for comparable work, burdened with domestic duties, and subject to male authority in the home, female urban dwellers used initiative and ingenuity to create and expand their economic opportunities. Circumscribed though they were, women of all classes played a vital role in the development of cities. At the same time, the vibrant life of the cities expanded women's horizons and altered their consciousness.

PART 3

FORCING THE PACE OF CHANGE

13 CHRISTINE DE PIZAN AND HER READERS

At a time when most Europeans spoke and understood only their mother tongue, the vast majority of manuscripts produced in Western Europe were written in Latin, the language of the Church. Over the years, however, literature written partly or wholly in the common language of the people began to circulate. The vernacular writings dealt with a variety of subjects: religion, of course, but also mathematics, science, medicine, history, philosophy, and love.

In Muslim Spain and Portugal, poets had been writing about love since the late 900's, but it was not until the final decades of the 1000's that love poems came to Christendom. For the next hundred years or so, men known as troubadours—and female poets termed trobairitz—composed and performed lyric poetry in Occitan (*langue d'oc*) for the entertainment of the lords and ladies of the aristocratic courts of southern France.

The troubadours' lyrics typically described a lovelorn knight's passionate devotion to an unattainable married woman, while the trobairitz lamented a woman's unrequited love for a man or, as in a few extant poems, for another woman. Thus, Bieiris (Beatriz) de Romans wrote, "if it please you, lovely woman, then give me/ that which most hope and joy promises/ for in you lie my desire and my heart." Another trobairitz, Castelloza, an aristocrat from the Auvergne, sang of her love for a man: "just once before I die/ of grief, show me/ your handsome face." In all, twenty trobairitz have been identified, but given the tendency of women's names and works to be lost and the fact that many troubadour poems are attributed to Anonymous, it seems likely that where twenty are known, there may have been others.[385]

As the Albigensian Crusade devastated Languedoc during the 1200's, many poets fled to other parts of Europe. In Germany and Austria, they inspired the Minnesingers, and in northern France, the *trouvères*. No female Minnesingers are known, but after many years of doubting the reality of female *trouvères*, historians now acknowledge their existence. Although the names of only a handful appear in surviving medieval manuscripts, Anonymous was probably sometimes a woman.[386]

The most prominent patrons of vernacular literature were Eleanor of Aquitaine, queen of France and then England, and her daughter, Marie of France, the Countess of Champagne.[387] It was at Marie's court that Chrétien de Troyes composed adventure stories in Old French about the legendary King Arthur and the Knights of the Round Table. In the introduction to *Lancelot*, Chrétien credited Marie with having inspired its composition: "Since my lady of Champagne wishes me to undertake to write a romance," he wrote, "I shall very gladly do so, being so devoted to her service as to do anything in the world for her." He claimed that she had supplied him with both "the material and treatment" for *Lancelot*. No doubt he exaggerated her contribution, but since he was dependent upon her largess, her preferences may well have influenced his choice not only of subject but also of language.[388]

In England, a writer known as Marie de France was instrumental in popularizing vernacular romances there. Little is known about her biography, other than that she resided for at least part of her life at the twelfth-century court of Henry II of England. Her surviving body of work consists of over a hundred fables and a dozen *lais* (stories in verse) written in Anglo-Norman, a form of French spoken in England at the time. The aristocratic English men and women who made up Marie de France's audience evidently were accustomed to hearing her tales read aloud, for according to a contemporaneous writer, the *lais* of a certain "Dame Marie" were much praised by the "counts, barons, and knights" of the court, who loved to hear them read and reread, as well as by "the ladies," who "listen to them joyfully and willingly, for they are just what they desire."[389] As the English translator of a twelfth-century Latin gynecological text attributed to the female physician Trota of Salerno (also known as Trotula) explained: "whomen of oure tonge [tongue] donne bettyr rede and undyrstande thys langage than any other."[390]

Dante Alighieri himself recognized the extent to which the needs of women had influenced European literature. Writing at the end of the thirteenth century, he observed, "The first poet to begin writing in the vernacular was moved to do so by a desire to make his words understandable to ladies who found Latin verses difficult to comprehend."[391] Ironically, when Dante wrote a treatise defending the use of the vernacular, he used Latin.[392] However, he composed his masterpiece, *The Divine Comedy*, in the Tuscan idiom, which he described as the humble speech in which women communicate.[393] The other supreme literary figures of the fourteenth century also wrote in their mother tongues. Francesco Petrarch used Italian for his poems about the woman he worshipped from afar, his beloved Laura, and Geoffrey Chaucer composed *The Canterbury Tales* in Middle English.

The fourteenth-century Italian, Giovanni Boccaccio, used the vernacular for his collection of ribald stories, *The Decameron*. But he apparently considered his compilation of female biographies, *Concerning Famous Women*, a more consequential work, for he wrote it in Latin. (It was translated into Italian almost immediately, and subsequently into French, German, and English.) *Concerning Famous Women* describes over a hundred extraordinary deeds performed by women. Boccaccio anticipated, as he said in the preface, "that the accomplishments of these ladies will please women no less than men." Yet he was hardly complimentary to the hoped-for female audience, for he went on to say that since women have "frail bodies and sluggish minds," they deserve special praise "when they take on a manly spirit [and] show remarkable intelligence and bravery." And evidently intending to flatter the countess to whom the book is dedicated, he wrote, "What nature has denied the weaker sex God has freely instilled in your breast."[394]

• • • •

There appeared at this moment in time Christine de Pizan, a secular woman who became a successful professional writer. Christine was brilliant and talented, yet her career would not have been possible if earlier women—the poets of al-Andalus, the trobairitz of Languedoc, Marie de France, and others—had not prepared the way by writing about love and other temporal subjects. And given Christine's sketchy knowledge of Latin, her genius would have remained hidden if authors like Dante and Boccaccio had not made it acceptable to write in a vernacular tongue.

Finally, if there were not a growing audience of secular women who were able to read, it is unlikely she would have chosen to become a writer.[395]

Christine was born in Venice in about 1364 to a Venetian mother and a father who was a graduate of the University of Bologna. Not long after her birth, he accepted a position as a physician and astrologer in the court of King Charles V of France, and his family followed him to Paris. Christine clearly obtained a basic education during her early years in Paris, but she always keenly regretted her educational deficiencies. At the age of 15 she wed a man ten years her senior who held a lifetime appointment as a royal secretary. The marriage was a happy one; but when she was only 25, her husband died, possibly during an outbreak of plague. Suddenly, she was thrust into the role of breadwinner for her three children and widowed mother. During this stressful period she may have worked in the commercial manuscript-copying industry in Paris while at the same time pursuing a decade-long program of independent study and reflection to prepare herself for a career as an author.[396]

Her initial literary efforts—poems that she later characterized as "short pieces in a lighter vein"[397]—won her the financial support of a number of aristocratic women and men whose patronage enabled her to provide for her family while devoting herself to her chosen profession. Over the next seven years, between about 1400 and 1417, there flowed from her pen some twenty works of poetry and prose, including a biography of King Charles V, a manual on arms and warfare, several volumes dealing with French politics, and two treatises in defense of women.

Christine first stepped forward as a champion of her sex in 1401, when she wrote a series of open letters to a group of male intellectuals who were publicly debating the literary merits of *The Romance of the Rose*, the most popular French book of the period. Christine was not concerned with the book as literature, however, but rather with the author's portrayal of women. "Let no one accuse me of unreason, of arrogance or presumption," she declared, "for daring, I, a woman, to challenge and answer back to so subtle an author . . . when he, one man on his own, has dared to slander and reproach the entire female sex without exception." Christine's open letters mark an important moment in the history of women, for they constitute the opening salvo of the *querelle des femmes*, a debate over the nature and capabilities of women which continued for the next three centuries.[398] Although the *querelle* did not in itself bring about change, it led people to think about women—a novel enterprise that ultimately affected the consciousness of people of both genders.

In 1405, Christine completed *The Book of the City of Ladies,* the first major text by a European woman to argue that women are morally and intellectually the equals of men.[399] It opens with the author brooding despondently over the low opinion of woman held by even the most esteemed philosophers. She confesses that although she has carefully considered her own character and that of other women—"princesses, great ladies, [and] women of the middle and lower classes, who had graciously told me of their most private and intimate thoughts"—she has been unable to uncover any "great faults" in the gender as a whole. Nevertheless, she is aware that many respected scholars have argued to the contrary, and she finally concedes that what these men have said must be so, that "God formed a vile creature when He made woman." Yet her surrender is not total, for she adds, "I relied more on the judgment of others than on what I myself felt and knew." Nor can she resist a sarcastic jab: "Alas, God, why did You not let me be born in the world as a man, so that . . . [I] would be as perfect as a man is said to be?"

Three resplendent ladies suddenly appear before Christine and introduce themselves as Reason, Rectitude, and Justice. They have come, Reason informs her, "to bring you out of the ignorance which so blinds your own intellect that you shun what you know for a certainty." Reason informs Christine that she has been selected to construct with their help a "city of ladies" whose walls will protect women from all detractors. This city, she adds, "will be extremely beautiful, without equal, and of perpetual duration in the world."[400]

The apparitions then describe scores of women whom they deem deserving of a place in the city. Among those admitted are illustrious queens, including Zenobia, Clotilde, and Fredegund; Amazon warriors; sibyls and prophets; Ulysses' faithful wife, Penelope; Xanthippe, wife of Socrates; noble ladies of ancient Rome; and heroines from literature, myth, and the Old and New Testaments. Christine asks Reason whether women are ever endowed with "high understanding and great learning," noting wistfully, "I wish very much to know this because men maintain that the mind of a woman can learn only a little." Responds Reason: "My daughter, ... you know quite well that the opposite of their opinion is true ... if it were customary to send daughters to school like sons, they would learn as thoroughly and understand the subtleties of all the arts and sciences as well as sons."[401]

Why is it then, Christine asks, that "one normally sees that men know more than women do." Reason explains that because women must stay at home and run the household, they are denied the instruction provided by a variety of experiences. She names a long list of women known for their intellect: the poet Sappho; the goddess Minerva, "who invented many sciences"; Ceres, the founder of the art of agriculture; and the Roman noblewoman Sempronia.

In choosing women to populate her fictional city, Christine borrowed freely from Boccaccio's *Concerning Famous Women*. However, she amended the Italian author's biographies when it suited her purpose. Thus, while Boccaccio branded Medea "the cleverest of witches," Christine stressed Medea's wisdom. She wrote that Medea "knew the powers of every and all the potions which could be concocted. ... It was thanks to the art of her enchantments that Jason won the Golden Fleece." *The City of Ladies* refrains from mentioning Medea's murder of her children.[402]

As she contemplates the existence of so many remarkable women, Christine cannot but wonder why "so many valiant ladies, who were both extremely wise and literate and who could compose and dictate their beautiful books in such a fair style, suffered so long without protesting against the horrors charged by different men when they knew that these men were greatly mistaken." Rectitude responds, "The composition of this work has been reserved for you and not for them. ... In the long run, everything comes to a head at the right time."[403]

Christine's second major book on women, *A Medieval Woman's Mirror of Honor: The Treasury of the City of Ladies*, was completed later that same year.[404] In this volume, she advised her readers how best to cope with the various stages of a woman's life, depending on the individual's social class. The wife of a great landowner, she counseled, should be ready to represent him at home during his absences. She must be able to take command of men in battle if necessary, be familiar with the legal rights and obligations of her locality, and be expert in all matters pertaining to farming and household management.

The wife of a man engaged in commerce ought to strive to avoid extravagance and pride, while the wife of an artisan should learn her husband's craft so well that she can direct the workmen if her husband is away and reprove them if necessary. Christine then addressed "the many women servants and chambermaids of Paris and other places" who toiled from dawn to dark and often went hungry; the prostitutes who were beaten, dragged about, and threatened by men, and whose very lives were daily in danger; and the wretched rural poor. For these sufferers, she could recommend only that they endure their situation patiently.[405]

In discussing married life, Christine, a supreme pragmatist, preached expediency. Aware that divorce was realistically impossible, she advised wives to behave lovingly toward their husbands no matter how abominable the man's conduct might be. When necessary, she counseled, a wife should go so far as to dissemble, pretending an affection she did not feel. The married woman ought to consider privately, "If I speak to him harshly, I will gain nothing. If he mistreats me, I am headed into a storm. . . . Alas, I am obliged to live and die with him, whatever he may be."[406]

Addressing herself to widows, Christine advised that they must learn to defend themselves against those "only too willing" to take advantage of them. Her own life had taught her that a widow must be self-assertive, "not crouching in tears like a simple woman, or like a poor dog who retreats into a corner when other dogs jump on him." She disparaged those widows who "have so little confidence in their own good sense that they will claim that they don't know how to manage their own lives." Since most marriages are observably unhappy, she argued, any mature widow able to survive financially on her own ought to remain single. For a widow in comfortable circumstances, "remarriage is complete folly."[407]

Many of Christine's insights are still remarkably relevant. Yet as the authors of a twentieth-century history of feminism remind us, she is "a companion in arms from an alien and distant world."[408] Clearly, the society in which she lived—a world of noble courts and peasant farms, of household manufacture, superstition, and shorter lifespans—was not one that could give birth to a modern feminist. The wonder is that she *does* still speak to us. Confident that most women were virtuous, intelligent, and praiseworthy human beings who were unjustly maligned, she was determined to say so.

. . . .

9. CHRISTINE DE PIZAN PRESENTS HER BOOK TO ISABEAU OF BAVARIA, QUEEN OF FRANCE, 1410-1414

Christine seems to have personally supervised the production of her books, for she commented in *The City of Ladies*: "I know a woman today named Anastasia, who is so learned and skilled in painting manuscript borders and miniature backgrounds that one cannot find an artisan in all the city of Paris—where the best in the world are found—who can surpass her.... And I know this from experience, for she has executed several things for me."[409] Some fifty manuscripts of Christine's books have corrections and notations written by one hand, presumably the author's.[410]

Each hand-copied manuscript represented a considerable outlay of time and money, but Christine was determined to immortalize her defense of women by distributing her books "throughout the world in various copies, whatever the cost might be." To this end, she ordered additional volumes and presented them to queens, princesses, and noble ladies. "This work will not remain unknown and useless but will endure in its many copies," she predicted.[411] Her prediction was not wrong, but she could not have imagined it would take so long, for although her pro-woman treatises were popular during her lifetime and for a century afterward, both books soon faded into obscurity. The first English translation of *The Book of the City of Ladies* appeared in 1521.[412] More than 450 years passed before there was another.

In the closing years of her life, Christine sought refuge from the Hundred Years' War in the French convent where her daughter resided. For more than a decade, her voice was silent. Then came her last known work, a paean to her countrywoman and contemporary, Joan of Arc. Overjoyed by Joan's military successes, she exulted, "Oh, what an honor to the female sex! Above all the brave men of the past, she must wear the crown."[413]

14   THE RENAISSANCE FOR WOMEN

They came to Italy from all over Western Europe, young men eager to be part of the intellectual life of the great fifteenth-century Italian universities. Excited by the new humanist curriculum, they explored Greek philosophy, Roman law, Arabic medicine, Hebrew ethical writings, Hellenistic mathematics. The Dutch philosopher Desiderius Erasmus studied at the University of Turin, and it was in Italy that the Polish scholar Nicolaus Copernicus first encountered the ancient writings that led him to formulate a heliocentric theory of the solar system, as opposed to the earth-centered model endorsed by the Church.[414]

Women, too, were in love with the new learning, yet their path to knowledge was never smooth. A young woman might, if she came from a wealthy family, study with a private tutor or at a convent school, but if she aspired to higher learning, she would have to struggle on alone. Barred from the universities, she would find her progress further hindered by discriminatory laws, crippling social customs, and in some cases, self-doubt. Moreover, she was apt to be married off in her teens to a man chosen by her father. Alternatively, if her father could (or would) not pay the exorbitant marital dowries that were usual, she might be sent to a convent.[415] Many girls were enrolled in religious communities as children and remained cloistered for the rest of their lives, without regard to their religious commitment.

A married woman theoretically owned her dowry, but in reality her husband controlled the funds. And since she had no work experience and no access to training in any profession, she could not hope to support herself beyond the bare necessities of life, if that. Thus, no matter how rich she might appear to be, how costly her jewels or palatial her home, she was dependent on her male relations. Understandably, most women chose to curry favor with their providers by cultivating those qualities men saw as the paramount virtues of female human beings: sexual modesty, domesticity, and obedience.[416]

Still, because of the substantial age difference between brides and grooms, widows made up a significant percentage of the female population.[417] And since a widow in most parts of Italy had the right to conduct essential business, including legal transactions, she was—according to a fifteenth-century advice manual—a "free woman." However, her alleged freedom had limitations, for the manual went on to stipulate that a widow must never show any interest in subjects that are the exclusive province of men, such as the natural world, the phases of the moon, or the courses of the planets. Nor should she venture to discuss politics, military engagements, statecraft, or "what the Turk is up to in Constantinople."[418]

The humanist educator Leonardo Bruni also believed that certain subjects were off-limits for women, but how much learning ought to be permitted depended on the woman's wealth and rank. Thus, he approved of instruction in Latin for the young noblewoman Battista Malatesta,[419] the scholarly daughter of the Count of Urbino, but advised against the full range of humanist studies. Rhetoric, in his view, was particularly inappropriate. Indeed, he wrote, if a woman were to emulate current oratorical fashion, that is, if she were to

> ... gesture energetically with her arms as she spoke and shout with violent emphasis, she would probably be thought mad and put under restraint. The contests of the forum, like those of warfare and battle, are the sphere of men.[420]

Battista Malatesta (who was a contemporary of Christine de Pizan) evidently did not take Bruni's admonition to heart, for when the Holy Roman Emperor Sigismund visited Urbino in 1433, the 50-year-old widow welcomed him with a public oration.[421]

A few elite families had a tradition of educating daughters. Battista Malatesta's female descendants, for example, included two granddaughters noted for their erudition and a great-granddaughter, Vittoria Colonna, who was a close friend of Michelangelo's and the best-known female poet of the Italian Renaissance. Similarly, the noble Nogarola family of Verona produced Angela, a respected poet in the early 1400's; her gifted nieces Ginevra and Isotta in the next generation; and Ginevra's granddaughter Veronica Gambara, a well-known poet.[422]

For a woman with scholarly aspirations, the prospect of wifehood was fraught with conflict. For while matrimony brought status, security, and the possibility of love and children, it often proved incompatible with study and creativity. The story of the Nogarola sisters, Ginevra and Isotta, is illustrative of the dilemma facing the Renaissance woman who dreamed of achieving great things. The sisters received an excellent education in the classics from private tutors, and both showed early promise. However, after Ginevra married at the age of 21, her literary activities ceased.

Her younger sister Isotta, who never wed, was determined to pursue further education on her own. She sent samples of her writing to an uncle and appealed to him for help in purchasing a copy of "the lovely, the most beautiful" *Decades* by the Roman historian Livy.[423] Later, her brother helped her by enlisting a fellow student at the University of Padua to advise her on a course of studies. The friend recommended mathematics, natural science ("living things and bodies in motion"), and history, but especially philosophy—Aristotle first, but also Thomas Aquinas, and the Islamic philosophers Avicenna (Ibn Sina), Averroes (Ibn Rushd), and al-Ghazali, all of whom were available in Latin translation.[424] To advance her reputation as an author and Latin scholar, Isotta carried on an extensive correspondence with well-known humanists—a common way to showcase one's erudition. Thus, without stepping out of her home, she was able to participate in the intellectual currents of the period. Still, she could not but be aware, as she wrote to her uncle in 1436, that there were men "who consider learning in women a plague and public nuisance":

> It seems to me that these men—who approve of nothing except what they themselves do and think—are themselves a different kind of plague, that of men envious of others' glory, which comes from ignorance and baseness of spirit.[425]

Yet despite these brave-sounding words, Isotta's ego was fragile. That same year, having learned that the illustrious teacher Guarino of Verona had commended her, she summoned the courage to write to him. But when he failed to answer, she wrote again, pleading for a response. Bitterly, she accused him of treating her with disdain because of her gender and claimed that his neglect had subjected her to contempt, particularly from women. You have "made me the butt of everyone's jokes," she lamented. When Guarino finally responded, he urged her to harden herself to criticism, to become, in effect, "a man within the woman."[426]

The slight from Guarino was insignificant compared to a subsequent assault on her reputation by an anonymous writer who accused her of sexual promiscuity and, worse, of incest with her brother, adding, "an eloquent woman is never chaste."[427] Nogarola, still in her early twenties, retreated into a room in her mother's home—a setting described by one acquaintance as a "book-lined cell"—and thereafter devoted herself primarily to studying and writing about religion.[428] Her best-known work is a dialogue in which a man and woman debate the comparative culpability of Eve compared to Adam. Her conclusion: "Adam's sin was greater than Eve's."[429] In her forties, she emerged from her "cell" several times to deliver public orations, including one in Rome before the pope and cardinals of the Church.[430]

. . . .

For the next generation of Italian women, the increased availability of printed books opened the gateway to knowledge. Laura Cereta of Brescia, for example, the daughter of a lawyer, was enrolled in a convent school at age 7, but when her formal education ended at the tender age of 11, she returned to her parents' home to study on her own. Stealing what time she could from domestic chores, she perused not only classical literature but also books on politics and war, religion, and the movements of the planets. Often she read all night. When she was 15, she married a Venetian merchant who, as she later recalled, "loved me even while I quietly pursued my studies in literature." But a year or so after they wed, he fell ill and died. After a period of incapacitating grief, Cereta again committed herself to scholarship. She never remarried but remained single for the rest of her brief life (she died at 30).

Isotta Nogarola had taken part in the intellectual life of her time only indirectly—that is, through her correspondence with great men—while Laura Cereta had attended public lectures and participated in scholarly salons. Yet as Cereta wrote to her father, her bold forays into the academic world had aroused the hostility of both "the ignorant public" and of certain men who, having "suddenly got learning of some sort," were jealous of her literary knowledge. The men's attacks, she confided, sometimes "made me so angry I was sick."[431]

Cereta was of stronger mettle than Isotta Nogarola, for when she was attacked, she counterattacked, vowing to use her pen to wage "a war of vengeance" against men who heaped abuse upon "the republic of women." But while casting her lot with others of her gender—she sometimes addressed female correspondents as "sister" and referred to "we women"—she also criticized those women who wasted time on frivolous pastimes and did not take advantage of the one freedom nature granted to all human beings equally, the ability to learn.[432]

Cereta composed two remarkable writings. In the first she argued that the institution of marriage as it was then constituted infantilized women and prevented them from fulfilling their talents. She pointed out that although both nature and the Church disposed women toward marriage and children, wedlock entailed "toil and duty," while motherhood brought "wailing and all night vigils." In the second, she lashed out at a fictitious critic, "Bibolo Semproni," emphatically denying his claim that her intellectual gifts made her an anomaly among women. If "Bibolo" had aimed his blows at her alone, she wrote, she might not have troubled to answer him; but he had implied that the whole of womankind was mentally deficient.

> Because of this, a mind thirsting for revenge is set afire; because of this, a sleeping pen is wakened. . . . Because of this, red-hot anger lays bare a heart and mind long muzzled by silence.[433]

A study conducted in 2008 by researchers at the University of Chicago found 130 works by women published in Italy during the sixteenth century. Among the authors were secular women and nuns; wives, single women, and courtesans; and women with various class and educational backgrounds. Writing in Latin as well as Italian, they produced letters, dialogues, orations, treatises, biographies, histories, and dramas. But poetry was by far their preferred genre.[434]

One poet greatly admired during her brief lifetime was Gaspara Stampa, the daughter of a distinguished Venetian humanist. Her beautiful singing voice and skill at the lute enchanted the men who gathered at her father's home, but her liberated lifestyle and sexually frank poetry put her at the outer margins of respectability. Evidently well educated, she alluded to classical history and myth in her poetry, and she was familiar enough with Copernican theory to write, "I love and I shall love you, while the spheres/ Turn round the sun." Few of Stampa's poems appeared in print during her lifetime, but after her death at the age of 31, her sister published a collection of her verse.[435]

Even further outside the bounds of polite society was the poet-courtesan Veronica Franco.[436] When a mother who was considering training her daughter to be a courtesan asked Franco for her opinion, Franco warned that the life of a courtesan often entailed misery, indignities, and the possibility of sexual abuse. In her will Franco set aside funds for poor girls in need of dowries, so they could marry rather than become prostitutes. Later, she asked the Venetian city council to establish a shelter for indigent wives and mothers.[437] Writing to a man who had publicly insulted a woman, she remarked that hers was an "unfortunate sex . . . always subjected and without freedom"; but, she added, "we have a mind and intellect" and "have given more than one sign of being greater than men."[438]

Renaissance women also made their mark as musicians, artists, and actors. An all-female choir in the court of the Duke of Ferrara reportedly sang like angels and also played instruments and danced.[439] As their fame spread, other Italian princes wanted their own singing ladies. The Ferrara consort was disbanded in 1597, but by that time similar choirs had been assembled at several other Italian courts, including that of the Medici in Florence.[440]

The first European woman to compose music that survives in printed form was Maddalena Casulana, whose collected madrigals were published in Venice in 1568 and 1570. Aware of her unusual achievement as a woman in music, she declared that it was her desire "to show the world . . . the vain error of men, who so much believe themselves to be the masters of the highest gifts of the intellect that they think those gifts cannot be shared equally by women."[441]

Nuns and abbesses had produced works of art throughout the medieval centuries, but when secular women attempted to join the ranks of professional artists, they found their way obstructed. Women were barred from most Italian art academies, they were excluded from the artists guilds, and their subject-matter was restricted by traditional notions of female modesty and propriety. In addition, they had to overcome the idea that women lacked creativity, just as they supposedly lacked generative power, which, according to Aristotle, resided solely in male sperm.

Art historians know of some thirty-five female artists in sixteenth-century Italy, and there doubtless were others.[442] Among the most skilled was the portraitist Sofonisba Anguissola of Cremona, who was so widely admired that she was invited to work in the court of King Philip II of Spain, Europe's most powerful monarch.[443] Anguissola is said to have inspired two younger women, Irene di Spilimbergo of Friuli and Lavinia Fontana of Bologna.[444] Although Lavinia Fontana had a long, successful career, Spilimbergo died young. A memorial volume published two years after her death in 1559 contains poems written by a dozen female poets.[445] The painter Artemisia Gentileschi, born in Rome in 1593, stands at the pinnacle of Italian female artists. Many of her fifty-seven known paintings are portraits of powerful women from scripture and myth. Confident of her own power as an artist, she promised a patron, "I will show Your illustrious Lordship what a woman can do."[446]

Paintings by Italian Renaissance women may be seen today in many leading museums, including Florence's Uffizi Gallery and Pitti Palace, Madrid's Prado, Rome's Galleria Borghese, New York's Metropolitan Museum of Art, Washington D.C.'s National Museum of Women in the Arts, and the Hermitage in Saint Petersburg, where Catherine the Great assembled one of the world's largest collections of works by women.[447]

Female actors were employed by several theater companies during the latter half of the 1500's.[448] Although a reputation for immorality clung to

10. SOFONISBA ANGUISSOLA, SELF-PORTRAIT AT THE EASEL, *1556*

most women who performed on the stage, Isabella Andreini of Padua, the prima donna of the leading *commedia dell'arte* group, was known to be a blameless wife and mother, and she was beloved by audiences. Not only a talented actor and improvisationist, she was also a linguist who spoke several romance languages, a scholar who knew Latin, and a talented poet and playwright.[449] The following speech from Act 4 of her pastoral drama *Mirtilla* shows that she understood current scientific theory. It displays wonderfully the Renaissance spirit that animated her:

> Is it not a great satisfaction
> to understand fully the course of the stars,
> the power of the planets . . . ;
> why the moon changes;
> why the earth often intervenes between the sun and his sister;
> why the days are short and why they are long
> according to when the sun stays away or draws near.
> And finally, is it not a great satisfaction
> to know how to investigate the deep secrets
> of nature and heaven? And that there's nothing
> that hides from our intellects?[450]

When Andreini died in Lyon in her early forties of complications resulting from an eighth pregnancy, she was given a large public funeral and was widely eulogized.

• • • •

At a moment in time when a few women were beginning to achieve a measure of intellectual renown and artistic success, the Church launched the Counter-Reformation, a program aimed at reinforcing Catholic orthodoxy in response to the advance of Protestantism in northern Europe. An *Index of Forbidden Books* (*Index Librorum Prohibitorum*) authorized by the pope and released in 1559 banned hundreds of volumes, including vernacular translations of scripture and Copernicus's treatise on the heavens.[451] Aristocratic girls were enrolled in convents in such large numbers between 1550 and 1660 that, according to one scholar, they were more likely to become nuns than wives.[452] Papal courts of inquisition were set up in several cities to investigate those whose religious practices did not conform to the Church's standards.

Amid pressing calls for moral reform, women were urged to embrace domesticity. Marriage manuals directed wives to obey their husbands and to engage in sexual relations solely for procreation,[453] while books on female deportment instructed women to limit their reading mainly to religious texts. Indeed, according to a cardinal of the Church, there was no need for most girls to learn to read at all.[454] Misogynist tomes spilled from the Italian presses. As one might have foreseen, a backlash developed.[455] In answer to a treatise that detailed the defects of women, Lucrezia Marinella, a Venetian writer, composed a book-length polemic entitled *The Nobility and Excellence of Women and the Defects and Vices of Men*. Published in 1600, it was a sharp departure from Marinella's three previous books, all of which had dealt with conventional religious themes in verse.[456]

Marinella informed her readers that women in Italy had fewer economic rights than women in several other European nations. In Spain, England, and France, she pointed out, wives and daughters could inherit estates, while in the prosperous cities of Germany, Flanders, and France women took part in commercial transactions "with a diligence that is unsurpassed by the foremost merchant in all of Italy." She portrayed Aristotle as an enemy of womankind whose view of the female as a defective human being defies all reason. As for his insistence that women must obey men everywhere and in everything, it was "a foolish opinion and cruel, pedantic sentence from a fearful tyrannical man." To prove that long-held opinions may be wrong—even those that come from respected sources—Marinella cited Copernicus's book on the revolution of celestial spheres. Although Copernicus was on the Church's *Index* of banned volumes, she audaciously asserted, "There are many people who believe that the earth moves and the sky remains still."[457]

Marinella praised notable women who had lived from antiquity to her own day. Although nearly 150 years had passed since the deaths of Isotta and Ginevra Nogarola, at least one of their countrywomen remembered and admired them as well as their successor, Laura Cereta. Marinella paid tribute to all three and also commended a number of her contemporaries, one of whom, Moderata Fonte, was, like her, a seasoned Venetian author.[458]

Moderata Fonte was the pen name of a respectable, convent-educated matron, the wife of a well-to-do lawyer, and the mother of three children. Until 1592, her published writings had consisted of a cantata and two verse narratives on the passion and resurrection of Christ. Then, at the age of 37, she wrote *The Worth of Women*.[459] Fonte's manuscript remained unpublished for eight years. When it finally appeared in print in 1600, the same year as Marinella's book, it had a dedication written by Fonte's daughter which explained that her mother had brought the volume "to the present stage of completion the very day before her death in childbirth."[460]

The Worth of Women is set in a garden where seven "noble and spirited women, all from the best-known and most respected families of the city," are gathered for two days of amusement and sociability. As the women chat, they revel in the lack of constraint they feel because they are out of the earshot of men. "To tell the truth," says one of the group, "we are only really happy when we are alone with other women." The friends decide to debate amongst themselves the relative merits of women versus men.

The characters in Fonte's book do not assume that male dominance was ordained by God or Nature. Rather, as one of them observes, men "set themselves up as tyrants over us, arrogantly usurping that dominion over us that they claim as their right." Another agrees, asserting that men did not acquire their sovereignty through merit but seized it by bullying, and then transformed their superior status into immutable laws and customs. The women berate those men who "refuse to allow women to learn to read and write, on the pretext that learning is the downfall of many women." And they criticize those who blame women for all sexual misbehavior.

One of the group notes that "in antiquity they used to punish women's transgressions extremely severely by law, while men went unpunished." Corinna, unmarried and the most scholarly of the company, has a ready explanation: "Men may be wicked but they aren't stupid, and since it was they who were making the laws and enforcing them, they were hardly going to rule that they should be punished and women go free." When one woman praises the civic leaders of Venice, another responds heatedly, "What on earth do magistrates, law courts, and all this other nonsense have to do with us women? Are not all of these official functions exercised by men, against our interests? Do they not make claims on us, whether we are obliged to them or not? Do they not act in their own interests and against ours? Do they not treat us as though we were aliens? Do they not usurp our property?"[461]

Cornelia, a young married woman, decries the fact that women do not have financial assets of their own. Some fathers, she complains, "leave everything, or the majority, to their sons, depriving their daughters of their rightful inheritance." Women are forced into prostitution in order to provide for themselves, while others "grow old at home under their brothers' rule, waiting on their nephews and nieces," virtually "buried alive." Some husbands, she notes, keep their mates so short of money that they lack the bare necessities. "Without having taken a vow of poverty, they have become nuns in all but habit."[462]

The women assign the largest responsibility for the unhappiness of their gender to matrimony. Virginia, the youngest member of the circle, suggests that she might prefer never to marry, but her mother, also present in the garden, quickly informs her that she has no choice in the matter since her uncles have decided that she *must* take a mate to protect her inheritance. Many wives, says Cornelia, "are kept like animals within four walls," or are expected to raise their husbands' illegitimate children. In addition, their husbands may shout at them, abuse them, "or even beat them over the most trivial matters." Finally, Corinna asks what a woman gains through marriage. Matrimony in her view is without redeeming features. "Instead of being her own mistress and the mistress of her own money, [the married woman] becomes a slave, and loses her liberty and, along with her liberty, her control over her own property. . . . Look what a good deal marriage is for women! They lose their property, lose themselves, and get nothing in return, except children to trouble them and the rule of a man, who orders them about at his will."

Through her spokeswoman, Cornelia, the author issued a clarion call: "Come on, let's wake up and claim back our freedom, and the honor and dignity they [men] have usurped from us for so long." Expressing her confidence in women's capacity to manage their own lives once they have achieved equality, Cornelia asks, "Do you think if we really put our minds to it, we would be lacking the courage to defend ourselves, the strength to fend for ourselves, or the talents to earn our own living? Let us take our courage into our hands and do it."[463]

· · · ·

Dazzling talent and intellectual brilliance alone were not enough to win a woman a place in the intellectual firmament or to assure her of artistic laurels. If she hoped to join a circle of learned men or build a career in the arts, she had to struggle against those who believed that the female mind was inferior to the male, and be prepared to face, at best, disapproval, at worst, ridicule and vilification. Still, some women persevered. And some men were eventually willing to concede the possibility, as one ungallant gentleman-scholar put it, that women were not "by nature stupid or consigned to dullness."[464] It was not much, perhaps, but it was a beginning.

15   DAUGHTERS OF THE WORLD

Through half a century, from 1553 to 1603, England was governed by women: Lady Jane Grey (who occupied the throne for only nine days), Mary I, and finally Mary's half-sister, Elizabeth I.[465] Each of the three was admired for her learning, but Elizabeth was also held up as proof of a woman's ability to rule. The sixteenth-century poet Mary Sidney praised Elizabeth's achievements in two hemispheres and marveled that even kings were forced "a woman to obay." A pseudonymous pamphlet signed "Ester Sowernam" spoke of "Elizabeth our late Soveraigne, not onely the glory of our Sexe, but a patterne for the best men to imitate." Writing more than three decades after the queen's death, a poet signed "Diana Primrose" termed her "Great ELIZA, Englands brightest Sun," an "Empresse of our Sex." Later still, the educator Bathsua Makin declared that the queen had "swayed the Sceptre of this Nation with as great honour as any man before her." And in the faraway colony of Massachusetts the English-born poet Anne Bradstreet asserted that Elizabeth had "wip'd off th' aspersion of her Sex,/ That women wisdome lack to play the Rex."[466]

In the course of Elizabeth's forty-four-year reign, tens of thousands of people streamed into London, swelling the population of the city and its suburbs from about 80,000 to about 250,000.[467] Among the new arrivals were many women of the middling sort—members of that large and vibrant stratum of urban society comprised of the families of professional men and civic functionaries; helpmates of retailers, brewers, and craftsmen; and widows and other single women who earned their livelihood as shopkeepers, food vendors, governesses, and similar occupations. Englishmen were unaccustomed to seeing women so actively involved in public life, and many heartily disapproved. Pamphlets and broadsides chastising ill-mannered domineering women and lampooning hapless husbands whose shrewish wives publicly cursed and scolded them poured from the London presses.[468]

The growing number of books that maliciously attacked women inspired a rebuttal titled *Jane Anger, Her Protection for Women*. The author—whose name is unknown but who was probably a woman—asks to be excused for the "choleric vain" of her counterattack because "It was ANGER that did write it."[469] Addressing herself to "all Women in General," she declares that though men abuse, vilify, and mistreat women, they are, in fact, "inferior unto us." She displays her own educational accomplishments by peppering her pamphlet with Latin phrases and allusions to classical and biblical literature. And she flatly denies the idea that women are sexually voracious, insisting that it is men who pursue women. "If we clothe ourselves in sackcloth and truss up our hair in dish clouts, Venetians will nevertheless pursue their pastime. If we hide our breasts, it must be with leather, for no cloth can keep their long nails out of our bosoms." She urges women to be wary of those men who aim to seduce and betray them. "Their fawning is but flattery; their faith, falsehood; their fair words, allurements to destruction."[470]

With the death of Queen Elizabeth in 1603, James I ascended to the English throne. The new monarch, who had previously ruled in Scotland as James VI, was fascinated with witchcraft. He had personally attended torture sessions of Scottish women accused of being witches and had written a book on the subject, *Demonology*. During his first year as king of England an edition of *Demonology* was published in London, and Parliament approved the death penalty for anyone convicted of conspiring with Satan. Sensationalized pamphlets describing the trials and executions of female witches sold briskly, and an English translation of portions of the *Malleus Maleficarum*—a handbook for witch hunters that is among the most odious anti-woman effusions ever set down on paper—was available from booksellers.[471] Before long London was a virtual battleground for a war of words about the nature and role of women.

One especially intemperate attack, *The Arraignment of Lewd, idle, forward, and inconstant women* was published in 1615 under a pseudonym, although the author, a London fencing instructor named Joseph Swetnam, was quickly found out. Crudely reasoned and badly written, the pamphlet portrayed wives as avaricious mercenaries who lead "a proud, lazy, and idle life," and warned of women who would not hesitate to "pick thy pocket and empty thy purse, laugh in thy face and cut thy throat." Widows, he added, are commonly "so forward, so waspish, and so stubborn that thou canst not wrest them from their wills. And if thou think to make her good by stripes, thou must beat her to death."[472]

Swetnam's diatribe was reprinted at least ten times over the next twenty years and provoked three refutations in a single year, 1617. The first, *A Muzel for Melastomus* (A Muzzle for Black Mouth), was penned by Rachel Speght, the author of several other extant writings. Speght denounced Swetnam as a monster and blasphemer and his pamphlet as "illiterate and irreligious." As befit the daughter of a cleric, she based her defense on Christian scripture, reinterpreting several biblical texts along lines favorable to women. Thus, she contended that Eve was made of finer material than Adam, who was fashioned from dust; and that Adam's sin in eating the apple was greater than Eve's since he was "the stronger vessel." Yet Speght hewed closely to gender conventions of the day. She accepted the traditional idea that women are morally weaker than men, and she endorsed the Pauline dictum that "the Man is the Woman's Head," with the proviso that a husband's superior position did not give him authority "to domineere, or basely command and imploy his wife, as a servant," but obliged him to defend and protect her.[473]

Both of the other answers were signed with pseudonyms: "Ester Sowernam" (a play on Swetnam) and "Constantia Munda" (a rejoinder to Swetnam's charge that women are "unconstant"). Although we do not know the identity of these writers or even their gender, it seems probable that they were, as they professed to be, women.[474] Sowernam, who evidently had some connection with the judiciary (perhaps she was a lawyer's wife or daughter), wrote that while in London for the fall term of the High Court of Justice, she attended a supper with friends.

> As nothing is more usuall for table-talke; there fell out a discourse concerning women, some defending, others objecting against our Sex: Upon which occasion, there happened a mention of a Pamphlet entituled *The Arraignment of Women*, which I was desirous to see. The next day a Gentleman brought me the Booke.

Finding Swetnam's volume "scandalous and blasphemous," she began to write a response, but laid it aside when she heard that another critique, presumably Rachel Speght's, was ready for the press. Yet after reading Speght's answer, she concluded that instead of defending women, it accused and condemned them, and she picked up her pen again.

Sowernam's pamphlet, *Ester Hath Hang'd Haman*, describes a trial in which Swetnam is arraigned before two "Judgesses," Reason and Experience. Acting the part of prosecutor, the author berates Swetnam and other writers who demean females: "It hath ever been a common custom amongst Idle and humorous Poets, Pamphleteers, and Rhymers ... to write some bitter Satire-Pamphlet or Rhyme against women." She concedes that it is usually best to ignore slanderers, but because Swetnam enjoys such exceptional public approval, she feels he must be opposed. Sowernam, who clearly has read widely in the literature of misogyny, cites anti-woman invectives from ancient Greece and Rome as well as contemporary works from which, she alleges, Swetnam stole many of his ideas. Why is such a poorly reasoned book so popular, she wonders, when women "laugh that men have no more able a champion"?

Sowernam points out that although men say that women "tempt, allure, and provoke" them, it is actually *they* who "solicit women to lewdness." To gain a woman's trust, one man "will pretend marriage; another offer continual maintenance." If the woman yields to the latter offer, her reputation is destroyed. If she refuses, she receives no material help. Thus, her options often come down to dependency in marriage versus a single life sustained by virtual or actual prostitution. Men will spend freely in bawdy houses, she charges, "but when will they bestow a penny upon an honest maid or woman, except to corrupt them?"[475] Sowernam's understanding that economic dependence makes women vulnerable to mistreatment and exploitation by men was an original and powerful contribution to the *querelle des femmes*.

Constantia Munda, author of the third response to Swetnam, was familiar with the efforts of Speght and Sowernam. Her offering, titled *The Worming of a Mad Dogge*, overflows with made-up words, puns, literary allusions, and quotations in Greek, Latin, and Italian. Like Sowernam, she deplores the fact that "every scandalous tongue and opprobrious wit" is able to successfully peddle his wares in the stationers' shops. "Printing, that was invented to be the storehouse of famous wits, the treasure of Divine literature . . . [and] of all Sciences, is become the receptacle of every dissolute Pamphlet." Thus, Woman, who should be "praised and glorified," is instead "most shamefully blurred and derogatively erased by scribbling pens of savage and uncouth monsters."[476]

A year or two after the publication of the anti-Swetnam pamphlets, an anonymous stage comedy titled *Swetnam the Woman-Hater Arraigned by Women* was performed at the Red Bull Theatre in London, a playhouse noted for its noisy, sometimes rowdy audiences of women and men. The script was subsequently published without disclosing the author's identity, which remains unknown today. The play opens with a prologue delivered by a female character:

> The Women are all welcome; for the men,
> They will be welcome: our care's not for them.
> 'Tis we poore women, that must stand the brunt
> Of this dayes tryall: we are all accused.
> The men, I know, will laugh, when they shall heare
> Us rayl'd at, and abused; and say, 'Tis well,
> We all deserve as much. Let um laugh on,
> Lend but your kind assistance; you shall see
> We will not be ore-come with Infamie,
> And slanders that we never merited.
> Be but you patient, I dare boldly say,
> (If ever women pleased) weele please to day.

As the prologue promises, women are vindicated in the play, for at the end Swetnam is groveling and repentant, having been declared "Guiltie of Woman-slander, and defamation" by an all-female court. The playwright clearly presumed that at least some members of the roughhewn audience were familiar with the controversy, for the script contains jesting references to Swetnam's pamphlet as well as to the three rebuttals.[477]

Although the pen was an effective and often eloquent weapon in the gender war, some London women experimented with another form of rebellion: dressing as men. For an individual woman to cross-dress when engaged in a stereotypically male activity was nothing new. The most famous example was the fifteenth-century French military commander Joan of Arc, who cropped her hair, donned leggings, and carried a sword. Seventeenth-century England had its own celebrated cross-dresser, the pickpocket and highway robber Mary Frith, alias "Moll Cutpurse." The title page of the script of *The Roaring Girle*, a stage play based on Moll's adventures, depicts her in breeches, smoking a pipe, and armed with a sword.[478] But while one eccentric woman might be seen as interesting, comic, or titillating, for ordinary women to parade about in men's garb seemed to many an unsettling, if not ominous, phenomenon. Outraged male writers censured the new fashion as if it were nothing less than a breach of Nature. Wrote poet William Averell: "Though they be in sexe Women, yet in attire they appear to be men . . . they are neither men nor women, but plaine Monsters."[479]

A leading clergyman claimed that women were seen even at church in garments "halfe male and halfe female . . . and
carrying a dagger." To some, women who dressed like men were undermining the very foundations of male supremacy. Where "Women-kinde the codpeeces did weare," warned one writer, "men to women Bow."[480] A private letter dated January 1620 reported that King James himself had disparaged the new fashion:

> Yesterday the bishop of London called together all his Clergie about this towne, and told them he had expresse commandment from the King to will them to inveigh vehemently against the insolencie of our women, and theyre wearing of brode brimed [broad-brimmed] hats, pointed dublets, theyre haire cut short or shorne, and some of them stilettoes or poinards [short swords] . . . the truth is the world is very far out of order, but whether this will mende it God knowes.

The same letter-writer later disclosed that not only the clergy but actors and ballad-singers too were denouncing women's mannish apparel.[481]

11. "MOLL CUTPURSE," TITLE PAGE, 1611

Two anonymous authors produced pamphlets in 1620 satirizing ambiguous clothing. The first, *Hic Mulier; or The Man-Woman*, charges that women of "all degrees . . . and all ages, from the Capitoll [London] to the Cottage" had donned men's garments and cut their hair. The second pamphlet, *Haec-Vir; or The Womanish-Man*, was published a week later. It describes an encounter between a man and a woman in which each mistakes the gender of the other. Apprised of his error, the foppish man is amazed. He berates the woman's manlike costume and behavior, and accuses her, among other faults, of being a slave to novelty. In response, she asserts her right to embrace change, "as becommeth a daughter of the world":

> I was created free, born free, and live free . . . we [women] are as free-borne as Men, have as free election, and as free spirits, we are compounded of like parts and may with like liberty make benefit of our Creations. . . .

When *Haec Vir* accuses her of having abandoned the "Customes of the Kingdome," she protests, "Custome Is an Idiot. . . . Oh for mercy sake bind us not to so hatefull a companion." The pamphlet ends with the "daughter of the world" and her opponent exchanging costumes and both promising henceforth to be "true men, and true women." [482] In real life, however, cross-dressing evidently continued. Eight years later the poet and pamphleteer Samuel Rowlands wrote, "Your Gallant is no man, unlesse his haire be of the womans fashion, dangling and waving over his shoulders; your woman no body, except (contrary to the modesty of her sexe) shee be halfe (at least) of the mans fashion. *O tempora! O mores!*" he exclaimed.[483]

. . . .

Charles I, who ascended to the throne in 1625, ruled a divided nation. On one side were Royalists, who favored an absolute monarchy; on the other were Roundheads, who supported Parliament, and Puritans, who wanted the Church of England "purified" of all Catholic practices. Charles's autocratic nature, his quarrels with Parliament, and his marriage to a Catholic princess had deepened the divide. Angry mobs formed in London at the slightest provocation, and aggrieved citizens from all walks of life deluged Parliament with petitions. With the nation on the brink of civil war, a new political constituency emerged: women.

On January 31, 1642, a delegation of women from London appeared at the House of Lords with a petition protesting shortages caused by "the present distractions and distempers of the state." Rebuffed by the Lords, the petitioners, about four hundred strong, returned the next day. Spotting the Duke of Lennox, they tried to hand the appeal directly to him, but he brushed them aside, alluding derisively to a parliament of women. Finally, the Lords permitted a dozen of the petitioners to state their grievances. Whatever transpired in the chambers, the women evidently were not mollified.[484] A private letter reported that a group of women joined by some workingmen had accosted the Duke of Lennox and other nobles as they exited Parliament.

Later that same week a delegation of female petitioners visited the House of Commons to protest the decline in trade and to ask that "Popish Lords" and bishops be ejected from the upper House. Although their petition was deferential, their demeanor was not. The Sergeant-Major on duty advised the Members of Parliament (MPs) that there were "great Multitudes of Women at the Houses, pressing to present a Petition to the Parliament; and their Language is, that where there is One Woman now here, there would be Five hundred To-morrow; and that it was as good for them to die here, as at home." The Commons refused to hear their petition and asked the guard "to pacify the Multitude, and send them Home in Quietness," since the House was "now in consideration of Matters of great Consequence."[485]

A few days later "Mrs Anne Stagg, a Gentlewoman and Brewer's wife," led a group composed largely of tradesmen's wives to Westminster to renew their protest against popish Lords in the upper House. Alluding to their "fraile condition" as women, they assured the MPs that they did not seek to equal themselves with men, "either in Authority or wisdom." They acknowledged that "It may be thought strange and unbeseeming our sex to shew ourselves by Way of Petition," but, they added, "Women are sharers in the common Calamities that accompany both Church and Common-Wealth."[486] John Pym, the leader of parliamentary opposition to King Charles I, promptly and courteously assured the women that their plea would be satisfied. This seeming victory, it later developed, was more the result of fortuitous timing than effective persuasion since Parliament had already drafted a bill calling for the unseating of all bishops.

In the summer of 1643, a year into the civil war, women staged a series of extraordinary peace demonstrations. Assembled before the House of Commons on August 8, their hats festooned with white silk ribbons, were "two or three hundred Oyster wives, and other dirty and tattered sluts," reported a London newspaper. While crying for peace, the paper commented tartly, they threatened to physically attack those MPs who opposed them. But another paper said that they "cryed for Peace, Comitted no great disorder," and then went home. Whatever the fact, there is no doubt but that the next morning women reappeared in far greater numbers—perhaps five or six thousand—and in a more combative mood. They filled the courtyard at Westminster and submitted a petition to the Commons that asked, above all, for an end to warfare. The Commons responded curtly that they too desired peace and would consider the women's petition, but meanwhile they should repair to their own homes. An MP noted in his diary that the women were displeased with this answer and "kepte knocking and beatinge of the outwarde door before the Parliament House," threatening to take hold of certain MPs and "caste [them] into the Thames." By afternoon, the petitioners had pushed past the sentries and were blocking the doors to the chambers so completely that no one could enter or exit. When the guards shot harmless powder from their muskets into the crowd, the women jeered at them and hurled bricks. The guards answered with bullets and drawn swords. What happened next is uncertain. One account said that that a troop of mounted soldiers attacked the departing women and killed three or four of them; another, that the women withdrew, vowing that "they would come againe the next day with greater strength and would have swords and guns likewise."[487] It was widely rumored that "Men of the Rabble in Womens Clothes" had incited the demonstration.[488]

Women affiliated with the radical Leveller movement submitted at least five petitions to Parliament during the turbulent years between 1649 and 1653. The first was brought to Westminster on a Monday morning in April by hundreds of women displaying a green ribbon, the Leveller symbol. Like an earlier petition submitted by Leveller men, it asked for the release of four imprisoned leaders of the movement. The women had collected an impressive number of signatures, about ten thousand according to some reports, but the MPs nevertheless refused to receive the petition. Undaunted, the women returned on Tuesday and again on Wednesday, at which point the legislators agreed to read the document. Their answer—delivered to the waiting throng by a guard—was that "the matter you petition about is of an higher concernment then you understand, that the House gave an answer to your Husbands; and therefore that you are desired to goe home, and looke after your owne businesse, and meddle with your huswifery."[489]

Contemporary accounts differ about what happened next. The petitioners may have gone home "very civilly," as one report had it; or they may have been forced down the stairs at the point of muskets, as another claimed. What we do know is that they were back again in early May. Thwarted and belittled in their previous attempt to plead the cause of incarcerated comrades, they now came before Parliament to plead on their own behalf. Their statement said in part:

> We cannot but wonder and grieve that we should appear so despicable in your eyes as to be thought unworthy to petition or represent our grievances to this honourable House. Have we not an equal interest with the men of this Nation in those liberties and securities contained in the Petition of Right and other good Laws of the Land?[490] Are any of our lives, limbs, liberties or goods to be taken from us more then from men, but by due processe of Law and conviction of twelve men of the Neighbourhood? And can you imagine us to be so sottish or stupid, as not to perceive, or not to be sencible when daily those strong defences of our Peace and wellfare are broken down and trod underfoot by force of arbitrary power?

In closing, they prayed that their plea would not be neglected because it was "presented to you by the weak hand of women." And they warned that posterity would judge the legislators harshly if they were to "deny us in things so evidently just and reasonable."[491]

In their next petitions to Parliament, Leveller women boldly demanded major legislative reforms. Declaring that they were speaking on behalf of "the poor, enslaved, oppressed, and distressed men and women of this land," they likened themselves to the biblical Esther, who had intervened with the Persian king on behalf of the Jews. And like Esther, they added, they had been emboldened by the justness of their cause.[492]

Denied the opportunity to express their views by voting or serving in the government, the female petitioners sought to exert political influence in the only way open to them: petitioning. They might endeavor to reduce the sting of their "unbeseeming" conduct by using conciliatory language and pleading the frailty of women. But they would not be put off nor would they give up. Confident and resolute, they came before the nation's rulers as freeborn English citizens who felt that they were entitled, in their own right, to seek redress of grievances.

16 ENTERPRISING WOMEN IN THE DUTCH REPUBLIC

The seventeenth-century Dutch Republic was a marvel of the age. Created in 1581 by seven provinces in the northern Netherlands that declared their independence from Spain, the young nation had prospered spectacularly. By 1600, it had become a center of international finance, a leading producer of textiles, and the world's foremost naval power. Before long, Dutch merchants had established trading posts on four continents.

With much of the male population engaged in building and defending the far-flung empire, women assumed many new commercial responsibilities. An English businessman visiting Holland in 1622 remarked in a letter that the Dutch matrons were "so well vers'd in Bargaining, Cyphering [arithmetic], and Writing, that in the absence of their Husbands in long Sea-voyages they beat the Trade at home, and their Words will pass in equal Credit."[493] Some seventeen years later, Dutch physician Johan van Beverwijk of Dordrecht noted proudly that "with us, many women, without forgetting their house, practice trade and commerce."[494]

Girls in merchant, shopkeeper, and artisan families acquired commercial know-how easily and naturally since workplace and living quarters often shared one roof. In addition, girls were taught the three Rs—plus a fourth, Religion—in publicly funded primary schools. French humanist scholar Joseph Scaliger, who lived in Leiden, was surprised to find that even servant girls could read.[495] In the view of a leading modern historian of the republic, "literacy among both men and women attained a level . . . wholly exceptional in Europe."[496] The seventeenth-century English writer Judith Drake envied her sisters in the Netherlands. In her own country, she remarked ruefully, women were brought up "ignorant of business," while in the Dutch Republic, they were "taught Arithmetick," and could be found "managing not only the Domestick Affairs of the

Family, but making and receiving all Payments as well great as small, keeping the Books, ballancing the Accounts, and doing all the business."[497]

Dutch law facilitated women's business dealings, for although the statutes of most of the provinces classified women along with children as legally incompetent, economic considerations often overrode gender bias. Thus, couples were able to own property jointly, and single women over the age of 25 were free to carry on trade independently.[498] Moreover, daughters often shared parental bequests equally with sons, and widows were legally entitled to at least half of a spouse's estate (in contrast, English widows were guaranteed only a third).[499]

Yet women's entrepreneurial activity and the authority it inevitably conferred were by no means universally approved. Dutch books and pamphlets presented a rogue's gallery of imperious, lascivious, deceitful amazons who tyrannized, cuckolded, and bankrupted their unfortunate husbands. Commented Leiden University professor Marcus Z. Boxhorn: "You will see not only grown and marriageable daughters, but also quite little girls sitting out all over the place to sell their delicacies. They suck in their desire for profit with their mothers' milk."[500]

To foreigners, gender relations in the Dutch Republic often seemed shockingly askew. An Englishman who visited in the mid 1600's declared, "The wives mostly wear the breeches." He thought it noteworthy that "the laws of the country . . . inflict punishments upon those that misuse their wives."[501] A "tragicomedy" by the English playwrights John Fletcher and Philip Massinger mocked Dutchmen for having supinely ceded authority to women. In one scene, Dutch wives tell an Englishwoman that in Holland,

> You may behold the general freedom
> We live and traffic in, the joy of women.
> No imperious Spanish eye governs our actions,
> Nor Italian jealousy locks up our meetings:
> We are ourselves our own disposers, masters,
> And those that you call husbands are our Servants.

The Englishwoman responds:

> Our country brings us up to fair obedience,
> To know our husbands for our Governors,
> So to obey, and serve 'em: two heads make monsters.[502]

Yet the "joy of women" applied to women of the middling sort, not to wage-earners. The most fortunate among the latter were teachers, midwives, and supervisors in hospitals, orphanages, and homes for the aged. But such positions were relatively few and the necessary training difficult to acquire. Most female wage-earners were domestic servants, and like servants in other European countries, those in the Dutch Republic were vulnerable to physical and sexual abuse. On the other hand, they had a measure of legal protection.[503] A French wine dealer who lived in Leiden marveled that anyone who struck a maid could be "condemned by the magistrates . . . to pay a fine and sometimes her full wage although she has not served her full term."[504] A German visitor commented that one could hardly tell servant girls from their mistresses because the attire and demeanor of the two were so similar.[505]

Considerably worse off than most servants were women who toiled in Haarlem's linen-bleaching fields or in Leiden's proto-capitalist textile industry as spinners and carders. Although they worked long hours in unhealthy conditions for low pay and had to contend with frequent layoffs, adult women competed for these jobs with children brought to Leiden from orphanages in Liège and other cities.[506] Still, real wages in the republic were the highest on the Continent, more than double those in the southern Netherlands (the present Belgium and Luxembourg) or the German states.[507]

Lower still on the economic ladder were sailors' wives, widows, and immigrant girls on their own. Lacking funds, skills, or families to assist them, they were forced to eke out a livelihood as best they could as peddlers, preparers and servers of food and drink, spinners, seamstresses, and laundresses—the same subsistence jobs that had been women's work since the beginning of urban life four centuries earlier. Some women performed hard physical labor as road-builders, grave-diggers, and warehouse workers; in Rotterdam, the majority of brick-makers and ironworkers were female.[508] And prostitutes were numerous, despite laws that made them subject to public flogging and incarceration in Amsterdam's *Spinhuis*, a female correctional institution.[509]

. . . .

Women contributed abundantly to the seventeenth-century Dutch Republic's golden age of art and literature. Among a dozen or more female artists who rose to the top of their profession, the best-known today are Rachel Ruysch and Judith Leyster.[510] Both were the wives of painters, the mothers of several children, and members of the painters guilds in their respective cities, Amsterdam and Haarlem. Ruysch left nearly a hundred signed works. Her exquisite renditions of flowers were greatly admired during her lifetime and may be seen today in Amsterdam's Rijksmuseum and the Norton Simon Museum in California, as well as in London, Prague, and Melbourne.[511]

Judith Leyster achieved the guild rank of master artist, which entitled her to run her own workshop and hire apprentices. Her canvases in major museums include a smiling self-portrait at Washington, D.C.'s National Gallery, a study of a young boy playing the flute at the national museum of Stockholm, the *Merry Drinker* at Amsterdam's Rijksmuseum, and depictions of family life at the Louvre and London's National Gallery. But in a familiar pattern, she produced no important paintings after her marriage.[512]

The artist and pioneer biologist Maria Sibylla Merian was born in Frankfurt, Germany, in 1647 to a family of artists, but spent much of her life in the Dutch Republic. Fascinated from childhood by butterflies and moths, she continued after her marriage to collect live specimens and draw them at different stages of their life cycles. Her two-volume work *The Caterpillars' Marvelous Transformation and Strange Floral Food* contains a hundred engravings. Merian's own lifespan was also marked by dramatic transformations. In 1685, she separated from her husband, who subsequently divorced her, and moved with her two daughters and widowed mother to the northern Dutch province of Friesland where she joined the Labadists, a dissident Protestant sect. For six years she adhered to the sect's abstemious lifestyle, then once again reinvented herself by moving to Amsterdam to earn her living as a painter. At age 52, Merian embarked on the great adventure of her life. Accompanied by her 21-year-old daughter, she sailed to the Dutch colony of Suriname on the northeast coast of South America (later, Dutch Guiana) to study its flora and fauna.[513]

A contemporary of Merian's was Anna Maria van Schurman, a gifted artist, writer, philosopher, and linguist.[514] Van Schurman read and wrote Dutch, Latin, Hebrew, German, Greek, Italian, French, and Arabic, yet the University of Utrecht refused to admit her on account of gender. Although the school finally relented and gave permission for her to attend lectures, she had to agree to sit behind a curtain, unseen and unheard by the other students. Writing to a friend, van Schurman criticized "the theory which would allow only a minority of my sex" to acquire wisdom, "the crown of all human achievement." Some people may believe, she added, "that the distaff and the needle supply women with all the scope they need, but I decline to accept this. ... They who would constrain us women have never tasted the harshness they wish to mete out."[515]

In 1638, van Schurman composed a Latin treatise in defense of women who, like her, wished to devote their lives to scholarship. A woman from a privileged family who had leisure time, she argued, ought to be permitted to pursue knowledge, provided she did not allow her studies to interfere with domestic duties or try to make use of her knowledge in the public sphere. The treatise, which was translated into English with the title *The Learned Maid or, Whether a Maid May Be a Scholar,* attracted considerable attention.

Taking advantage of her celebrity, she embarked on a letter-writing campaign to promote "our cause," that is, access to higher education for women from the upper strata of society. To each of her correspondents— female scholars and writers in England, Sweden, Germany, France, Ireland, and Denmark—she sent words of sisterly friendship and encouragement.[516] For though she had never met most of them, she considered them kindred spirits who, like her, had fought against and overcome the obstacles that blocked women's path to knowledge.

To the 75-year-old Frenchwoman Marie de Gournay, author of the 1622 tract *The Equality of Men and of Women* (*L'Egalité des hommes et des Femmes*), van Schurman sent a Latin verse she had composed in her honor. It said in part:

> Anna Maria van Schurman congratulates
> the great and noble-minded heroine of Gournay,
> strong defender of the cause of our sex. . . .
> Lead on, glory of Gournay,
> we shall follow your standard,
> for in you our cause advances.[517]

12. ANNA MARIA VAN SCHURMAN SELF-PORTRAIT, 1633

Van Schurman predicted that her own fame would not endure since "the reader of history finds no more record of [women's] names . . . than a ship leaves traces of her course through the waves."[518] That was indeed the fate of Judith Leyster, whose paintings were misattributed to Franz Hals for more than two centuries. However, it seemed, at least for a time, that van Schurman might be an exception. She was celebrated during her lifetime by the women who frequented the Paris salons,[519] and was admired in the eighteenth century by the learned Englishwomen known as bluestockings.[520] Even the minister Cotton Mather in far-off Massachusetts was aware of her work.[521]

Yet sixty-four years after van Schurman's death, Dorothea Erxleben—the first woman licensed to practice medicine in Germany and herself the author of a treatise advocating higher education for women—complained that the Dutch scholar's book "was not to be had." (Ironically, fifty years after that, another female proponent of education for women complained that Erxleben's treatise was "no longer available.")[522] Women's participation in the commercial and cultural life of the Dutch Republic was similarly ephemeral. For when the economic boom that had supported and facilitated female enterprise declined, women's participation was no longer encouraged. Those who could afford not to work withdrew into the domestic sphere, which had been defined throughout the boom period as woman's ideal milieu, the one for which Nature had designed her. Still, the Dutch female trader did not disappear from the stage of history, for in the rough-and-tumble Dutch colony in North America she once again had an opportunity to take part in the founding of a new state.

17   SHE-MERCHANTS

Soon after he stepped ashore in New Netherland in the summer of 1626, Isaack de Rasière discovered that several women in the colony were buying and selling animal skins in open violation of the Dutch West India Company's fur-trading monopoly. De Rasière, the company's representative in New Netherland, immediately sent a letter to his employers reporting the offense. He provided details: "The wife of Wolfert Gerritsen came to me with two otters, for which I offered her three guilders, ten stivers. She refused this and asked five guilders, whereupon I let her go, this being too much. The wife of Jacob Lourissen, the smith, knowing this, went to her and offered her five guilders, which Wolfert's wife again told me. Thereupon, to prevent the otters from being purloined [from the company], I was obliged to give her the five guilders."[523]

The company had hired the women and their families to raise crops in New Netherland and, in the words of the company charter, to advance "the peopling of those fruitful and unsettled parts."[524] However, it was soon obvious that employers and employees alike were more interested in profit than peopling—specifically, exploitation of North America's lucrative natural resources: beaver, otter, and mink.

That autumn the governor of New Netherland, Peter Minuit, met with representatives of the Lenni Lenape, an Algonquian-speaking Native American tribe that inhabited the northeastern woodlands, including Manhattan island. Minuit believed that when he paid sixty guilders worth of trade goods he had purchased Manhattan. But to the Native American way of thinking, Mother Earth could no more be the possession of any one group of people than could the air they breathed, or the waterways they traveled and fished, or the deer they hunted.[525] Minuit, oblivious to such subtleties, renamed his supposed acquisition New Amsterdam and moved some of the colonists to its southern tip.[526]

Two years later, New Amsterdam was still a far cry from its Old-World namesake since few people were interested in leaving the prosperous Dutch Republic for an uninviting colonial backwater. The town's non-native population in 1628 consisted of only 270 Europeans,[527] plus about fifteen enslaved women and men from Angola who had been taken from a captured Portuguese vessel. Their slave-names—Simon Congo, Antony Portugese—attested to life stories of abduction and bondage.[528] Commonly referred to collectively as "the company's Negroes," they supplied much of the labor for Manhattan's first structures: a fort, some houses, a windmill, roads, and a gallows.

To encourage immigration, the West India Company offered a grant of land—described as "a perpetual fief of inheritance"—to any person who agreed to transport at least fifty Europeans over the age of 15 to the colony and settle them on the property. The prospective landlords were promised military protection, a supply of African slaves, and political and judicial privileges equivalent to those enjoyed by feudal lords in the Middle Ages.[529] Of the several estates claimed in the next few years, the most successful was Rensselaerswyck, located in the Hudson Valley north of Manhattan. But as its owner, or patroon, Kiliaen van Rensselaer, soon discovered, the proud and independent seafaring people of the northern Netherlands made intractable vassals. Van Rensselaer protested to his agent in New Netherland that the people he engaged to live on his estate "contract with me here [in Holland] only *pro forma* and on their arrival there do as they please." Particularly aggravating were single women whose passage he had paid but who quickly married in Manhattan and never proceeded upriver.[530]

Van Rensselaer had ordered his colonists not to "barter any peltry with the savages," but the meager rewards of tenant farming could not compete with the easy money to be made in the fur trade. Whether justly or not, the patroon blamed women for breaking the rules. Thus, when goods went missing, he speculated that the wife, mother, and sister of one of the settlers had taken them to barter for furs. And when Wolfert Gerritsen asked to be released from his contract as a farm overseer ahead of time, van Rensselaer faulted Gerritsen's wife, the same woman who a few years earlier had driven a sharp bargain over the sale of two otter skins.[531] Yet there was nothing the patroon could do to stop such offenses, for despite his pretensions, he was not a feudal nobleman, the colonists were not medieval bondsmen and women, and New Netherland was not fourteenth-century Europe.

With immigration still proceeding at too slow a pace, the West India Company in 1640 relinquished its fur-trading monopoly (which had proved unenforceable in any event) and offered land to settlers on more generous terms than formerly. But no sooner had the colony begun at last to flourish than a party of Dutch soldiers raided a Lenape village located in the present Jersey City, New Jersey, and brutally massacred more than a hundred of its residents. The attack united the Algonquian-speaking peoples of the surrounding region and precipitated "Kieft's War," a bloody conflict named for the Dutch general who had led the initial attack. So many Europeans abandoned New Netherland during the two years the war lasted that the colony came close to total collapse.

While the war with the Algonquian nations raged, Dutch merchants in the north maintained close commercial and personal contacts with the five indigenous tribes that then made up the Iroquois Confederacy (or more accurately, the Haudenosaunee, meaning People of the Longhouse): the Cayugas, Mohawks, Oneidas, Onondagas, and Senecas. Among the Iroquois, women were at the center of family life. Children were considered descendants of their mother, land was passed down from mother to daughter, husbands lived in their wives' communal longhouse, and the women of the longhouse controlled the distribution of food and other supplies. Women also played important roles in Iroquois religious rites and political councils.

Geographical proximity had not, however, brought understanding. Even the Reverend Johannes Megapolensis, who was fluent in the Mohawk language, judged Iroquois gender customs by European standards. He wrote:

> They generally live without marriage; and if any of them have wives, the marriage continues no longer than seems good to one of the parties, and then they separate, and each takes another partner.... And, though they have wives, yet they will not leave off whoring; and if they can sleep with

another man's wife, they think it is a brave thing. The women are exceedingly addicted to whoring; they will lie with a man for the value of one, two, or three, schillings, and our Dutchmen run after them very much.... The women are obliged to prepare the land, to mow, to plant, and do everything; the men do nothing, but hunt, fish, and make war upon their enemies.[532]

The perspective of Mary Jemison—an Englishwoman who had been captured by the Senecas when she was about 13 and had lived among them for decades—was quite different. In 1824, when she was over eighty, she recounted her experiences, including her marriage to a Seneca man whom she loved and who, she said, treated her with generosity, tenderness, and kindness. She further claimed that the workload borne by Indian women was not severe, for although they were responsible for planting, tending, and harvesting corn, there was "no master to oversee or drive us, so that we could work as leisurely as we pleased." She also pointed out that since they wore animal skins, women were spared the tedious labor of spinning, weaving, and knitting.[533] "During Jemison's lifetime," wrote a historian of Native American captivity narratives, "Seneca women had rights possessed by few women in white or black America."[534]

After Kieft's War finally subsided in 1645, immigration to New Netherland rapidly resumed. Families, who made up about 70 percent of new arrivals,[535] generally settled on farmland in Brooklyn, Staten Island, New Jersey, or the Hudson Valley, while more mercantile types came to the colony's capital, Manhattan. Within the narrow confines of Manhattan island there resided Native American, African, Dutch, German, Scandinavian, French Huguenot, English, Flemish, and Walloon men, women, and children. Religious groups on the island included several Christian denominations whose presence was only grudgingly tolerated by the Calvinist majority, and an even less welcome minority: twenty-three Jews who had fled, penniless, from Brazil after the Dutch lost their Brazilian settlement to Portugal.[536] While the Native American population had declined drastically,[537] the number of enslaved Africans had multiplied.[538]

13. NEW AMSTERDAM, c. 1653

Enslaved African-American women and men were forced to labor without pay and were denied fundamental personal freedoms. Still, slavery Dutch-style offered a few concessions that were not available at the time in Massachusetts or Virginia or in the Spanish or Portuguese colonies to the south, including the right to sue in court, join a church congregation, and contract legal matrimony. The marriages of twenty-six couples of African descent and the baptisms of scores of infants born to Black parents are recorded in the archives of New Amsterdam's Dutch Reformed Church.[539]

In addition, the West India Company awarded a few faithful, long-serving slaves parcels of land and freedom, or, more accurately, a sort of half-freedom. This hybrid status, unique to New Netherland, required the payment of an annual fee plus the performance of certain duties as demanded by the company. When the Dutch traveler Jasper Danckaerts visited Manhattan in 1679, he noted in his journal that there were "many habitations of Negroes, mulattoes, and whites" along Broadway, a street that followed the north-south route of a Lenape trail. Danckaerts wrote that the Negroes were company slaves who had "obtained their freedom and settled themselves down . . . on this road, where they have ground enough to live on with their families."[540]

Half-freedom had a deeply painful proviso: children did not inherit their parents' semi-emancipated status. The white population of the colony sent a protest to the home country in 1650, arguing that it was "contrary to the laws of every people that anyone born of a free Christian mother should be a slave and compelled to remain in servitude."[541] But the company countered that only three youngsters were affected by the rule, one of whom, Lysbet Antonissen, was a "wench with Martin Cregier, who hath reared her from a little child at his own expense."[542] Twenty years after her parents' manumission, Lysbet Antonissen, still a slave, was convicted of setting fire to the home of the man she had worked for since childhood. She was sentenced to be strangled and then burned at the stake. But unbeknown to her, a postscript to the order of execution directed that "all the preparations for strangling and burning her be made, and then that she be pardoned and returned to her master."[543]

In the New World, as in the Old, women were excluded from religious and political offices and from the legal and medical professions, midwifery excepted. On farms, they cared for the livestock and poultry and cultivated kitchen gardens. In cities, they worked mainly as domestic servants, street vendors, seamstresses, and laundresses—the same low-status, low-paid jobs allotted to women in their home countries. Sometimes their houses did double duty as retail shops or taverns. Yet despite the diversity of nationalities, the gender customs and laws of New Netherland were predominantly Dutch, which meant that women had the right to engage in commercial activities.

In a 1654 New Amsterdam court proceeding, for example, Jan Harmensen, who was accused of nonpayment of a debt, testified that since "his wife has gone to Fatherland, and he does not know if she has paid plaintiff, he requests delay until his wife's return." In another New Amsterdam legal case a few years later, the plaintiff's wife appeared in court on his behalf. She accused the defendant, a furniture maker, of not paying for some land he had purchased. The defendant, who was present in court, acknowledged the debt but pleaded for more time to pay since *his* wife was currently upriver trading chairs for beaver pelts.[544]

Jasper Danckaerts' journal has this description of a Dutch female trader:

> She is a truly worldly woman, proud and conceited, and sharp in trading with *wild* people [Native Americans], as well as *tame* ones.... This trading is not carried on without fraud, and she is not free from it, as I have observed. She has a husband, which is her second one.... He remains at home quietly, while she travels over the country to carry on the trading. In fine she is one of the Dutch female-traders, who understand their business so well."[545]

A record from Schenectady, north of Albany, says that Hilletje van Slijck, the daughter of a Dutch man and a Mohawk (or part-Mohawk) woman, was a translator and agent in the fur trade.[546] And a letter written by Jeremias van Rensselaer of Rensselaerswyck (the first patroon's son) mentions a woman named Tryn Claas who refused to pay the 65 guilders she owed him, although "She has plenty of money, for at present she is a great trader."

In another letter, Jeremias van Rensselaer commented that he had gone into the brewery business for the sake of his 17-year-old bride, Maria van Cortlandt, since "in her father's house she always had the management thereof, to wit, the disposal of the beer and helping to find customers for it." After Jeremias's death, Maria took over the day-to-day management of the 750,000-acre manor at Rensselaerswyck.[547] The diarist Jasper Danckaerts, who visited her there, observed, "She is still in possession of the place, and still administers it as patroonesse."[548]

One of the most successful New Netherland businesswomen was Margaret Hardenbroeck, who arrived in New Amsterdam alone in 1659 at age 22, and soon married. When her husband died shortly after they were wed, she took charge of his small shipping business and expanded it enormously. Although she married again—her second husband was Frederick Philipse, a wealthy slave-trader and real-estate speculator in the Hudson Valley—she continued to operate her own fleet of merchant ships, occasionally traveling back to the Netherlands on one of her ships to supervise the cargo.[549]

• • • •

The Dutch lost their New World colony in 1664 when New Netherland surrendered without bloodshed to a superior English force.[550] Changing the name of the colony to New York was easily accomplished but making it over in the image of the home country—with English laws, customs, and language—proved more difficult. Some churches continued for decades to conduct services in Dutch,[551] and couples continued to draft wills that were "written after the ancient Dutch form," that is, joint wills that gave at least half of the estate to the surviving spouse and did not privilege eldest sons.[552]

A historian who examined wills written by individuals of Dutch descent in five upstate New York counties from 1664 until 1754 found that 73 percent were written in Dutch.[553] And in 1678, an Englishman who remarked "what a heap of wealth" the son of Frederick Philipse would inherit was informed that "the daughter must go halves for so was the manner amongst them."[554]

New laws were enacted to further the process of Anglicization. Divorce, infrequent enough in the Dutch colony (only three cases were recorded between 1655 and 1664), became impossible. After 1675, no divorce was granted anywhere in New York for more than a century.[555] And in 1683 the New York legislature adopted the *Charter of Libertyes and Priviledges*, a document that is often praised for its broad guarantees of civil and religious freedoms but which deprived women of many rights they had enjoyed under Dutch governance. Most harmful was the introduction of English common-law provisions that nullified the legal existence of married women and slashed the inheritance rights of wives, daughters, and widows. One clause, for example, allotted a widow only forty days after her husband's death to "tarry" in her home before the property passed to her late husband's (male) heirs.[556] Another law passed the next year grouped married women with children, criminals, and individuals of unsound mind—a classification that must have seemed strange, even laughable, to those who had dealt with Dutch female traders.[557]

Nor did the misnamed *Charter of Libertyes* offer any liberties to African Americans, an omission that was especially egregious since the number of slaves imported from Africa and the Caribbean increased so rapidly that at the turn of the century enslaved women and men made up 14 percent of the population of the province. In 1702, the New York legislature passed an *Act for Regulating Slaves*, which prohibited enslaved persons from assembling in groups of more than three, conducting independent business dealings, leaving their owner's property without a signed permit, or testifying in court against a free person. Moreover, a Dutch statute that had made it unlawful for a master to whip a slave without first obtaining official permission was replaced by a new law that gave owners the right to punish slaves in whatever manner they chose, provided the punishment did not result in the death or maiming of the victim. Free Blacks, who made up a small proportion of the African-American population, also suffered setbacks. Freedoms they had previously possessed—including the right to own land, contract marriage, and engage in business—were gradually curtailed.

The breaking point came a few months after a slave market was set up in Manhattan at the foot of Wall Street. In April 1712, a group of more than twenty African-born slaves planned and carried out a carefully coordinated revolt which resulted in the deaths of nine white residents of New York City. Twenty-one Blacks were apprehended, six of whom committed suicide. The others were convicted and brutally executed. One of those sentenced to death was a pregnant woman who was allowed to live long enough to deliver her child.[558]

• • • •

In spite of many changes in custom and law, New York retained aspects of its Dutch character well into the eighteenth century, especially in the northern part of the province. A prominent lawyer observed in 1757 that Dutch was still so commonly spoken in upstate New York "that the sheriffs find it difficult to obtain persons sufficiently acquainted with the English tongue, to serve as jurors in the courts of law." He added, "The manners of the people differ as well as their language."[559]

An early eighteenth-century arithmetic textbook that belonged to a little girl named Sarah Dubois who lived in the upstate New York community of New Paltz is revealing. Although the book is written in English, its contents imply an ongoing tradition of female participation in trade, for it has questions on weights and measures, currency exchange, simple and compound interest, and computation of discounts—skills Sarah had to master if she wished to follow in the footsteps of her Dutch mother, who helped to run the family retail store.[560]

In January 1734, Peter Zenger's *New York Weekly Journal* ran a letter that had purportedly been sent to the paper by a group of widows but had actually been written by men who were opposed to the current government. Its humor depended upon readers recognizing a familiar denizen of the city, the Dutch "she-merchant." It said:

> We the widows of this city, have had a meeting and as our case is something deplorable we beg you will give it place in your *Weekly Journal*. . . . most of us are she merchants, and as we in some measure contribute to the support of government, we ought to be entitled to some of the sweets of it.[561]

The persistence of the female trader is charmingly illustrated in a 1724 letter Cadwallader Colden, a prominent Manhattan physician and politician, sent to an English merchant. He wrote that he was enclosing some money for the purchase of goods that he wished to use for a "small adventure" he had in mind. He explained: "I send it to please a little Boy and Girl who want to be merchants . . . like their play fellows the Dutch Children here.[562]

18 DISSENT AND DEFIANCE IN NEW ENGLAND

After more than two months at sea, the *Mayflower* made landfall at Plymouth, Massachusetts, on a wintry day in 1620. Twelve years earlier many of its 102 passengers had left their English homeland and immigrated to the Dutch Republic in search of freedom of worship. Now, disillusioned by the materialism of Dutch society and fearing its corrupting influence on their children, these stalwart Pilgrims had decided to abandon the Old World. Here in the virgin wilderness of North America they hoped to create a community where they would be able to live in strict conformity with God's holy ordinances—as they interpreted them.

A decade later a second wave of English religious nonconformists embarked on the perilous North Atlantic crossing. Fleeing persecution at the hands of King Charles I, these refugees, known to history as the Puritans, also wished to create a society based on biblical precepts. Their leader, John Winthrop, described their new home as a "city upon a hill" to serve as a model of righteousness for all of Christendom.[563]

By 1640, about 20,000 people had left England for New England. But in contrast to Virginia, New Netherland, New France, and New Spain, where the first European settlers were largely male, the New England colonies were settled from the beginning by many family groups.[564] Indeed, families were central to the Puritans' holy endeavor, for as the General Court of Connecticut explained, "The prosperity and well being of Common weles [Commonwealths] doth much depend upon the well government and ordering of particuler Familyes."[565] A Connecticut minister instructed his congregation that "the foundation of all societies is laid in families," while a Massachusetts preacher declared that God himself had chosen "to lay the foundations both of State and Church, in a family, making that the Mother Hive, out of which both those swarms ... issued forth."[566] Several colonial legislatures issued decrees that made family life virtually compulsory.[567] Although women in northwestern Europe often postponed matrimony until their late twenties, in New England nearly every female married, married young, and if widowed, quickly remarried.[568]

The model Puritan family was a fixed constellation at the center of which was a patriarch whose authority was affirmed by Scripture, law, and custom. The Reverend John Robinson, the beloved pastor of the Pilgrims during their sojourn in the Dutch Republic, took it upon himself to instruct women on their marital obligations. The married woman, Robinson asserted, must behave with "reverend subjection in all lawful things to her husband." He in turn "ought to give honor to the wife, as to the weaker vessel"; but if he failed to do so, she still must not "shake off the bond of submission, but must bear patiently the burden, which God hath laid upon the daughters of Eve."[569]

In practice, however, the ideal of wifely subjection promulgated by the Reverend Robinson was difficult to sustain in early New England, where humility was a less useful female trait than capability. At a time when every household had to function as its own infant nursery, primary school, hospital, food preparation center, and manufactory of clothing, candles, and soap, families depended upon the skill and labor of women who, like the virtuous wife of the Old Testament, rose at dawn and ate not the bread of idleness.[570] The Massachusetts minister who advised his congregation, "tho' the Husband be the Head of the Wife, yet she is an Head of the Family" was only stating what was obvious to everyone.[571]

Moreover, since the exigencies of pioneer life sometimes required wives to act in place of husbands, English laws that restricted women's agency had a tendency to wither and lose their force when transplanted to the hardscrabble soil of New England. Especially impracticable was the common-law doctrine of *feme covert,* which forbid married women to sign contracts, negotiate business deals, or testify in court.[572] As historian Richard Morris observed, there was a "substantial advance" in the legal position of the wife in colonial New England.[573]

Finally, the female colonists themselves were part of the problem. A historian who analyzed the archives of Plymouth colony found that wives were accused of "abusive carriage" toward their mates about as frequently as husbands.[574] And while the earliest Massachusetts legal code, the *Body of Liberties*, protected wives from "bodilie correction or stripes by her husband," it added a significant proviso: "unlesse it be in his owne defence upon her assa[u]lt."[575] Clearly, the daughters of early modern Europe were not cast in the mold of Patient Griselda, the longsuffering medieval wife in Boccaccio's *Decameron*. The Reverend Robinson himself ruefully acknowledged, "Many proud women think it a matter of scorn and disgrace, thus to humble themselves to God and their husbands." Such women, he declared, choose "a sin of rebellion."

In truth, even a wife who sincerely wished to comply with the severe mandate laid down by New England clerics might find it problematic. For the ministers counseled on the one hand that female subordination was divinely ordained; on the other, that women, no less than men, were accountable for their own behavior. To reconcile two such fundamentally irreconcilable principles required the wisdom of a Solomon.

John Winthrop, the first governor of the Massachusetts Bay Colony, knew that he was fortunate to have a spouse, Margaret Tyndal Winthrop, who was an exemplary Puritan helpmate. Writing to her in 1629 as he was preparing to immigrate to North America, he thanked God for having blessed him with "a wife who is such a helpe and incouragement to me in this greate worke, wherein so many wives are soe great an hindrance to theirs."[576] Winthrop had personal experience with one such hindering woman in his sister, Lucy Winthrop Downing, who confessed to him that she was loath to submit to her husband's wish to move to Massachusetts because she dreaded "the hazards of the sea with our little ones shrinking about us" and the deprivations of pioneer life. "From extremities good Lord deliver me!" she implored.[577] Lucy held out for two years, but finally agreed to sail in 1638.

Also reluctant to travel to the New World was Elizabeth Mansfield Wilson. Her husband, the Puritan minister John Wilson, had embarked in 1630 without her or their four children. When his letters urging her to join him had no effect, he re-crossed the Atlantic to entreat her in person. Her obdurate refusal must have been the talk of the Puritan community. Margaret Winthrop, who was readying her own departure at the time, mentioned in a letter to her stepson that the Reverend Wilson had visited her. "He cannot yet persuade his wife to go," she reported, "for all he hath taken this pains to come and fetch her. I marvel what mettle she is made of. Sure she will yield at last." But in a subsequent letter, Margaret revised her prediction. "If he [the Reverend Wilson] goe, it must be without his wife's consent, for she is more averce [adverse] than ever she was." Wilson had to make a second return voyage before Elizabeth relented. She finally arrived in Boston in 1635, five years after her husband.[578]

As earnestly as New England's founding fathers wished to resurrect the Old Testament world of the ancient patriarchs, their ability to do so was limited. Many factors thwarted their goal, not least of which were the material conditions of life in early America and the consciousness of the women whose cooperation they counted on to help build, support, and populate their city on a hill.

. . . .

A bitter controversy in which a woman was the central figure erupted in 1636, tearing the Massachusetts colony apart and threatening to topple the established order. According to a minister who had experienced the crisis at first hand, the woman and her supporters had undermined the three main pillars of society: "in Church and State, and in families, setting division betwixt husband and wife!" The rebels, he later commented, were so imbued with "a spirit of pride, insolency, [and] contempt of authority" that it was "a wonder of mercy that they had not set our Churches on a fire, and consumed us all therein."[579]

The individual who lit this near-conflagration was Anne Marbury Hutchinson, a 43-year-old Englishwoman who had arrived in Massachusetts in September 1634 with her husband of twenty-two years, William Hutchinson, and their eleven surviving children. The daughter of a minister, Anne was profoundly religious and thoroughly grounded in theology. Her decision to leave England had been motivated by the recent departure for the New World of her religious mentor, the Reverend John Cotton.[580] The Hutchinsons settled in Boston and were admitted to the church.

The Reverend Cotton later recalled that Anne initially "did much good in our Town." She proved "skilfull and helpfull" to women during childbirth, he observed, and would make use of such occasions to engage the women present in the birthing room in fruitful discussion of their spiritual condition.[581] Governor Winthrop, however, discerned a sinister side to Anne's seemingly benevolent care of women, noting that soon after joining the church, "shee began to go to work, and being a woman very helpfull in the times of child-birth, and other occasions of bodily infirmities . . . shee easily insinuated her selfe into the affections of many."[582]

It was common practice in Boston for church members to meet in private residences for religious discourse, and Anne Hutchinson opened her home to a regular weekly gathering of women. At first, only a half-dozen or so attended, among them her sister, Katharine Scott; Jane Hawkins, then Boston's chief midwife; and Mary Barrett Dyer, the young wife of a cloth merchant.[583] So long as her listeners were few and female, the Boston authorities raised no objection. But they became concerned when she organized a second weekly lecture that included men as well as women, an unease that increased as sixty to eighty people crowded into the Hutchinson parlor each week—this in a town whose adult population in 1636 numbered about five hundred. Worse yet, although Hutchinson disingenuously claimed that "wee do no more but read the notes of our teachers [ministers] Sermons, and then reason of them by searching the Scriptures," she apparently also ventured to criticize the views of certain clergymen and put forward her own contrary beliefs.[584]

What Hutchinson believed, in broad outline, was that an inner experience of grace is the truest indication that an individual is among "the elect," that is, has been singled out by God for salvation. Traditional Puritans considered this doctrine, known as antinomianism, a heresy that was likely to lead to a breakdown of moral standards, for it implied that persons whom the Holy Spirit blessed (or "justified," in the vocabulary of the period) were not obliged to follow the dictates of the ministers. Yet this was the very aspect of Hutchinson's ideas that some people found particularly attractive, for it offered any believer, however low in social status, lacking in formal education, or derelict in religious observance, the possibility that she or he might be among those destined to attain Paradise.

By the beginning of 1637 people were choosing sides in the dispute. Supporting Hutchinson were the new governor of the colony and a substantial number of merchants and artisans, who felt that the policies of the colony's present leaders were stifling commercial growth. Aligned against her were several of the colony's most eminent men, including former governor Winthrop and John Wilson, the pastor of the First Church of Boston and the husband of the recalcitrant Elizabeth Wilson.

The Hutchinsonians soon comprised a majority of the members of the Boston church. Men who backed Hutchinson often interrupted the Reverend Wilson's sermons with queries and objections,[585] while her female followers took to standing and exiting the meetinghouse when Wilson was in the pulpit. The exodus of female parishioners could not be prevented, Winthrop later acknowledged, for if questioned, they could say that they had to care for a baby or a sick child.[586] It would be fascinating to know how, when, and where the female walkouts were planned, but the written record is silent on the matter.

Edward Johnson, an anti-Hutchinsonian, penned a lively account of the controversy without mentioning Hutchinson by name. "The weaker Sex." he wrote, "prevailed so farre, that they set up a Priest of their own Profession and Sex [presumably Hutchinson]." These "Sectaries," he added,

> . . .had many prety knacks to delude withall, and especially to please the Femall Sex. . . . Come along with me, sayes one of them, i'le bring you to a Woman that Preaches better Gospell then any of your black-coates that have been at the Ninneversity, a Woman of another kinde of spirit, who hath had many Revelations of things to come.[587]

In spring 1637, the General Court censured Hutchinson's brother-in-law, the Reverend John Wheelwright, and replaced the present governor, a Hutchinson supporter, with John Winthrop. An assembly of ministers, not to be outdone, issued a resolution declaring Hutchinson's meetings disorderly and illicit.[588] More than sixty Hutchinsonians signed a petition protesting the censure of Wheelwright, and Hutchinson defied the ministers' rebuke by continuing to hold meetings. "The case," Winthrop wrote, "was now desperate."[589]

Winthrop's own wife, the consummate Puritan helpmate Margaret Winthrop, was in turmoil. Margaret must have known Anne well since the two lived across the street from one another in Boston. Moreover, they had a great deal in common. Both were mature women in their forties, deeply religious, educated, and the mothers of large families. In a letter to her husband, Margaret confided, "Sad thoughts possess my spirits and I cannot repulce them, which makes me unfit for anythinge, wonderinge what the Lord meanes by all these troubles amonge us." She had discovered in herself, she added enigmatically, "an aferce spirit, and a tremblinge hart, not so willinge to submit to the will of God as I desyre."[590]

In early November the Massachusetts General Court summoned Anne Hutchinson for questioning. The ensuing two-day interrogation, a stenographic transcript of which survives, shows that she did indeed possess the "nimble wit and active spirit" that Governor John Winthrop attributed to her.[591] Winthrop, who presided over the examination, accused her of promoting erroneous opinions and conducting gatherings that were not "fitting for your sex." When he asked her by what scriptural rule she defended her public meetings, she cited Titus 2, "where the elder women are to teach the younger." Winthrop objected that she had misinterpreted Titus; she should have counseled the younger women "to love their husbands and not to make them to clash."[592] He countered her reference to Titus with the injunction in I Timothy, "I permit not a woman to teach."[593] Hutchinson alluded to Joel: "It is said, I will poure my Spirit upon your Daughters, and they shall prophesie. If God give mee a gift of Prophecy, I may use it." When Winthrop insisted that she still had not shown a Scriptural rule, she shot back:

> *Hutchinson:* I have given you two places of Scripture.
> *Winthrop:* But neither of them will sute your practise.
> *Hutchinson:* Must I shew my name written therein?

As the hearing wore on, Hutchinson grew rash, claiming that the Lord had shown her "which was the clear ministry and which the wrong."[594] When asked how she knew that it was the Lord who had informed her, she shocked her judges by asserting that, like the biblical Abraham, she had received "an immediate revelation" directly from God. Imprudently, she threatened, "if you go on in this course . . . you will bring a curse upon you and your posterity." At this, Winthrop proposed that she be banished from Massachusetts on account of "the troublesomeness of her spirit and the danger of her course amongst us." Most of the court agreed. Anne, still defiant, threw down a parting challenge:

> *Hutchinson:* I desire to know wherefore I am banished.
> *Winthrop:* Say no more, the court knows wherefore and is satisfied.

Some Massachusetts residents may have been less satisfied than the magistrates, however, for the court later reported "great disorders growing in this common welth" and ordered that "whosoever shall openly or willingly defame any court of justice, or the sentences or proceedings of the same, or any of the magistrats or other judges... shall be punished."[595] In Roxbury, several Hutchinson supporters refused to renounce their alleged errors and were excommunicated.[596] Massachusetts military commander John Underhill reported that he heard daily complaints from women "that New England men usurpe over their Wives, and keep them in servile subjection." Underhill, a Hutchinsonian, urged: "Let no man despise [the] advise and Counsell of his wife, though shee be a woman."[597]

Meanwhile, Hutchinson was detained in the home of a Roxbury clergyman until the weather was more favorable for her journey out of the colony. Finally, in March 1638, some four months after her court appearance, she was called to Boston for a hearing before the ministers. The church was crowded, but Hutchinson's husband and many of her chief defenders were absent, having moved to Rhode Island.

Hutchinson advised the ministers through a spokesman that the physical weakness caused by her long detention made her unable to endure a protracted examination. Nonetheless, the hearing went on from morning until eight o'clock at night. The ministers clearly were worried about Hutchinson's influence on women. The Reverend Shepard called her "a most dayngerous Spirit" who was "likely with her fluent Tounge and forwardnes in Expressions to seduce and draw away many, Espetially simple Weomen of her owne Sex."[598] And the Reverend Thomas Weld of Roxbury later explained that false prophets like Hutchinson "commonly laboured to worke first upon women, being (as they conceived) the weaker to resist . . . and if once they could winde in them, they hoped by them, as by an Eve, to catch their husbands also, which indeed often proved too true."[599]

The clergymen were also concerned that her doctrine would unleash rampant sexual promiscuity. She was asked if she held "that foule, groce [gross], filthye and abominable opinion held by Familists, of the Communitie of Weomen," that is, free love. The Reverend John Cotton—the man she had so esteemed that she had followed him to the New World—rebuked "the Sisters of our owne Congregation, many of whom I fear have bine too much seduced and led aside by her." He predicted that her ideas would necessarily lead to "promiscuus and filthie comminge togeather of men and Woemen without Distinction or Relation of Marriage."[600]

The ministers summoned Hutchinson again a week later to pronounce the formal order of excommunication. Although her demeanor was now more contrite, her judges were implacable. The Reverend Wilson commanded her "as a Leper to withdraw your selfe out of the Congregation." As she turned to walk toward the meetinghouse door, Mary Dyer, an early and faithful ally, rose to help her. Putting her hand through the older woman's arm, Dyer supported her as she made her way out.[601]

Reflecting on the crisis, the Reverend Wilson and John Winthrop were of one mind. To the minister, Hutchinson was "a dayngerus Instrument of the Divell raysed up by Sathan," while to Winthrop, she was "an instrument of Satan . . . fitted and trained to his service."[602] But although the leaders of the colony longed for harmony, it eluded them. "The devil would never cease to disturb our peace and to raise up instruments one after another," Winthrop lamented. And all too often, those instruments were female. "Amongst the rest," he wrote, "there was a woman in Salem, one Oliver his wife."

Mary Oliver made her first appearance in Winthrop's *Journal* in the troubled year of 1638. He reported that she stood in church and insistently argued with the minister (unfortunately, he did not reveal what she said). Charged with disturbing the peace, she was unapologetic and was sentenced to prison. Winthrop commented, "She was (for ability of speech, and appearance of zeal and devotion), far before Mrs. Hutchinson, and so the fitter instrument to have done hurt, but that she was poor and had little acquaintance." A few years later, Goodwife Oliver was whipped for reproaching the magistrates in court. Reported Winthrop: "She stood without tying, and bared her punishment with a masculine spirit, glorying in her suffering." Later still, a cleft stick was placed on her tongue to stop her from scolding the church elders.[603]

Also pursued by the Massachusetts General Court was Hutchinson's friend Boston midwife Jane Hawkins. Warned by the court in 1638 "not to meddle in surgery, phisick, drinks, plaisters, or oyles, nor to question matters of religion," she was subsequently ordered to leave the colony. Noted Winthrop, "It was known that she used to give young women oil of mandrakes and other stuff to cause conception; and she grew into great suspicion to be a witch."[604] Hawkins and her husband joined other Hutchinsonians in Rhode Island.

Anne Hutchinson's husband, who had remained loyal throughout her Boston ordeal, died in 1641. Afterward she emigrated with her six youngest children to New Netherland, where she and all but one of the children were killed by a Native American war party during Kieft's War between the Dutch and the Algonquians.[605]

• • • •

In 1656, two Quaker missionaries, Mary Fisher and Ann Austin, sailed into Boston Harbor. The Massachusetts authorities, dismayed by the arrival of these representatives of what they deemed another dangerous heresy, had the women apprehended, searched for witchmarks, and imprisoned. After holding them in isolation for five weeks, the officials charged them with witchcraft and sent them back to England. The following year Hutchinson's devoted supporter Mary Dyer—who had joined the Religious Society of Friends (the Quakers) during an extended visit to England in the 1650's—sailed for Boston with the intention of proselytizing in the colony. She too was seized and held incommunicado. Her husband finally managed to secure her release by promising that she would go directly to Rhode Island without talking to anyone in Massachusetts.

Before long, however, Dyer openly defied a recently enacted law that authorized the death penalty for any Quaker who reentered the colony after having previously been ejected.⁶⁰⁶ She was immediately arrested and sentenced to death. Once again, her husband managed to obtain her release.⁶⁰⁷ But when she returned a third time, the sentence was carried out. She was hung in Boston on May 31, 1660.

. . . .

Today monuments honoring both Anne Hutchinson and Mary Dyer stand on the grounds of the Massachusetts State House in Boston. The statue of Dyer, inscribed "Witness for Religious Freedom," was dedicated on the

14. ANNE HUTCHINSON AND DAUGHTER, 1922

tricentennial of her execution. The one of Hutchinson was commissioned by the Anne Hutchinson Memorial Association and the State Federation of Women's Clubs in 1920, the year female citizens of the United States won the vote. It bears the tribute, "Courageous Exponent of Civil Liberty and Religious Toleration."

Few American women have been as feared in their lifetimes as were Mary Dyer and Anne Hutchinson. Neither set out to protest gender inequity, but each insisted upon her right to speak and act according to her own conscience and understanding—powerful assertions of moral and intellectual independence.

PART 4

WOMEN MAKING HISTORY

19 REVOLUTIONARY WOMEN IN AMERICA

On the last day of March 1776 Abigail Adams wrote a letter to her husband, John Adams, who was then in Philadelphia attending the Second Continental Congress. Abigail was an enthusiastic supporter of the American Revolution, but now she had a different revolution in mind— one in which she hoped to enlist John's aid. Prudently, she cloaked the radical nature of her request in lighthearted banter. "By the way," she began, "in the new Code of Laws I suppose it will be necessary for you to make I desire you would Remember the Ladies, and be more generous and favourable to them than your ancestors."

> Do not put such unlimited power into the hands of the Husbands. Remember all Men would be tyrants if they could. If perticuliar care and attention is not paid to the Laidies we are determined to foment a Rebelion, and will not hold ourselves bound by any Laws in which we have no voice, or Representation. That your Sex are Naturally Tyrannical is a Truth so thoroughly established as to admit of no dispute, but such of you as wish to be happy willingly give up the harsh title of Master for the more tender and endearing one of Friend. Why then, not put it out of the power of the vicious and the Lawless to use us with cruelty and indignity with impunity. Men of Sense in all Ages abhor those customs which treat us only as the vassals of your Sex.

John made light of his wife's "saucy" remarks, while firmly denying her request:

> As to your extraordinary Code of Laws, I cannot but laugh. We have been told that our Struggle has loosened the bonds of Government every where; that Children and Apprentices were disobedient—that schools and Colledges were grown turbulent—that Indians slighted their Guardians and Negroes grew insolent to their Masters. But your Letter was the first Intimation that another Tribe, more numerous and powerfull than all the rest, were grown discontented. . . . Depend upon it, we know better than to repeal our Masculine systems.

To this, Abigail responded soberly, a note of sarcasm perhaps indicating her displeasure:

> I cannot say that I think you are very generous to the ladies; for whilst you are proclaiming peace and good-will to men, emancipating all nations, you insist upon retaining an absolute power over wives.[608]

Margaret Livingston of New York City also remarked on the contradiction between the high-flown rhetoric of the period and the status of women. In a letter to a niece written in October of 1776 she confided that she was not persuaded by the "romantic notions" about the goddess of liberty currently in vogue. "You know," she commented, "that our Sex are doomed to be obedient in every stage of life, so that we shant be great gainers by this contest."[609] However, many of Mistress Livingston's female compatriots would not have agreed with her, for more than a decade of patriotic propaganda had made them steadfast devotees of the goddess of liberty.

The propaganda campaign had begun in 1764, the year Britain imposed the first of a series of taxes on English imports to America. Merchants in the New England and Middle colonies retaliated by calling for boycotts of British goods. Since women were major consumers of several of the taxed items (sugar, tea, salt, clothing), their cooperation was essential to the success of the boycott. Thus, the fair sex—formerly instructed not to trouble themselves about matters outside the private sphere of home and family—were now being urged to demonstrate their patriotism. Women must not buy "gaudy, butterfly, vain, fantastic, and expensive Dresses brought from Europe," admonished the *Pennsylvania Journal,* but should wear instead "decent plain Dresses made in their own country."[610] And Maryland lawyer Daniel Dulany wrote: "Let the Manufacture of America be the Symbol of Dignity, the Badge of Virtue, and it will soon break the Fetters of Distress." A homespun garment made with patriotism, he added, "is more honourable and attractive than all the Pageantry and the Robes … of an emperor."[611]

By 1766 Benjamin Franklin was able to tell the British House of Commons that the colonists had already made "surprising progress" toward clothing themselves.[612] The English governor in New York confirmed his claim. "The Custom of making these Coarse Cloths [that is, homespun] in private families prevails throughout the whole province," he reported to the British Board of Trade, "and almost in every house a sufficient quantity is manufactured for the use of the family."[613] In Boston, the pro-British judge Peter Oliver later recalled, "Women and Children, both within Doors & without, set their Spinning Wheel a whirling in Defiance of Great Britain." It was, he commented caustically, "a new Species of Enthusiasm . . . the Enthusiasm of the Spinning Wheel."[614]

Communal spinning marathons in which young women assembled with their spinning wheels on village greens were held in many New England towns. Historian Laurel Thatcher Ulrich found almost fifty such events reported in local newspapers between 1768 and 1770.[615] Most of the newspaper stories emphasized the spinners' religious and charitable motives, but a few of the spinning bees evidently had a political purpose as well. The April 7, 1766, edition of the *Providence Gazette,* for example, described a gathering at Newport, Rhode Island, at which eighteen "Daughters of Liberty" displayed a "spirit to save their sinking country." But even events that had no obvious political objective reinforced the patriot cause by promoting homespun. Moreover, the spectacle of a bevy of pious maidens dressed in white doing gender-appropriate work under the watchful eye of a minister linked the revolutionary cause with traditional social values.

In rural households women who were already in the habit of making their own clothing stepped up production to create a surplus for sale. An eighteenth-century historian reported that "large quantities of coarse and common cloths were brought to market" and were preferred over finer British imports.[616] Market days and fairs, which had been commonplace in the seventeenth century, were revived in New York and Philadelphia for the distribution of homemade textiles. In Boston, a merchant advertised that he "takes in all Sorts of Country-made Cloths at his Store."[617]

In 1769, William Molineaux, a Boston merchant and ardent patriot, opened a spinning school where, he later boasted, three hundred women and children were taught to spin "in the most compleat manner."[618] According to a Boston newspaper, "the laudable practice of spinning is almost universally in vogue among the female children of this town."[619] In 1775, the United Company of Philadelphia for Promoting American Manufactures advertised for local women to pick up cotton, wool, and flax at the company headquarters to take home for spinning. The ad noted the importance of spinning at "this time of public distress,"[620] but when addressing potential investors, the company president highlighted the advantage of using low-wage employees. Speaking with unselfconscious candor, he pointed out, "The expense of manufacturing cloth will be lessened from the great share women and children will have in them."[621] In New York City, a charitable society founded several cloth-producing establishments, providing a source of income to "numbers of distressed women, now in the poor-house."[622]

Although tea was less central to British economic interests than textiles, it too was the object of propaganda directed toward women. In 1770, Philadelphia poet Hannah Griffitts penned a verse entitled "The Female Patriots" in which she urged women to abstain from tea and other taxed goods. "Let the Daughters of Liberty nobly arise," she wrote, "And tho' we've no Voice but a negative here,/ The use of the Taxables, let us forebear." In Boston, three hundred "Mistresses of Families"—among them, according to the *Boston Evening Post*, "Ladies of the highest rank and influence"—signed a statement in which they vowed not to drink tea until the "unconstitutional" British taxes were repealed.[623]

Women in the New England and Middle colonies had been boiling the sap of maple trees as a substitute for imported sugar, processing seawater for salt, making their own homespun clothing, and brewing tea from sage and raspberry leaves for nearly a decade before boycotts were advocated in the South. In 1774, minister William Tennent III addressed a letter to "The Ladies of South Carolina," entreating them "to lend their hand to save America from the Dagger of Tyranny" by giving up imported tea, a beverage that "has now become a political plague." He added: "If you thought you could do anything to save your Country, I am sure you would do it."[624] Fifty-one women in Edenton, North Carolina, pledged to give up tea and imported clothing. "We cannot be indifferent on any occasion that appears nearly to affect the peace and happiness of our country," they declared.[625]

In the past, women in prosperous southern families had disdained spinning and weaving, preferring to purchase garments of foreign manufacture. Now the South found itself without a pool of skilled clothmakers. Patriots in Virginia and Maryland took steps to remedy this deficit by putting African-American women to work spinning. In early 1775, the wealthy Virginia plantation-owner Robert Carter acknowledged, "The time is now come requiring all people here, who have slaves and plantations, to make Cloathing for their Negroes and Families." He instructed the steward at one of his estates to "set apart Ten Black Females, the most Expert Spinners belonging to me, they to be Employed in Spinning Solely." At another plantation he set up a textile manufactory where African-American women and girls—especially older women who were no longer useful as agricultural workers—would do nothing but spin.[626] The Williamsburg Manufacturing Society in Virginia announced plans to open a factory with a spinning school for African-American girls.[627] Charles Carroll, a planter in Maryland, made use of white indentured servants as well as enslaved African Americans for spinning and weaving.[628] George Washington set up a spinning shed at Mount Vernon where enslaved women were put to work spinning flax and wool into thread and yarn.

As military engagements escalated, women who supported the revolution found additional ways to aid the cause. They carried messages for the Continental forces, spied on British troop movements, and like the possibly fictional Molly Pitcher (tentatively identified as Mary Ludwig Hays of New Jersey), they ventured up to the battle lines to supply the soldiers with ammunition and water.[629] Some women took up arms themselves. In the best-documented of several such instances, Deborah Sampson of Massachusetts donned masculine dress, enlisted under the name "Robert Shurtliff," and fought with the Fourth Massachusetts Regiment for seventeen months. Although her true gender was revealed when she fell ill and was hospitalized, she was honorably discharged at the end of the war and was subsequently awarded a pension.[630] Less dramatic, but no less essential, was the contribution to the war effort made by women who maintained family farms, supplying essential provisions to soldiers and civilians through years of danger and uncertainty.

European military forces were traditionally accompanied by a body of women who served the troops as cooks, nurses, and laundresses, and the Continental Army was no different. Many of the women who followed the troops were the wives and widows of soldiers. Their numbers varied from year to year and from regiment to regiment, but averaged about one woman to every thirty or thirty-five men. Also treading in the footsteps of the rebel soldiers was a scraggly collection of destitute homeless women, some prostitutes (probably fewer than is commonly supposed), and vendors of food and other items.[631] In August 1777, General George Washington complained that "the multitude of women in particular, especially those who are pregnant, or have children, are a clog upon every movement." He ordered women to march behind the lines with the baggage wagons, but many continued to walk alongside the men. Brigade commanders were instructed to "use every reasonable method in their power to get rid of all such [women] as are not absolutely necessary." Yet some four hundred camp followers accompanied the troops to Valley Forge, where they shared the hardships of that famously bitter winter. Washington later acknowledged that the presence of women was essential to the morale of the men; if the female entourage departed, he admitted, the army would probably lose "some of the oldest and best Soldiers In the Service."[632]

About a third of white Americans were opposed to the revolution. Among these Loyalists, or Tories, were Quaker pacifists as well as people with strong personal and business ties to Britain. Thousands of Loyalist families moved to New York City, which was in British hands through much of the war, and thousands more emigrated to Canada, the West Indies, or England. Some Loyalist wives followed husbands who were serving in pro-British colonial militias, and some remained in their homes to protect their property, enduring insults and abuse from neighbors and former friends. Loyalist women sheltered families fleeing rebel advances, interceded on behalf of men imprisoned as traitors, and surreptitiously supplied food, medical care, and information to British troops.

African Americans, both free and enslaved, made up about a fifth of the population of the thirteen colonies. Eager to win their support, two British officers issued proclamations promising freedom to any enslaved person who aided the Crown.[633] Thousands of Black women and men responded to the offer. Traveling on foot or in makeshift boats through the swamps and forests of the interior, they made their way to British army encampments or to seaports that were under British control.[634]

After the British surrender, several thousand "Black loyalists" were stranded in New York City. American authorities demanded custody of them, but the British decided to honor their pledge to free those who had aided them by conveying them to Nova Scotia. A brief description of some of these individuals was entered in a registry titled "The Book of Negroes."[635] The entries are frustratingly meager, but they nonetheless offer fascinating snapshots of African-American women and girls in the era of the revolution.

Peg Boden, in her twenties, and her husband, Cato Boden, both born free, had lived before the war on John's Island, South Carolina. During the conflict they had worked for a British regiment, he as a carpenter, she as the servant of an officer. Dinah Mitchel, 30, a "stout healthy negress," formerly a slave in Charleston, had made her way to New York with a babe-in-arms and a 10-year-old son. Another evacuee, "Joyce," 12, was apparently on her own since her father had died "in the King's service" and no mother or sibling is mentioned. "Nancy," 40, was the subject of an affidavit submitted by a slave-owner who claimed her as "his property." That claim was denied, but another fugitive slave, "Betty," was returned to her former master, Thomas Smith, "to be disposed of by him at his pleasure." Eleanor Hicks, 13, born free in "Rockaway," New York, had been an indentured servant for five years of her young life. Betsey Collins, 30, a "stout wench," had run away from her master in Hackensack, New Jersey. Catherine, 66, born free at Norwalk, Connecticut, was "worn out." Free-born Elsia Daughty, 30, was "half Indian." Cathern and Cornelius Van Sayl had escaped from a slave-owner in New Jersey with their newborn daughter, Mary; their son, Peter, now two months old, had been born while they served "within the British Lines."

Blacks who left America during or immediately after the war were eventually scattered across the globe, from the West Indies to London, from Florida to Nova Scotia. Some lived out their lives as free persons, but many were re-enslaved in their new homes, often under harsher conditions than formerly. About a thousand of those who went to Nova Scotia ultimately undertook a further journey in their search for freedom and opportunity. At their request, they were "repatriated" to Africa, a continent many of them had actually never set foot on before. They were among the African-American settlers—former slaves as well as free-born women and men from America and the Caribbean—who helped to found the city of Freetown, Sierra Leone.

Only about a tenth of America's postwar Black population lived in New England and the Middle colonies.[636] Some had gained their freedom when their Tory masters abandoned America and left them behind, while others benefited from a growing sentiment in the North that slavery was morally incompatible with the ideals of the new republic. In 1777, the Vermont and New Hampshire constitutions banned human bondage outright, while in Massachusetts, a series of court judgments made it virtually impossible to enforce slave laws there. Pennsylvania, Connecticut, Rhode Island, New York, and New Jersey all enacted laws in the postwar decades that mandated the "gradual emancipation" of slaves, but many years were to pass before slaveholding was eliminated in those states.[637]

Two landmark court cases in Massachusetts involved African-American women from northern states. The first was brought by Elizabeth Freeman (also known as "Mum Bett"), who had been born into bondage in upstate New York. In 1781, an abolitionist attorney in Boston represented her in a suit for freedom. Her petition (joined to that of an unrelated Black man) cited the Bill of Rights of the Massachusetts

Constitution, which asserted that "all men are born free and equal." Assuming that the word "men" encompassed "women," she claimed that it effectively outlawed slavery. A jury found in her favor, and she lived out her days as a free person.[638]

The other case was based on a petition submitted to the Commonwealth of Massachusetts in 1783 on behalf of a 70-year-old former slave known only as "Belinda." Having obtained her freedom by default when her Loyalist owner left the country without her, Belinda requested a "morsel of that immense wealth" he had accumulated—partly as a result of her stolen labor. Her suit was successful, and she was awarded a small annual income as reparation for years of work performed without any compensation.[639]

A rare surviving African-American female voice from the eighteenth century is that of poet Phillis Wheatley, who endured the middle passage from Africa to America in early childhood and was purchased by John Wheatley of Boston as a gift for his wife, Susanna. Phillis's exceptional intelligence quickly became apparent, and the Wheatleys' daughter taught her to read. After only about four years in America, she was already proficient enough to compose poetry in her adopted language. A friendship developed between mistress and slave, underpinned by their shared Christian piety.

In 1773, when Phillis was nineteen, a volume of her verse—*Poems on Various Subjects, Religious and Moral*—was published in England. She was emancipated shortly after her book came out, but a planned second volume of her work never appeared, and she died in poverty at about 30 years of age.[640] Wheatley's poetry is graceful and heartfelt; her references to slavery, though restrained, acknowledge the sufferings of "our sable race." Her best-known lines speak of her abduction from Africa:

> I, young in life, by seeming cruel fate
> Was snatched from Affric's fancied happy seat:
> What pangs excruciating must molest,
> What sorrows labor in my parent's breast?
> Steel'd was that soul and by no misery moved
> That from a father seized his babe beloved:

Such, such my case; And can I then but pray
Others may never feel tyrannical sway?[641]

The ambivalence expressed by the phrases "*seeming* cruel fate" and "*fancied* happy seat" reflects the poet's belief that her kidnapping, harsh though it was, had nonetheless brought her the blessing of Christianity. Still, her hatred of slavery was unequivocal. To Samson Occom, a Native American (Mohegan) minister, she wrote: "In every human Breast, God has implanted a Principle which we call love of Freedom; it is impatient of Oppression and pants for Deliverance." She condemned those "whose Avarice impels them to countenance and help forward the Calamities of their Fellow Creatures."[642]

15. PHILLIS WHEATLEY, FRONTISPIECE, 1777

In a postwar letter to John, Abigail Adams remarked that American women had demonstrated a devotion to the revolution that was nothing short of remarkable. For though deprived of a voice in legislation, obliged to submit to laws they had no part in formulating, denied control of their own property, and subject to the authority of husbands, they had unreservedly aided the cause. "Patriotism in the female Sex," she concluded, "is the most disinterested of all virtues."[643]

An observer as discerning as she may also have been aware that women's wartime experiences had instilled in some a wider vision of their place in the world. When Eliza Wilkinson of Charleston, South Carolina, wrote in 1782, "Surely we may give our opinions . . . without being reminded of our spinning and household affairs," she was voicing a hope that many women shared.[644] Groups of women hailed George Washington and scattered flowers in his path as he made his way from Virginia to New York City for his inauguration as first president of the United States. Women demonstrated their support of the goals of the French Revolution by donning "liberty caps," displaying tri-color ribbons, and singing patriotic songs; they re-enacted a ceremony honoring Liberty that had recently taken place in Paris; and a few even signed themselves "citizeness," an Anglicized version of *citoyenne*.[645] When Thomas Jefferson sent a letter to his friend Anne Willing Bingham criticizing the women of France for involving themselves in civic affairs and praising American women for being "too wise to wrinkle their foreheads with politics," she begged to differ. "The Women of France interfere in the politics of the Country, and often give a decided Turn to the Fate of Empires," she countered. Therefore, we in America "are bound in Gratitude to admire and revere them, for asserting our Privileges."[646]

As the eighteenth century drew to a close, women joined in a public debate in newspapers and magazines on the pros and cons of educating girls. An early entry in the controversy, "On the Equality of the Sexes," by Judith Sargent Murray of Gloucester, Massachusetts, appeared in *Massachusetts Magazine* in 1790 (but was probably written as much as a decade earlier). "Is it reasonable that women should at present be so degraded, as to be allowed no other ideas, than those which are suggested by the mechanism of a pudding, or sewing the seams of a garment?" Murray asked. It was especially important in a republic, she pointed out, for female citizens to be "sensible and informed," so they could bring up their children intelligently. Moreover, they ought to be trained in practical skills that would enable them to support themselves, making marriage a choice rather than a necessity for survival. If women's judgment and achievements seem inferior to men's, Murray wrote, the fault was not in the natural endowment of the sexes but rather in the difference in educational opportunities.[647]

With the publication of Mary Wollstonecraft's pioneering book, *A Vindication of the Rights of Woman*, the debate on female education became broader and more substantive. First printed in England in 1792, the *Vindication* was published in America immediately afterward and was excerpted in the first issue of *The Lady's Magazine and Repository of Entertaining Knowledge*, a Philadelphia periodical addressed to "female patronesses of literature."[648] Wollstonecraft criticized the state of ignorance and servility to which women were condemned and advocated equal education for girls and boys. She conceded that women were obligated to fulfill their domestic duties but insisted that "the grand end of their exertions should be to unfold their own faculties."[649]

The *Vindication* received generally favorable reviews in the United States and was widely read and discussed. But while agreeing with the author's support of female education, American women often took exception to more radical aspects of her argument. Annis Boudinot Stockton of Princeton, New Jersey—an accomplished poet and a member of a circle of female and male literati—wrote to her daughter: "I have been engaged these two days with reading the rights of women. . . . I am much pleased with her [Wollstonecraft's] strength of reasoning, and her sentiment in general." However, she added, "I do not think any of that Slavish obedience exists, that She talks so much of—I think the women [in America] have their equal right of every thing, Latin and Greek excepted. . . . [It is] accommodating ourselves to our situation, that adds dignity to the human character."[650] Sixty-one-year-old Philadelphia Quaker, Elizabeth Sandwith Drinker also had some reservations about Wollstonecraft's argument. She noted in her diary that "in very many of her sentiments, she . . . *speaks my mind*, in some others, I do not, altogether, coincide with her—I am not for quite so much independence."[651] But nineteen-year-old Eliza Southgate of Scarborough, Maine, expressed no such hesitation. She wrote to a male cousin, "I confess that I admire many of her [Wollstonecraft's] sentiments." Although Mistress Southgate was "aware of the censure that will ever await the female that attempts the vindication of her sex," she pronounced herself ready "to brave that censure that I know to be undeserved."[652]

When a male acquaintance asked Susan Bull Tracy of Connecticut, a former schoolteacher, her opinion of the Wollstonecraft book, she replied thoughtfully that although she agreed with the author's proposals for educating women, she believed that even with improved education, it would take many years, perhaps a century, before women were "completely emancipated from the chains of ignorance, & consequent folly; or men from their passion to tyrannize."[653]

The debate over female education was fast becoming moot since schools for girls had begun to open in towns and cities across the country—and girls were flocking to enroll in them. Moreover, the nation's first chartered institution of higher education for female students, the Young Ladies' Academy of Philadelphia, had already welcomed its first classes. The new academy offered a wide range of courses, but not Latin or Greek, the quintessential signs of a superior education.[654]

Guests at the Young Ladies' Academy's 1793 commencement ceremony may have been startled, or even offended, by the Wollstonecraft-like opinions expressed by Priscilla Mason, the salutatorian. Mistress Mason boldly declared, "[O]ur high and mighty Lords . . . have denied us the means of knowledge, and then reproached us for the want of it. . . . They doom'd the sex to servile or frivolous employments, on purpose to degrade their minds, [so] that they themselves might hold unrivall'd, the power and pre-eminence they had usurped." Although she acknowledged that access to schooling had improved, she saw this as only a first step. "Where shall we find a theater for the display of [our talents]?" she asked. "The Church, the Bar, and the Senate are shut against us." Yet she urged her fellow graduates to remain hopeful. "Let us by suitable education, qualify ourselves for those high departments; they will open before us."[655]

The writer Judith Sargent Murray was equally optimistic about women's future. Noting approvingly in a 1798 volume titled *The Gleaner* that "Female academies are everywhere establishing,"[656] and sensing that the consciousness of the new generation of women was changing, she exulted: "Yes, in this younger world, the Rights of Women begin to be understood; we seem, at length, determined to do justice to THE SEX." With what proved to be remarkable prescience, she observed, "I may be accused of enthusiasm; but such is my confidence in THE SEX, that I expect to see our young women forming a new era in female history."[657]

20 CITOYENNES

Thousands of women from Paris's working-class quarters—fishwives and fruit vendors, seamstresses and laundresses, shopkeepers, domestic servants, and homemakers—set out on foot for the royal palace at Versailles on the morning of October 5, 1789.[658] Bread had been in short supply in the city for months, but the situation was now desperate, and the women were determined to do something about it. It was by no means the first time hunger had brought Frenchwomen into the streets, but this time they had an additional purpose: to demonstrate their support for the reforms that in just five months had undermined the power of the monarchy.

Women had joined the general rejoicing over the extraordinary events of the previous spring and summer. In May, they had hailed the convening of the first national legislature in 175 years; on the fourteenth of July they had participated in the storming of the Bastille; and they had cheered in August when the reorganized legislature issued the *Declaration of the Rights of Man and of the Citizen* (*Déclaration des droits de l'homme et du citoyen*). By October, however, soldiers with rifles were having difficulty restraining crowds of distraught women clamoring to buy bread at the bakeries.

Early on the fateful morning of October 5, an angry, largely female crowd assembled in front of Paris's city hall, the Hôtel de Ville. A group of women, joined by male allies, forced their way into the building. While accusing city officials of having done nothing but produce worthless reports, they scooped up armfuls of government papers and threatened to set fire to them.[659] Meanwhile, those outside the building milled about uncertainly until a plan finally took shape: They would go to Versailles, where Louis XVI and Marie Antoinette resided in regal splendor, to confront the king face to face and demand that he do something to relieve the city.

The idea quickly won acceptance, and detachments of women immediately started out. Passing through market districts and working-class neighborhoods to recruit additional marchers, they assembled six or seven thousand strong in the Champs Elysées and headed for Versailles. Accompanying them was a contingent of men from the National Guard, a recently created citizens' militia. A contemporaneous engraving shows a column of grim-faced women carrying upraised pitchforks, pikes, and axes; a few brandish swords; in the foreground, several drag a large

16. WOMEN'S MARCH TO VERSAILLES, OCTOBER 5, 1789

cannon on wheels while an unhappy woman dressed in finery tries to move out of the way.

The marchers reached Versailles late that afternoon. Louis XVI granted an audience to a delegation and gave his word that Paris would soon be more adequately provisioned, but the women massed outside in a heavy downpour were in no mood to trust vague promises. Tired, wet, and hungry, they invaded the meeting-place of the national legislature and in effect occupied the hall. Some stretched out on benches and fell asleep. Others went up to the front, interrupted the proceedings, and insulted the deputies. Playing at being statesmen, they introduced bogus motions and conducted mock votes.

When thousands more National Guardsmen arrived at Versailles the next morning, a group of women and soldiers forced their way into the royal château, killing two sentries who tried to block their entry. While the throng in the courtyard below yelled taunts and threats, the intruders cornered Louis in his private chambers and demanded that he immediately move his court to Paris. Faced with the likelihood of further violence if he refused, he agreed. The royal family was unceremoniously hustled into carriages and, virtual captives of the guards and the women, embarked on an ignominious one-way journey to Paris. Wagons filled with flour confiscated from storerooms at Versailles brought up the rear of the extraordinary line of march.

The caption on a contemporary illustration says in part, "Our modern Amazons, glorying in their victories, return on horse and with cannons along with the gentlemen of the National Guard." The women in the print are clearly in a triumphant mood. They wave branches of "liberty trees," and one coquette, perched atop a cannon, cozies up to a guardsman seated in front of her. Another depiction of the homeward procession, however, is less lighthearted. In what seems an ominous portent of what was to come, it shows a column of guardsmen, two of whom hold pikes upon which are impaled the heads of the murdered palace sentries.

Once situated in the capital where revolutionary passions churned menacingly on his doorstep, the king saw the wisdom of finally ratifying the *Declaration of the Rights of Man and of the Citizen*. Although most people enthusiastically approved the declaration, a few women publicly questioned its references to *citoyen* (male citizen*)*. Was that word intended to encompass *citoyenne* (female citizen) as well? they wondered. Among the doubters was a group of women in Paris who submitted a petition to the national legislature. They pointed out that the declaration of rights ignored "the oldest and most general of all abuses," the one that denied women dignity, position, and honors. They congratulated the delegates for granting equal rights to all male citizens, "the poor villager . . . the timid soldier . . . the modest priest . . . the black African," but asked: "Will we [women] be the only ones who will not participate in this astonishing regeneration?"[660]

Yet Frenchwomen in general simply assumed that the declaration's assertion of human rights embraced the female half of humanity. They joined patriotic clubs and many for the first time took an active interest in local politics. The national legislature was inundated by petitions from women urging the delegates to enact reforms of special importance to wives and mothers: legalization of divorce, improved education of girls, abolition of arranged marriage, and more equitable marital-property laws.[661] A women's club in Beaune protested to Paris that municipal authorities had prevented them "as female citizens (*citoyennes*), wives, and mothers" from participating in a public pledge administered on the first anniversary of the attack on the Bastille. In Bordeaux, a speaker at a women's club rejoiced that wives were no longer "reduced to housework and the education of our children," or "deprived of the benefits of the law," or consigned to "abject obscurity, painfully enduring our degradation."[662]

The Enlightenment philosopher and mathematician Nicolas de Condorcet reiterated his support of women's rights in an essay titled "On the Admission of Women to the Rights of Citizenship." "Have not philosophers and legislators violated the principle of natural rights by unthinkingly depriving one-half of humanity of the rights of citizenship?" he asked. "Why should temporary indispositions occasioned by motherhood render women any less capable of exercising these rights than the periodic attacks of gout, bronchitis, and other ailments suffered by men"?[663]

During its two-year existence the National Assembly passed several measures that did some good for women—albeit serendipitously. Most significantly, it placed limitations on laws which for generations had disinherited daughters along with younger sons. However, the draft constitution presented to the nation in September 1791 gave the wealthiest third of men (whom it designated "active citizens") the right to vote and serve in the legislature, withheld these privileges from the remaining two-thirds of men (termed "passive citizens"), and assigned women to neither category, evidently assuming that it went without saying that no female was entitled to citizenship at any level.[664]

A newly formed Paris club, the Fraternal Society of Patriots of Both Sexes, condemned the constitution's "truly humiliating distinction between active and passive citizens."[665] A member of the club, the playwright and human rights advocate Olympe Gouges, was moved to issue a *Declaration of the Rights of Woman and Female Citizen* (*Déclaration des droits de la femme et de la citoyenne*). Using the *Declaration of the Rights of Man* as a model, de Gouges' declaration proclaimed, "Woman is born free and lives equal to man in her rights." It argued that all female and male citizens ought to have a say in the formulation of the nation's laws, and it advocated repeal of statutes that discriminated against daughters and wives in inheritance, gave husbands control of marital property, and permitted arranged marriages.

In closing, de Gouges implored women to open their eyes to their true situation:

> Woman, wake up; the tocsin of reason is being heard throughout the whole universe; discover your rights. . . . Oh, women, women! When will you cease to be blind? What advantage have you received from the Revolution? A more pronounced scorn, a more marked disdain. . . . Regardless of what barriers confront you, it is in your power to free yourselves; you have only to want to."[666]

Among the members of the Fraternal Society of Patriots of Both Sexes were also a pioneer female journalist,[667] the wife of a well-known artist, and three women who would soon emerge as champions of their gender. Each of the three had at least a measure of financial independence, and two of them had led unconventional, sexually uninhibited lives. Théroigne de Méricourt, for one, was a former courtesan, concert singer, and *saloniste*. Born in Belgium, she left home at a young age and traveled widely in Western Europe with various lovers before arriving in Paris in 1789, on the eve of the revolution.[668] Etta Palm d'Aelders, a 46-year-old Dutchwoman, had been separated from her husband for many years. After moving to Paris in 1773, her adventuresome life featured several lovers and work as a clandestine political agent for the French government. The third, Pauline Léon, was just 21. She lived in Paris with her widowed mother and worked in the family chocolate business.[669]

Etta Palm was the most politically sophisticated and self-assured of the group. In addition to the Fraternal Society of Patriots of Both Sexes, she was affiliated with the Friends of Truth, a Paris club in which the philosopher Condorcet and his wife, Sophie de Grouchy Condorcet, were active. Speaking before about four thousand people at a December 1790 meeting of the Friends of Truth, Palm protested laws that "everywhere ... favor men at the expense of women, because everywhere power is in your [men's] hands."

Aware that the revolution had created an unprecedented moment of opportunity for the women of France, Palm endorsed a broad feminist agenda. She declared that "justice, the sister of liberty, calls all individuals to equality of rights, without discrimination of sex." In her passionate speeches and writings, she focused upon legal rights ("the laws of a free people must be equal for all beings, like the air and the sun"), but also advocated women's participation in government, improved education for girls (with fewer lessons devoted to "legends of the saints"), "equal and separate" powers for husband and wife in the home, legalization of divorce, decriminalization of female adultery, egalitarian inheritance laws, public assistance of indigent women, and protection of the health of wet nurses.[670] An organizer as well as a theoretician and orator, she founded an all-female branch of the Friends of Truth in Paris, "to the success of which I have pledged all my attention and my entire life." And she endeavored, with limited success, to establish a nationwide federation of women's clubs.[671]

Before long the young chocolate-maker Pauline Léon had found her voice. Standing at the head of a delegation of Parisian women on March 6, 1791, she announced to the National Assembly, "We are *citoyennes*, and we cannot be indifferent to the fate of the homeland." She then read aloud a petition that asked for the establishment of an armed female militia. And she threw down a challenge: "You cannot refuse us . . . unless you pretend the Declaration of Rights does not apply to women." This petition, which the National Assembly promptly denied, was signed by over 300 women.[672]

Later that month, the former singer Théroigne de Méricourt told a club in a Paris neighborhood, "It is finally time that women emerge from their shameful nullity, where the ignorance, pride, and injustice of men have kept them enslaved for such a long time." De Méricourt—who now often appeared in public in martial garb, a pistol at her waist and a sword at her side—demanded that women be admitted to the National Guard.[673]

The following spring, Mary Wollstonecraft's pathbreaking volume *A Vindication of the Rights of Woman* appeared in French translation. Evidently hoping to influence events in France, Wollstonecraft had dedicated the *Vindication* to Talleyrand, the former bishop of Autun, whose recent official report on education in France had failed to mention women. "I dedicate this volume to you," she had written, "to induce you to reconsider the subject. . . . I plead for my sex—not for myself." A fifteen-page section of the book was devoted to refuting the educational theories of Jean-Jacques Rousseau. For although Wollstonecraft agreed with the French philosopher's criticisms of absolutism in politics and orthodoxy in religion, she opposed his views on women, especially the assertion in his 1762 treatise *Emile, or On Education*, that "Woman is made for man's delight," and his recommendation that a girl's education ought to prepare her for her primary role in life: to please and be useful to men.[674]

In August 1792 a bloody anti-monarchist insurrection in Paris resulted in the dethroning of Louis XVI and the founding of the First French Republic. Three women were awarded civic honors for acts of heroism in the uprising: Louise-Reine Audu, a fruit-seller who had been a prominent participant in the women's march to Versailles; Claire Lacombe, a young actor recently arrived in the city; and Théroigne de Méricourt, the flamboyant advocate of a regiment of Amazons.[675]

During this critical period of transition from a constitutional monarchy to a republic, leftist deputies in the moribund legislature pushed through a law that for the first time legalized divorce throughout France. The new law was remarkably evenhanded. It gave wives as well as husbands the right to initiate divorce proceedings; sanctioned divorce on several grounds, including incompatibility and mutual consent; and granted mothers automatic custody of children below the age of seven. Historian Dominique Godineau estimated that 71 percent of the decrees handed down in Paris in the eighteen months after January 1, 1793, were initiated by wives. One of these wives wrote to the national legislature to thank it for the "holy law of divorce." Her letter said that she had formerly "trembled under the empire of a despotic husband," but was now "restored to dignity as an independent woman." She enclosed her wedding ring, the "symbol of my slavery."[676]

The legislature of the First French Republic, known as the National Convention, ordered and carried out the execution of Louis XVI in January 1793, and nine months later, of Marie Antoinette. Monarchs across Europe, shocked and horrified by this turn of events, feared that France's revolutionary fever would prove contagious. Within weeks of the execution of Louis, the fledgling republic was at war with a coalition comprised of Austria, Prussia, Great Britain, the Netherlands, and Spain. More than a few Frenchwomen—no one knows how many—enlisted in the army disguised as men. Although the National Convention issued an edict barring women from the military, those who were determined to bear arms defied the law.[677]

In the capital, food prices had risen and shortages of essential commodities like flour, sugar, candles, and soap were causing hardship. Some of the scarcity was undoubtedly due to wartime disruptions in distribution. However, among the *sans-culottes*—a derisive term for lower-class women and men, who wore ankle-length pantaloons rather than the silk knee-length pants favored by upper-class men—there was widespread suspicion that the shortages were caused chiefly by market manipulators who were attempting to destroy the republic by starving the people. And starvation *was* indeed claiming lives in the most poverty-stricken Paris neighborhoods.[678] In late February a delegation representing a few hundred *sans-culottes* women appeared before the National Convention to demand that monopolizers be punished, and a group of laundresses asked the Convention to impose the death penalty on hoarders and speculators who, they believed, were responsible for shortages of soap. The legislators tabled the women's requests for two days, prompting one of the protesters to comment, "When our children ask us for milk, we don't adjourn them until the day after tomorrow."

In the next few months France experienced demoralizing military defeats abroad and counterrevolutionary uprisings at home. Bands of desperate women (sometimes egged on and supported by men) raided the shops of suspected hoarders and price-gougers. As the police stood by, unwilling or unable to intervene, the crowd seized merchandise and sold it at whatever price they deemed just.[679] A hundred women from Versailles led by a drummer entered a session of the National Convention to demand price controls on grain. That same day a contingent of Parisian women appeared before the Convention and declared that if price controls were not enacted, their neighborhood, the Faubourg Saint-Antoine, would rise in protest. When the deputies hurriedly attempted to adjourn the meeting, the women threatened to remain until their demand was met. They eventually agreed to leave, and three days afterward the deputies imposed price controls on grains and flour.

On May 10, 1793, an all-female political association, the Society of Revolutionary Republican Women (SRRW), was formally organized in Paris. In a rare instance of class unity, the SRRW leadership, made up principally of women from the bourgeoisie, established a close working relationship with *sans-culottes* women. Attired in trousers and red "liberty caps" and armed with pistols and daggers, women from both groups policed the streets together and kept an eye on the bakeries to ensure that price controls were not violated.

Although the SRRW's primary concern was not women's rights, the issue was not ignored either. In the sole surviving account of a regular SRRW meeting, the club's president, former actor Claire Lacombe, announced to the sixty-seven women in attendance (among them, Olympe de Gouges) that the topic of the evening was the role of women in a republican government. A tradeswoman delivered an address in which she presented historical evidence showing that women were as capable of leading armies and governing nations as men, perhaps more so.

The SRRW's broad-based membership gave the organization considerable political clout. As individuals, Frenchwomen had little or no authority in the political sphere, but united, they made up a formidable bloc. When political discord arose within the National Convention, the SRRW and their *sans-culottes* allies threw their support behind the Jacobins, the more radical faction. From the spectators' galleries of the Convention hall, women heckled and shouted down speakers who sided with the opposing Girondins, and they forcibly prevented Girondin partisans from claiming gallery seats. Feelings ran so high that Théroigne de Méricourt, who backed the Girondins, was attacked by a group of women and cruelly beaten. In early June, an insurrection broke out in Paris that resulted in the arrest of Girondin deputies and the subsequent execution of twenty-two of them.

Although women were now commonly referred to in the press and legislature as *citoyennes*, the National Convention drafted a new constitution that did not provide for female suffrage. Women's clubs in the towns of Besançon, Le Mans, Nancy, and Beaumont sent messages to Paris protesting the exclusion of women from a scheduled nationwide referendum on the constitution. The petition from Beaumont, in the Dordogne, insisted, for example, that "*citoyennes* also have the right to ratify an act to which they have so effectively contributed."[680] A speaker representing female residents of Paris's Beaurepaire section appeared before the Convention to voice their opposition to the constitution:

> Citizen legislators, you have given men a Constitution; now they enjoy all the rights of free beings; but women are very far from sharing these glories. Women count for nothing in the political system. . . . as the Constitution is based on the Rights of Man, we now demand the full exercise of these rights for ourselves.[681]

On July 13, a prominent Jacobin spokesman, Jean-Paul Marat, was stabbed to death by Charlotte Corday, a 25-year-old Girondin sympathizer.[682] Corday's deed proved to be a turning point for women, for the fact that one of their gender had committed the murder—and that she had done so in support of a political ideal—had a decidedly chilling effect on the public's attitude toward activist women. Although the members of the SRRW devoted most of the rest of the month to mourning Marat and excoriating Corday, her bloody deed evidently conjured for many Frenchmen archetypal fears of massive social disarray caused by female passions run amok.

To make matters worse, the SRRW threw its support to the Enragés, a group of radical revolutionaries who opposed the Jacobins and backed the demands of the most extreme factions of the working class. (Actor Claire

Lacombe was linked romantically with an Enragés leader, and chocolate-maker Pauline Léon married him.) The SRRW's alliance with the Enragés proved disastrous, for as the club's bourgeois leadership drew closer to the male radicals, the group's collaborative relationship with *sans-culottes* women deteriorated. The stage was set for the annihilation of the SRRW and for the long-term defeat of the aspirations of Frenchwomen.

On September 5, 1793, the National Convention formally inaugurated the Reign of Terror under the Jacobin deputy Maximilien de Robespierre. A few weeks later, a speaker at a Jacobin Society meeting denounced the SRRW and its president, Claire Lacombe, as counterrevolutionaries. When Lacombe, who was present in the spectators' gallery, requested an opportunity to defend the SRRW, a near-riot broke out. She later reported that some women seated close to her in the gallery had cried "Down with the new Corday," and "Get out, miserable woman, or we will tear you to pieces." A motion to place her under arrest was passed, and she was immediately surrounded by guards and conducted to the headquarters of the Committee of General Security, a feared enforcer of the Terror. The committee took no action, however, and for the time being, she was let go.[683]

In late September the Convention issued an order requiring all women to wear a cockade—a tricolor rosette of ribbons—as a sign of their support of the republic. The SRRW enthusiastically endorsed the order and even attempted to enforce it, but their former *sans-culottes* allies did not agree. Disillusioned with the revolution, which had brought them so much hardship and so little gain, marketwomen were heard to object that only whores and Jacobins wore cockades, and women "should be concerned only with their households and not with current events." Fights erupted between those who had affixed a cockade to their bonnets and those who had not.[684]

A delegation representing the marketwomen brought a petition to the National Convention charging that a previously unknown freedom, the "freedom of costume," had been abridged and recommending the abolition of all women's clubs, "because it was a woman [Charlotte Corday] who had brought about France's misfortunes." Two weeks later, André Amar, a zealous Jacobin, presented a report from the Committee of General

Security to the deputies of the National Convention. Amar summarized a number of questions that the committee had considered: "Should meetings of women gathered together in popular societies in Paris be allowed? ... Can women exercise political rights and take an active part in affairs of government? Can they deliberate together in political associations or popular societies?" The committee's conclusion, he stated, was that women lack the moral and mental characteristics required for the duties of citizenship since they are prone to excessive excitement and intense passions, emotional states that are "deadly in public affairs" and are often found to produce "errors and disorder." Indeed, he added, women are "destined by their very nature" to devote themselves to private concerns. What had started as an attack on a political club had segued into a censure of womankind in general.

The Convention endorsed the committee's recommendations and issued a draconian decree: "Clubs and popular societies of women, whatever name they are known under, are prohibited."[685] One Convention deputy objected, "I do not know on what principle one could lean in taking away women's right to assemble peaceably. ... Unless you are going to question whether women are part of the human species, can you take away from them this right which is common to every thinking being?" But his protest fell on deaf ears. After an existence of less than six months, the first female political organization in France was outlawed. The women themselves had made mistakes, but the broadness and vitriol of the Convention's condemnation leave little doubt that it was the idea of Woman as a citizen actively engaged in the issues of her time that was under attack.

Thousands of French women and men lost their lives to the guillotine and hundreds of thousands more were imprisoned for counter-revolutionary thoughts and deeds. Etta Palm left France in January 1793 and returned to her native Netherlands, but several of her coworkers felt the fury of the Terror. Théroigne de Méricourt suffered an emotional breakdown and was confined in the Salpêtrière hospital for the insane, where she died at the age of 55. Olympe de Gouges was beheaded in Paris in November 1793. Although she was charged with royalist sympathies (she had backed the constitutional monarchy), a French journal accused her of a more nebulous crime: "She wanted to be a statesman, and it seems

17. OLYMPE DE GOUGES EXECUTION, 1793

the law has punished this conspirator for having forgotten the virtues that suited her sex."[686] Claire Lacombe and Pauline Léon were imprisoned in April 1794. Léon was released in a few months, but Lacombe was held for over a year.

Disunited, denied freedom of assembly, and forbidden to organize, female activists were effectively silenced. The Napoleonic Code adopted in 1804 gave husbands the right to control all family assets, prohibited widows from inheriting land owned by their deceased mates, barred married women from participating in legal or business transactions, limited women's access to divorce, and required wives to obey their husbands. Frenchwomen did not win the right to vote until after World War II, decades after most other European women.

Yet in the narrow streets and broad market squares of working-class Paris, pride in women's part in the great eighteenth-century revolution lived on. In the midst of an anti-monarchist uprising in Paris in 1848, a feminist newspaper, *La Voix des femmes* (*The Voice of Women*) reminded readers, "The history of our first revolution is ringed by a dazzling halo of great women who honored their sex and their country."[687] During the Paris Commune of 1871 a young woman implored several hundred female Communards to follow in the footsteps of the women who had marched from Paris to Versailles "in the name of the people and justice."[688] And at a Paris women's club that year, a speaker urged the audience to heed the example of their revolutionary foremothers. "Let us not cause their shades to blush for us," she exhorted, "but be up and doing, as they would be if they were living now."[689]

21   FIRESIDE TO FACTORY

Women have clothed humanity through all recorded time. Bronze Age clay tablets inventory female textile workers; Iron Age female graves contain spindle weights; Homer sang of women who "weave the webs" and "turn the distaffs"; the Old Testament praises wives who work with wool and flax; Greek vases depict women weaving. The age-old division of labor by gender was neatly summed up in a fourteenth-century verse: "Adam delved and Eve span."

With the introduction of the "putting-out system" in the seventeenth century, however, the process of making cloth entered upon a centuries-long transition from domestic chore to commercial activity. Under the new system, men from the rising class of merchants supplied home-based spinners and weavers with raw materials and purchased the finished product at minimal piecework rates.

The invention of the spinning jenny in England in 1764 quickened the pace of change. The jennys were a boon to domestic spinners at first since they could fabricate high-quality thread and yarn at previously unimaginable speed. But when design improvements made them too bulky and expensive for the fireside, entrepreneurs set up centralized spinning workshops, the largest of which employed thousands of girls and women.

With the development of water-powered spinning frames in 1769 cotton mills proliferated in England's northwest, where there were fast-flowing rivers to supply power and a seaport, Liverpool, to which raw cotton from slave plantations in the West Indies and the American South could be shipped.[690] Conveniently, northwest England also had a ready workforce comprised of dispossessed rural families whose farms had been appropriated by large landowners. Thus, Europe's first female proletariat was made up of Englishwomen from landless peasant households working for wages at machines they did not own and producing goods that no member of their family would use. In many parts of Britain, wrote historian Ivy Pinchbeck in her pioneering study *Women Workers and the Industrial Revolution,* women were "forced by unprincipled employers to accept starvation rates."[691]

As spinning became increasingly mechanized, female unemployment soared and pay rates plummeted. Workers in several textile-producing districts attempted to turn back the clock by attacking the machinery itself. In 1779, thousands of men and women in Manchester and nearby towns smashed hundreds of machines—an attack as futile and misdirected as Don Quixote's tilting against windmills. Local militia were called out to put down the uprising, but before it was over, two demonstrators were killed, eight wounded, and four arrested.[692] Afterward, the protesters—who became known as Luddites after a possibly legendary leader, Ned Ludd—defended their actions in a pamphlet entitled *An Impartial Representation of the Case of the Poor Cotton Spinners in Lancashire.* The pamphlet said in part that "thousands of women, when they can get work, must make a long day to card, spin, and reel . . . and for this they have four-pence or five-pence and no more. . . . Prompted by want and poverty, we pulled down and demolished several of these Machines, the causes of our calamitous situation."[693]

The appearance in 1789 of a still faster and more efficient spinning machine—a hybrid of the jenny and the water frame popularly known as the mule—delivered a final blow to female spinners. For since the mule was too heavy for most women to operate, men gradually took over what for millennia had been women's work. Forced to seek alternative means of earning a livelihood, some women reverted to domestic service, still the principal female occupation; others found occasional employment as farm laborers or turned their hands to minor cottage industries, such as plaiting straw for bonnets, fashioning gloves, or making lace. But what finally relieved female unemployment was the development of water-powered weaving machines that could be operated by women and girls.

By the mid 1820's, the majority of power-loom operators were female. Many wives and mothers toiled twelve to fourteen hours a day, six days a week, while continuing to carry the main burden of cooking, cleaning, and caring for children. Family life deteriorated. Children, many of whom also worked long hours in the mills, were often malnourished and poorly educated. Working-class neighborhoods became crowded, squalid, and unhealthy. Poet William Blake's allusion to England's "dark Satanic mills" was tragically apt. Studies of one aspect of workingwomen's lives, their ability to read, reveal that in the largest of the English mill towns, Manchester, female literacy declined from about 29 percent in the 1750's (before the spinning jenny) to 19 percent in the 1820's.[694]

Women's subordinate position in the family was replicated in the workplace, where female operatives were consigned to lower-level jobs and were paid half or less of what men received. To add insult to injury, workingwomen were accused of neglecting the domestic duties for which Nature had designed them. A London newspaper proposed that "females of any age" be barred from working in the mills. In response, "The Female Operatives of Todmorden" (an industrial town near Manchester) pointed out that "there is scarcely any other mode of employment for female industry." If barred from factory work, the women asked, "What is to become of them?"[695]

After the defeat of Napoleon at Waterloo in 1815, unemployment in Great Britain's manufacturing districts became so severe that some areas experienced outright famine. Male factory operatives formed political-action associations aimed at improving workers' lives through legislation. Women soon founded similar groups of their own—the first such organizations ever created by Englishwomen. It was clearly a development whose time had come. The Female Reform Society of Manchester, for example, enrolled a thousand members in its first week. However, the women's groups did not advocate on their own behalf, but rather strove to back up the men and, to quote the Blackburn Female Reform Society, "to instill into the minds of our children a deep and rooted hatred of our corrupt and tyrannical rulers."[696]

A rally at Peter's Field in Manchester in August 1819 drew more than 60,000 supporters of political rights for (male) workers. Among those present were representatives of the new female political associations, many of whom had marched to Manchester at the head of processions from neighboring towns. Dressed in white, the women held aloft colorful silk banners embroidered with mottoes. "Success to the Female Reformers of Stockport," said one. "Let Us Die Like Men and Not Be Sold Like Slaves," exhorted another. Declared a third, "Annual Parliaments and

Death to Those in Authority Who Oppose Their Adoption." Yet despite the combative slogans, the mood on Peter's Field was peaceful, almost festive, until mounted cavalrymen brandishing sabers suddenly charged into the crowd, followed by infantrymen armed with bayonets and local constables with truncheons. Of 654 people stabbed, bludgeoned, and trampled, 168 were women, 4 of whom died. The event became known as the "Peterloo Massacre," a sardonic allusion to the battle at Waterloo.[697]

Parliament enacted in quick succession the Reform Act of 1832, which failed to enfranchise propertyless men; the Factory Act of 1833, which aided children but did little for adult workers; and the Poor Law of 1834, which consigned indigent women and children to Dickensian workhouses. Bitterly disappointed, many working-class women and men lost faith in mainstream politics and turned instead to the radical economic and social programs advanced by the utopian socialists Robert Owen and Charles Fourier, whose goals included the emancipation of women. In the "new moral world" envisioned by Robert Owen, for example, sexual relations were based on love rather than legal right; girls and boys had equal educational opportunities; divorce was easily accessible; workers received comparable pay irrespective of gender; and domestic duties were shared by all members of the collective community. "Women will no longer be made the slaves of, or dependent upon men. . . . They will be equal in education, rights, privileges and personal liberty," he declared.[698]

Among the promoters of Owenite socialism were Frances and James Morrison of Birmingham. James, a former house painter, edited an influential radical newspaper, *The Pioneer,* to which Frances, the daughter of a farm laborer, contributed letters on women's rights under the pseudonym A Bondswoman.[699] "Be slaves no longer" the Bondswoman urged female readers, "but unite and assert your just rights!" "A Page for the Ladies" in *The Pioneer* provided a forum to air grievances and promote gender solidarity. It was later renamed the "Woman's Page" because "ladies" was deemed "shockingly aristocratic and unequal."[700]

Women workers who wished to organize politically often encountered resistance from an unexpected source: their husbands. It seemed that however radical a man might otherwise be, he could be conservative when it came to his wife gadding about to public meetings. Moreover, women's male co-workers, even those who were staunch proponents of workers' rights, often viewed female workers as competitors for "men's jobs." When a tailors union in London called a strike aimed at eliminating women from the trade because their lower wages undercut men's pay, James Morrison published a thoughtful editorial in *The Pioneer* which argued that the long history of undervaluing female labor had accustomed employers to paying women less. The solution: "to make the two sexes equal, and to reward them equally." But few men were willing to surrender male supremacy in the workplace—or to accept its implications in the home. The collapse of the tailors' strike was a defeat for both sexes since afterward men were pushed out of the needle trades, while the pay of female seamstresses and tailors sank to bare subsistence.[701]

The struggle for workers' rights during the latter half of the 1830's and early 1840's was centered in the Chartist movement. By 1836 there were over a hundred female Chartist associations in England and some two dozen in Scotland. The average membership was about fifty, but more than two thousand women belonged to the Birmingham group. Chartist women usually acted behind the scenes, raising money, boycotting uncooperative merchants, organizing social events, and sewing banners (some of which were embroidered with emotional appeals like "Our children cryeth for bread").[702] In addition, women were active participants in the movement's principal activity, a massive petition campaign demanding "universal suffrage," or more accurately, universal male suffrage.

The author of an early draft of the Chartist petition acknowledged that excluding women from the vote was unreasonable and unjust, but, he insisted, it was politically necessary.[703] The Female Radical Association of Elland generally accepted this explanation, stating in a letter to the Chartist paper *The Northern Star* that it was women's duty "to co-operate with our husbands and sons in their great work of regeneration." The Female Radicals of Ashton agreed, if somewhat less unreservedly, commenting wryly that they looked forward to the day when intelligence would be the qualification for voting, "and then sisters, we shall be placed in our proper position in society, and enjoy the elective franchise as well as our kinsmen."[704] The Ashton female radicals might have been surprised to learn that it would take nearly a century and a national campaign that entailed much suffering and sacrifice before adult women in the United Kingdom would finally win the vote in 1928.

The Chartist petition garnered more than a million signatures in England, Scotland, and Wales, but when submitted to Parliament in 1839, it was denied a hearing. A second Chartist petition in 1842 won even more phenomenal popular backing—over three million signatures—but was similarly rejected without a hearing. Desperate textile workers launched a wave of militant strikes that brought the mills to a virtual standstill. As thousands of operatives paraded through the streets of many towns, often led by a contingent of women, worried government officials mobilized troops to counter what seemed a potentially revolutionary situation. About fifteen hundred Chartist activists were arrested, hundreds were sentenced to prison terms, and fifty were transported to Australia. A third Chartist petition in 1848 was discredited for allegedly including fraudulent signatures. Chartism died out soon afterward, a victim of government hostility, disputes among Chartist leaders, and the rise of trade unions that adopted key Chartist demands.

· · · ·

Across the Atlantic, industrialization was delayed, first, by the American Revolution and then by British laws that forbid the exportation of textile-manufacturing technology. As late as 1791, the U.S. Secretary of the Treasury, Alexander Hamilton, remarked on the "vast scene of household manufacturing" in the newly independent nation. In some districts, he reported, "two-thirds, three-fourths, and even four-fifths of all the clothing of the Inhabitants are made by themselves."[705] But when an enterprising Englishman memorized the design of a water-powered spinning frame and brought it to the United States, industrialization advanced rapidly. By 1812, there were thirty-three small mills producing cotton thread in Rhode Island and twenty in Massachusetts.[706] Children made up a majority of spinners in the earliest New England mills, while weaving was done mainly by rural girls and women in their homes. In the South, where industrialization was slower, enslaved African-American women spun and wove much of the fabric produced domestically, including the material known as "Negro cloth." This coarse homespun was usually a combination of linen and wool known as linsey-woolsey. Left undyed, it was used to make the white shirts and breeches commonly worn by field hands.

In 1814 a power loom modeled on the British machines was constructed in the United States and installed in a factory in Waltham, Massachusetts. Textile mills across New England soon acquired the new loom. In 1821, a group of capitalists in Boston financed the construction of a manufacturing center at a rural site on the Merrimack River in Massachusetts. This site became the city of Lowell, whose population exploded from 2,500 to 18,000 in just fifteen years.[707]

Power looms were too complicated for children to operate and most New England men were occupied with agriculture, so agents for the mill owners combed the countryside for women whom they could recruit as factory workers. Thousands of New England's daughters seized the opportunity. Traveling by stagecoach and canal boat to Lowell and other mill towns, they entered a world utterly different from the one they had grown up in. Their daring leap into the unknown required no little courage, but as former mill worker Harriet Hanson Robinson explained in her late-life memoir, *Loom and Spindle*, the countryside had little to offer them. Before the factories, Robinson recalled, "If [a woman] worked out as servant, or 'help,' her wages were from fifty cents to one dollar a week; if she went from house to house by the day to spin and weave, or as tailoress, she could get but seventy-five cents a week and her meals. As teacher her services were not in demand, and nearly all the arts, the professions, and even the trades and industries, were closed to her."[708] Little wonder that the wages at Lowell, which averaged about two dollars a week after room and board, were attractive to many.

The Yankee mill girls, unlike their counterparts in Britain, came for the most part from land-owning families; thus, they did not see themselves as permanent members of an industrial working class, but tended to view their time in the mills as an interlude before marrying. Nor were the New England factory towns as unhealthy and demoralizing as those abroad since the industrialists who founded Lowell expressly sought to avoid the worst abuses of the British labor system. They built schools, churches, and boarding houses and provided for employees' limited leisure time with concerts, lectures, evening and Sunday classes, and a free lending library.

From their meager salaries, mill girls put money aside for a bridal trousseau, sent funds home to their families, indulged a love of fashionable clothing, or saved to realize a dream. Ann Swett Appleton wrote to her sister from Lowell of her pleasure in being financially independent: "The thought that I am living on no one is a happy one, indeed." A young factory worker we know only as Lucy Ann wrote to her cousin that she had "earned enough to school me awhile." She confided that she planned to travel to Ohio and enroll in Oberlin, the nation's first co-educational college. There she hoped to "forget all those long wearisome mill days" and perhaps "prepare myself for usefulness in this life."[709] Another mill girl, Lucy Larcom, reported that after a short visit home, she had been glad to return to Lowell. At Lowell, she wrote, she felt that she "belonged to the world, that there was something for me to do in it, though I had not found out what. Something to do: it might be very little but still it would be my own work."[710]

Harriet Robinson wrote in her memoir that the female residents of Lowell boarding houses discussed the books they read, debated religious and social questions, compared their thoughts and experiences, and advised and helped one another. . . . [They] knew all about the Mexican war, and the anti-slavery cause had its adherents among them. Lectures on the doctrine of Fourier were read. . . . The [Fourier-based] Brook Farm experiment in communal living was familiar to some of them. . . . Mrs. Amelia Bloomer, one of the early pioneers of the dress reform movement, found followers in Lowell." When the abolitionist speakers Sarah and Angelina Grimké came to Lowell in 1837, some 1,500 people, many of them mill workers, heard them denounce the evils of slavery.[711]

The New England mill towns quickly gained a reputation as healthy, happy places where respectable young women were enriched not only monetarily but also intellectually, culturally, and spiritually. This rosy view was burnished by stories, articles, and poems published in *The Lowell Offering,* a literary journal written and edited by the mill girls and subsidized by the mill owners.

Yet conditions for female workers were never that idyllic. Only men were hired as factory supervisors; the spinning and weaving floors where most women and children worked were poorly lighted, noisy, and badly ventilated; employees, including children, toiled from five a.m. to seven p.m. (with two half-hour breaks for breakfast and dinner); and the women's boarding houses were rigidly regimented and overcrowded.[712] A worker accused of a serious infraction, such as insubordination or sexual misconduct, could be discharged on the spot and her name entered on a blacklist that disqualified her from future employment at any mill.[713]

In 1824 the owners of eight cotton mills in Pawtucket, Rhode Island, colluded to extend the employees' workday by an hour and cut their piecework rates by 25 percent. The *Providence Gazette* claimed that the new pay scale was still "generally considered to be extravagant wages for young women," but the women did not agree, and they and their male co-workers joined in a "turnout," or strike. Lacking organization and perhaps discouraged by the unsympathetic local press, they returned to work after only a week.[714]

Three years later, mill girls in Dover, New Hampshire, organized an all-female turnout. The Dover women objected to several "obnoxious regulations" management had recently introduced, including a ban on talking while at work. Predicted the *Philadelphia National Gazette*, "By and by the Governor may have to call out the militia to prevent a gynecocracy [*sic*]."[715] A local newspaper applauded the mill owners for attempting to silence notoriously loquacious females. Criticized and belittled by the press and unsupported by popular opinion, the protesters quickly capitulated. Also unsuccessful were groups of self-employed "seamstresses and tailoresses" who attempted to organize. The *Boston Evening Transcript* termed a group of needlewomen in New York who were demanding a living wage "clamorous and unfeminine" and told them to stick to "their scissors and pincushions."[716]

When factory owners in Dover, Lowell, and several other mill towns simultaneously announced pay cuts in 1834,[717] their female employees joined forces in a work stoppage. The *Boston Evening Transcript* reported that one of the strike leaders at Lowell "mounted a pump, and made a flaming Mary Wollstonecroft [*sic*] speech on the rights of women and the iniquities of the 'monied aristocracy,' which produced a powerful effect on her auditors."[718] The strikers circulated a petition headed "Union Is Power," but when management fired the leaders and threatened other reprisals, the women ended the walkout.[719]

The first major American labor federation, the National Trades Union—an all-white, all-male organization—issued a report in 1835 which declared that labor was debasing to women and condemned women's "destructive competition with the male labourer."[720] Just a year later, however, the union did an about-face. Announcing its support of the Lowell mill girls, who were again protesting a pay cut, the union not only praised the strikers but also urged local labor organizations "to do all in their power to aid either by money or otherwise the females" who were "standing out against the oppression of these soulless employers."[721] Harriet Robinson recalled that the Lowell strikers had marched through the city, singing:

> O! isn't it a pity, such a pretty girl as I
> Should be sent to the factory to pine away and die?
> O! I cannot be a slave,
> I will not be a slave,
> For I'm so fond of Liberty
> That I cannot be a slave.[722]

The mill owners offered a compromise that benefited only a minority of employees, but it was a rare victory, and the women accepted it and returned to work.[723]

In December 1844 six Lowell mill girls founded the Lowell Female Labor Reform Association (LFLRA). Its constitution reflected pride in the heritage "our brave ancestors bequeathed to us, and sealed with their blood," but pointed out that even in "the land where Democracy claims to be the principle by which we live," we "see the evil daily increasing which separates . . . the favored few and the unfortunate many." Sarah Bagley of New Hampshire, 38 years old, was the LFLRA's first president.[724]

The LFLRA's membership grew exponentially. In a whirlwind initial year, it ran picnics and fairs, sponsored anti-slavery rallies, presented lecturers, and published a series of pamphlets titled *Factory Tracts*. Among the problems tackled by the *Factory Tracts* were the fourteen-hour workday and the overcrowded boarding houses. One issue likened female factory operatives to chattel slaves, and mill owners to "the dealers in human flesh at the South."[725] Bagley traveled through New England and west to Pittsburgh, Pennsylvania, helping women workers organize and forging alliances with male trade unionists.

In 1845 the LFLRA in partnership with the newly formed New England Workingmen's Association launched a petition campaign for a ten-hour workday. The women collected so many signatures that the Massachusetts state legislature made the unusual gesture of inviting five female factory operatives, including Bagley, to testify at public hearings. However, possibly influenced by the fact that the majority of the petition's signers were women, who could not vote, the legislators took no action. (The British Parliament established a ten-hour workday for women in 1847; Massachusetts had no comparable statute until 1874.)

The *Voice of Industry*, a labor newspaper started by the Workingmen's Association, moved to Lowell in the fall of 1845, and Bagley became one of a three-person publishing committee. She inaugurated a Women's Department whose aim, she announced, was to defend woman's rights. In a letter to the new department, a female factory worker in Manchester, New Hampshire, commented, "I am heartily glad when any thing is done to elevate that class to which it is my lot to belong. We are a band of sisters—we must have sympathy for each other's woes." Another contributor asserted that for women, marriage was "almost the only *business* in which there is any chance of success. . . . It may be, that most women are so dwarfed and weakened, that they believe that dressing, cooking, and loving . . . make up the whole of life; but Nature still asserts her rights, and there will always be those too strong to be satisfied, with a dress, a pudding, or a beau." The letter-writer herself was certainly one of the strong, for she bravely inscribed her full name, Ellen Munroe.

Another correspondent, identified only as an Operative, fumed:

> Woman is never thought to be out of her *sphere*, at home; in the nursery, in the kitchen, over a hot stove cooking from morning till evening—over a wash-tub, or toiling in a cotton factory 14 hours per day. But let her once step out . . . and plead the wrongs of her slave sister of the South or the operative of the North . . . and a cry is raised against her, "*out of her sphere.*"[726]

Bagley took a job at a telegraph station in Lowell in 1846. She continued to write for the *Voice of Industry* through most of that year, but by the next year her byline was gone and her name had disappeared from the public press.[727] The 2016 edition of the *Encyclopedia Britannica* reported that there was no record of her existence after 1847. However, she is one of many lost women whose life stories have been recovered by contemporary historians. Thus, we now know that she married in her mid-forties, worked with her husband as a homeopathic healer, and died in about 1889 in Philadelphia.[728] Three letters she wrote to a well-known artist named Lily Martin Spencer (also known as Angelique Martin) have surfaced.[729] The two women had not met, but they had much in common, for both were advocates of Fourier socialism, opponents of slavery, and supporters of women's and workers' rights. The most interesting of the letters is dated March 13, 1848. Bagley, then in charge of the telegraph office in Springfield, Massachusetts, confided:

> I am sick at heart when I look into the social world and see woman so willingly made a dupe to the beastly selfishness of man. . . . Well, the world is quite satisfied with the present arrangement, and we can only protest against such a state of things, and strive to arouse the minds of others to their state of servitude and dependence on the caprice and whims and selfishness of man. . . . To labor year after year and have only an ungrateful return from those you are striving to bless is truly discouraging. But it is the way of the world. . . . Let us trust on and try to leave a little seed on earth that shall bear fruit when we shall pass away.[730]

Bagley had no way to know that in just four months a seed would be planted in Seneca Falls that would take root and grow into a worldwide campaign for the emancipation of women. An experienced organizer who had struggled for more than a decade alongside working-class women, she never played a leadership role in the emerging feminist movement.

22 FREE WOMEN

Forty years after a revolutionary tribunal crushed the French campaign for women's rights it unexpectedly revived. The seedbed for resurgent French feminism was the semi-religious socialist movement inspired by the political theorist Claude Henri de Saint-Simon. After Saint-Simon's death in 1825, the movement split. When the leader of one faction, Barthélemy Prosper Enfantin, embraced a program that emphasized the emancipation of the female sex, many women joined him, and some rose to positions of influence in the organization. But before long, Enfantin concluded that efforts on behalf of women would have to be postponed—supposedly temporarily, but actually, permanently. Saint-Simonism became increasingly mystical and otherworldly, and issues of importance to women were sidelined. A spokesman went so far as to declare that "woman is today legitimately excluded from public life." In 1832 Enfantin announced that women had been entirely eliminated from the movement's hierarchy.[731]

Ironically, it was not Saint-Simonism's adoption of a feminist agenda but the cancellation of that agenda that gave birth to the nineteenth-century women's movement in France. For afterward, a circle of Saint-Simonian women in Paris who wanted to continue to work for gender equity came together in an informal feminist-socialist network. Two among them—Marie-Reine Guindorf, a 20-year-old chambermaid, and Desirée Véret, 22, a seamstress—conceived an ambitious project: the publication of a weekly journal devoted to the liberation of women.[732] The first issue, titled *La Femme libre* (*The Free Woman*), appeared in August 1832.

The Free Woman occupies a unique place in the history of feminism as the first women's-rights periodical in Europe or North America published exclusively for and by women. A total of thirty-one issues appeared at irregular intervals over the next two years. The staff, some of whom remained comrades and co-workers for decades,[733] experimented

1·· NUMÉRO.

On souscrit, rue du Caire, n. 17, à l'entresol.

PRIX : 15 C.

Chaque exemplaire.

Pour les renseignemens tous les jours de midi à 4 heures.

LA FEMME LIBRE.

APOSTOLAT DES FEMMES.

APPEL AUX FEMMES.

Lorsque tous les peuples s'agitent au nom de *Liberté*, et que le prolétaire réclame son affranchissement, nous, femmes, resterons-nous passives devant ce grand mouvement d'émancipation sociale qui s'opère sous nos yeux.

Notre sort est-il tellement heureux, que nous n'ayons rien aussi à réclamer? La femme, jusqu'à présent, a été exploitée, tyrannisée. Cette tyrannie, cette exploitation, doit cesser. Nous naissons libres comme l'homme, et la moitié du genre humain ne peut être, sans injustice, asservie à l'autre.

Comprenons donc nos droits; comprenons notre puissance; nous avons la puissance attractive, pouvoir des charmes, arme irrésistible, sachons l'employer.

* Le second numéro paraîtra le 25 août.

18. LA FEMME LIBRE, AUGUST 1832

with several titles and subtitles: *La Femme L'avenir (The Woman of the Future), L'Apostolat des femmes (The Women's Apostle),* and *La Femme nouvelle (The New Woman).* Finally, the editors decided on a non-ideological name, *Tribune des femmes (Women's Tribune),* because "the cause of women is universal and not only Saint-Simonian."[734] The journal announced that articles by men would not be accepted and that only the first names of contributors would be published. "If we continue to take men's names, we shall be slaves without knowing it," explained "Jeanne-Desirée" (Desirée Véret). A woman who takes her husband's name might as well brand her forehead with his initials "so that she may be known by all as his property," wrote "Jeanne-Victoire" (Jeanne Deroin).[735]

The *Tribune* targeted injustices that affected women of all classes, especially inequality in education, employment, and marriage. It endorsed the Rousseau-like concept of Woman as the moral compass of family and society but maintained that unjust customs and laws could be defeated only by united action by women themselves.

An introductory editorial titled "*Appel aux Femmes*" ("Appeal to Women") invoked the revolutionary battle cry—Liberty, Equality, but significantly, not Fraternity. It said in part:

> Until now woman has been exploited and tyrannized. This tyranny, this exploitation must cease. We are born free, like man, and half the human race cannot, without injustice, be in servitude to the other half. . . .
>
> We demand equality in marriage. We prefer celibacy to slavery! . . . Liberty, equality—that is to say, a free and equal chance to develop our faculties: this is the victory we must win, and we can succeed only if we unite in a single group. Let us no longer form two camps—that of the women of the people and that of privileged women. Let our common interest unite us. . . .
>
> Women of every class, you can exercise a powerful action; you are called upon to spread the notion of order and harmony everywhere. Turn to the advantage of society-at-large the irresistible charm of your beauty, the

sweetness of your convincing words, which can make man march toward the same objective.[736]

The *Tribune* quickly acquired an international following. Copies were available at Saint-Simonian bookstores and reading rooms and were circulated hand to hand by socialists, feminists, and other progressives in Western Europe and the United States. The English abolitionist Anne Knight translated passages from its pages and forwarded them to associates in the anti-slavery movement. And the widely distributed Owenite paper, *The Crisis*, reprinted the "Appeal to Women" in an English translation prepared by Anna Doyle Wheeler.[737]

Anna Wheeler, an Irish socialist-feminist, was a key figure linking women's-rights activists on both sides of the Channel. During a three-year sojourn in Paris in the 1820's she hosted a salon in her home where people interested in social issues—including her friend the French utopian socialist Charles Fourier—met and traded ideas.[738] Later she returned to Paris to help put out the *Tribune*; and when several women associated with the paper subsequently visited London, she introduced them into radical circles there.[739] Wheeler was a bold innovator. A treatise she coauthored with fellow socialist William Thompson not only advocated political and educational rights for women but even ventured to discuss such taboo topics as birth control, female sexual pleasure, and the sexual double standard.[740]

When the *Tribune* ceased publication in 1834, the women who had been associated with it scattered. Desirée Véret went to England, where she married Jules Gay, a translator of Robert Owen's work.[741] Jeanne Deroin, who also married at about this time, earned a teaching certificate and helped run a school for working-class girls and boys.[742] A woman close to the group, Flora Tristan, traveled to Peru, her birthplace, and to London, where she attended a General Convention of the workers' organization, the Chartists. When she died suddenly in 1844, her friend and comrade Pauline Roland, herself a single mother, assumed responsibility for Tristan's sons and her 19-year-old daughter, Aline.[743] (The painter Paul Gauguin was Aline's son.) Another *Tribune* co-worker, Eugénie Niboyet, founded a feminist weekly in Lyon. Returning to Paris in 1836, she started a new newspaper, the *Gazette des femmes* (*Women's Gazette*), as well as a feminist collective to help support it.[744]

• • • •

The anti-monarchist uprisings of 1848 gave women's-rights activists in several European states an opportunity to advocate on their own behalf. In Hungary a twenty-four-point petition entitled "Demands of the Radical Hungarian Women" asserted women's right to participate in civic affairs.[745] An anonymous pamphlet published in Vienna made a similar demand. "We claim the equality of political rights," it argued. "Why should women not be elected to the Reichstag?"[746] In Berlin, women attended meetings of the (all-male) Democratic Club and founded an affiliated women's club. In Hamburg, a newly organized political club advocated higher education for women.[747] At least four German-language feminist periodicals appeared during 1848 and 1849. The best known were Louise Dittmar's *Soziale Reform* (*Social Reform*) and Louise Otto's *Frauen-Zeitung* (*Women's News*). The latter, despite government opposition, survived for four years, longer than any other European feminist publication of the period. Like Jeanne Deroin, Otto appealed to women to unify. "My sisters," she wrote, "unite with me, so that we do not remain behind, when everything and everyone about us ... presses forward and struggles."[748]

In France, a mass uprising in early February 1848 toppled the monarchy and inaugurated the Second French Republic. Energized by the swirling rhetoric of freedom and equality, a group of feminists, including some formerly associated with the *Women's Tribune*,[749] came together in Paris to rededicate themselves to the struggle. Yet they must have wondered, too, how—or indeed if—the current political revolution, which had abolished slavery in France and its colonies, would also free women. Would the Second Republic be more generous to women than the First? Would voting rights be extended to *citoyennes* this time? Would the National Workshops created by the new government to relieve spiraling unemployment provide aid to suffering workers of both sexes? Answers were not long in coming. None of the new workshops admitted women. And when Pauline Roland attempted to vote in a local election, her ballot was rejected, indicating that "universal suffrage" still meant men only.[750]

Paris's workingwomen, unable to find jobs and excluded from the National Workshops, took to the streets in spontaneous demonstrations. Veterans of *The Free Woman*, the *Women's Tribune*, and the *Women's Gazette* were at the forefront of the protests. The former seamstress Desirée Gay (she now used her husband's last name) organized female textile workers; Suzanne Voilquin, a certified midwife, founded a Society of United Midwives and organized wet nurses; Eugénie Niboyet helped to unite domestic workers.

Hundreds of women's clubs were founded in cities around the country. Most were cultural or social in purpose, but some had a women's-rights agenda.[751] Among the latter were the *Société pour l'émancipation des femmes* (Society for the Emancipation of Women), which petitioned the provisional government for female suffrage, access to divorce, and other reforms, and the *Comité des droits de la femme* (Committee of the Rights of Woman), which based its claims on women's role as mothers.[752] Another club, the *Société de la Voix des femmes* (The Society of the Voice of Women), was formed to support a new publication, *La Voix des femmes*. At the helm of this paper—the first ever woman-centered daily[753]—was the experienced editor Eugénie Niboyet.[754]

The Voice of Women described itself as "a socialist and political newspaper representing all women's interests." It promoted woman suffrage, equal legal rights for female entrepreneurs, educational opportunities for girls and women, and repeal of the repressive marriage and divorce laws. Desirée Gay emerged in its pages as a champion of workingwomen, advocating passionately for the establishment of National Workshops for women and for communal restaurants and laundries "where the people will find inexpensively healthy food . . . and clean linens that they can procure, not in isolation, but as united women."[755] All of the agitation bore fruit. At the end of March 1848, just two months after the establishment of the Second Republic, the government authorized the creation of women's workshops and also set up food distribution centers at various Paris locations. The women in one of the new workshops elected Desirée Gay to represent them in negotiations with municipal authorities.[756]

The media chose to blame the proliferating women's groups for the unsettled political climate. "Club women, great God! Our mothers, our virgins, our sisters! It is absurd, it is monstrous, it is unheard of," charged one publication.[757] Unruly bands of men invaded women's meetings, disrupting the proceedings, jeering at members, and even pursuing them through the streets.[758] A play parodying the *clubistes* opened at Paris's *Théâtre de Vaudeville*.[759]

In early April, Eugénie Niboyet made an audacious foray into the political arena. At a time when Frenchwomen could not vote and no woman had ever held a national political office, she announced the nomination of the celebrated novelist George Sand as a candidate in the National Assembly election scheduled for later that month.[760] It may have seemed to Niboyet and her colleagues at *The Voice of Women* that the campaign for women's rights had sufficient public support to justify the move, but if so, they badly underestimated the opposition. More serious still, they neglected to obtain the consent of the candidate herself.

The choice of George Sand was not unreasonable, for she had defied gender norms in her own life by abandoning an unhappy marriage and living as a free woman and an independent artist. Moreover, her best-selling novels implicitly advocated the legalization of divorce and the repeal of laws that gave men mastery over women. But unlike Jeanne Deroin—who wrote in *The Voice of Women*, "We are all sisters and we should extend our hands to each other"[761]—Sand evidently felt little sisterly solidarity. She immediately fired off an open letter deriding her nomination and attributing this "ridiculous presumption" to a newspaper edited by women she did not know who wanted her to become a mouthpiece for principles she did not support.[762] A disheartened Eugénie Niboyet remarked, "Woman will not be truly strong until she becomes, in good faith, the friend of her own sex."[763]

In June, the police shut down the club that supported *The Voice of Women*, and the paper ceased publication soon afterward. Desirée Gay was accused by government officials of inciting dissension and was removed from her elected position as leader of a women's workshop. On June 22, the government announced the closure of all National Workshops, and the next day Paris's working-class quarters erupted. Women stood alongside men at hastily erected barricades and were among the multitude killed and wounded during six days of bloody street-fighting. Thousands of women and men were arrested, tried, and sentenced to deportation to Algeria. The National Assembly issued a decree barring "women and minor children" from joining or attending meetings of any club and forbidding all political activity by women. Explained one Assembly delegate, "The suitable and appropriate place for women is in private life." Referring to women's role in the 1789 revolution, he commented darkly that "historic memories of the presence of women in political assemblies suffice to exclude them."[764]

In the spring of 1849 Jeanne Deroin announced her candidacy in the forthcoming election of national legislature delegates. To publicize her views, she revived the journal *L'Opinion des femmes* (*The Opinion of Women*), one issue of which she and Desirée Gay had put out the previous year. In the journal's pages she defined woman's social role in spiritual terms reminiscent of Saint-Simonian theory—"Woman's mission in the present ... is apostolic," she wrote; "... its goal is to realize the kingdom of God on earth." But she also presented an overarching argument for women's rights. "The abolition of the privileges of race, birth, caste, and fortune cannot be complete and radical unless the privilege of sex is totally abolished," she asserted. "It is the source of all the others, the last head of the hydra. . . . Women must constantly demand the right of citizenship."[765]

Predictably, it was not so much Deroin's opinions but her gender that opponents attacked. One of the sharpest rebuffs came from a man whom she might have expected to support her candidacy, the journalist and politician Pierre-Joseph Proudhon. Proudhon—an anarchist who famously proclaimed, "property is theft"—contended that civic freedoms were rightfully denied to women. "Political equality of the sexes, which is to say the presumption by women of the male prerogative of public office," he wrote, "is one of the fallacies that defies not only logic but even more so human conscience and the nature of things."[766]

The renowned artist Honoré Daumier, known for his biting social satire, had previously lampooned female intellectuals in a series of drawings called "*Les Bas-Bleus*" ("The Bluestockings"). Now he again employed his talent to disparage women's aspirations. In ten lithographs titled "*Les Femmes socialistes*" ("The Socialist Women"), he caricatured feminists as viragos who emasculated their husbands and neglected their homes and children. Captions on four drawings specifically mentioned

Jeanne Deroin, whose name alone was enough to raise the specter of female rebellion.

In the May 1849 election, half of the (all-male) electorate voted for the monarchist "Party of Order"; and although socialists won nearly 30 percent of the seats in the national legislature, only a handful of ballots were cast for Deroin. Her candidacy marked the last hurrah of that era's women's movement in France. Suppressed by a totalitarian government, unable to win the support of male radicals and artists and even of many women, and demonized by a popular culture fiercely opposed to any social change that encroached upon male privilege, the French activists were politically isolated: friendless and powerless.

The year 1851 found Deroin and Pauline Roland serving a term in Paris's Saint-Lazare prison for the crime of organizing workers. Shortly before their scheduled release they composed two valedictory letters in which they passed the torch to sisters-in-struggle abroad. One letter went to the Sheffield Female Political Association, an English Chartist group, the other to a National Women's Rights Convention in the United States. The latter said in part:

> Dear Sisters:
>
> Your courageous declaration of Woman's Rights has resounded even to our prison, and has filled our souls with inexpressible joy. . . . The darkness of reaction has obscured the sun of 1848. Why? Because the revolutionary tempest, in overturning at the same time the throne and the scaffold, in breaking the chain of the black slave,[767] forgot to break the chain of the most oppressed of all—of Woman, the pariah of humanity. . . .
>
> Sisters of America! Your socialist sisters of France are united with you in the vindication of the rights of woman to civil and political equality. We have, moreover, the profound conviction that only by the power of association based on solidarity—by the union of the working classes of both sexes to organize labor—can be acquired,

completely and pacifically, the civil and political equality of woman, and the social right for all.

It is in this confidence that, from the depths of the jail which still imprisons our bodies without reaching our hearts, we cry to you, Faith, Love, Hope, and send to you our sisterly salutations.[768]

By the end of the next year the French monarchy had been restored with Louis Napoleon at its head. Niboyet, Deroin, and Voilquin went into exile, followed a few years later by Desirée Gay. Pauline Roland was dead, having succumbed to the aftereffects of deportation to Algeria. The French feminists had succeeded in raising public awareness of gender inequities and had built a solid base of support among the laboring women with whom their strongest sympathies always lay. Although the movement they had created ultimately did not survive, they understood that they had forged a link in the centuries-long chain of women's protest, and they rejoiced in the knowledge that others would carry the cause forward.

The American women who took up the fight were more favorably positioned than their French predecessors. They were (with a few notable exceptions[769]) middle-class, native-born, and white. They had learned to withstand ridicule and animosity in what Elizabeth Cady Stanton aptly termed "the school of anti-slavery." And crucially, they did not live in a repressive monarchy but in a republic with a constitution that guaranteed freedom of speech and assembly. Thus, it was they who were able to create the world's first sustained feminist movement.

19. HONORÉ DAUMIER, 1849
(".... It is my right to throw you out the door of your own house.... Jeanne Derouin [sic] proved it to me last night.")

CODA

The inaugural meeting of the International Council of Women—held in Washington, D.C., in the spring of 1888—was timed to coincide with the fortieth anniversary of the Seneca Falls convention. Many of the speakers in the weeklong program highlighted the remarkable achievements of the women's-rights campaign in the United States. The principal of a girls' school in Indiana recalled that in 1848 no institution of higher education had admitted women, but 473 colleges and universities now had female students. A journalist reported that women had formerly worked in just seven paid occupations but were now employed in hundreds of different industries and professions. A writer and suffrage activist commented that the provisions of English common law that had once negated the legal existence of wives had been modified in most states.[770] Elizabeth Cady Stanton observed in her welcoming address that public approval of woman suffrage had increased markedly. And Frederick Douglass noted that in 1848 the women's movement "was wrapped in obscurity; now it is lifted in sight of the whole world."

A less rosy assessment might have pointed out that Douglass's reference to the "whole world," like the word "international" in the new organization's name, was aspirational rather than actual. The conference delegates came from only nine countries. Neither Africa nor Latin America was represented, while a single individual, an Indian woman who was not an official delegate, stood in for the vast and various continent of Asia. Moreover, the tragic racial divide in the American movement was evident throughout the meeting. The only African Americans listed as speakers were the pioneer anti-slavery and women's-rights activists Frederick Douglass and Robert Purvis, and the noted writer, abolitionist, and suffragist Frances Ellen Watkins Harper. There were no Native Americans on the program, but a white woman representing the Woman's National Indian Association had been invited to address the session on

"Philanthropy." She delivered the opinion that "civilization, education, citizenship, and Christianity can alone solve the Indian problem."[771]

Yet with all its serious limitations, the campaign for women's rights had undoubtedly improved the lives of many women, and in the next two or three decades the pace of improvement quickened. In spite of its precarious beginnings, the International Council of Women not only survived but flourished; it serves today as an umbrella organization for women's groups in seventy countries. African-American women had countered the exclusionary policies of the Stanton-Anthony suffrage organization by working for both racial and gender justice—sometimes alongside white suffragists, sometimes in their own organizations. In 1896, a number of local clubs merged to form the National Association of Colored Women, which was led for several years by the distinguished educator and suffrage activist Mary Church Terrell. Finally, Stanton's claim that public sentiment about female suffrage had changed for the better was borne out over the next few decades. In 1893, New Zealand became the first self-governing state to grant women full suffrage, and although equivalent voting rights took many years in most of the world, women cast ballots in Wyoming, Colorado, Utah, and Idaho before 1900; in four Scandinavian nations between 1906 and 1915;[772] and in a great many local elections before World War I.

One may search all 471 pages of the transcript of the international conference without finding the word "feminism," but by the end of the nineteenth century it had entered the vocabulary of most Western languages. The nameless idea that had inspired women through so many generations had succeeded at last in sparking a powerful movement for social and political justice.

・・・・

The primary focus of the American women's movement since the Civil War had been the fight for the vote. But in her later years Elizabeth Cady Stanton frequently spoke about broader goals. Addressing a meeting in San Francisco in 1871, for example, she had suggested that suffrage was virtually won, and that it was time to consider "more vital questions of this reform," questions having to do with marriage, divorce, and the role of women in the family. These issues, she made clear, had no quick solution, for the elimination of men's authority over women in the home would require "a social revolution greater than any political or religious revolution that the world has ever seen, because it goes deep down to the very foundations of society."[773]

Later, at the international conference, Stanton again pondered the enormity of the task the women's movement faced. She was now 72. Together with Susan B. Anthony and thousands of other women, she had made the struggle for gender justice her life's work, but she was well aware that she would not live to see the fulfillment of the "deep yearnings of [women's] souls for freedom." She confessed to feeling "a peculiar tenderness for the young women on whose shoulders we are about to leave our burdens." But she took a long view of history. She knew that the journey is not defined by how it has ended but by how far we have traveled and what has changed for the better along the way.

What she said then remains so for us today: "The true woman is as yet a dream of the future."[774]

ACKNOWLEDGMENTS

A book that has been as long in the making as this one incurs many debts. First among those to whom I owe thanks are the librarians who aided me in my search for the hidden history of women. A brief perusal of the endnotes will make clear how much I am indebted to them.

Many people kindly agreed to read drafts of chapters. I especially want to thank Cynthia Fuchs Epstein, Nina Miller, Robin Morgan, Carol Sicherman, and Catherine Silver for their helpful criticism, advice, and encouragement. Colleagues in a Columbia University seminar heard and usefully commented on an early version of the chapters on women in the Dutch Republic and New Netherland. Members of my family history group—Martha Driver, Dorothy Helly, Sarah Pomeroy, and Alison Smith—reviewed the introduction and several other chapters, and generously offered me the benefit of their deep scholarship. Of course, I alone am responsible for any misstatements. Thanks also to Conrad Gries, Aimee Kron, and John Trotti for help with translations.

Heartfelt gratitude goes to my family for their loving support over the years. My husband and writing partner, Walter Schneir, was with me every step of the way until his death in 2009. My son Nicholas Schneir gave every chapter a thorough, intelligent reading. He asked probing questions, helped to solve a number of knotty writing problems, and made many creative suggestions—including the title *Before Feminism*. My daughter, Frances Schneir, read every word of the manuscript. She caught innumerable typos and made valuable stylistic suggestions that greatly improved the readability of the text. My older son, Jason Schneir, was unfailingly interested in what I was working on, looked out for my wellbeing from thousands of miles away, and always kept me smiling.

Finally, I want to thank friends in Pleasantville, San Miguel de Allende, East Hampton, New York City, Tucson, upstate New York, Mississippi, and Montclair. They listened to my seemingly endless discourse on the history of women and never asked when in the world I would ever finish That Book.

LIST OF ILLUSTRATIONS

1. Minoan "snake goddess" statuette from Knossos, faience, Heraklion Archaeological Museum, Crete. *15*
2. Tiryns fresco, National Archaeological Museum, Athens. *27*
3. Oil flask, terracotta, from Athens, attributed to the Amasis painter, Metropolitan Museum of Art, New York City. *30*
4. Mother goddesses, limestone relief, Corinium Museum, Cirencester, England. *40*
5. Isis nursing Horus, anhydrite statuette, Egypt, Metropolitan Museum of Art, New York City. *50*
6. Sequana, bronze statuette, Musée Archéologique de Dijon. *64*
7. Guda, illumination on parchment, Saint Bartholomew homiliary, *Universitätsbibliothek*, Frankfurt am Main, Germany. *76*
8. Cathar expulsion from Carcassonne, illumination on parchment, attributed to fifteenth-century Master of Boucicaut, *Grande Chronique de France*, British Library, London. *114*
9. Christine de Pizan, paint and gold leaf on parchment (detail), British Library, London. *140*
10. Sofonisba Anguissola, oil on canvas, Museum of Fine Arts, Boston, Massachusetts. *150*
11. "Moll Cutpurse," woodcut, title page of *The Roaring Girle* by Thomas Dekker and Thomas Middleton. *163*
12. Anna Maria van Schurman, engraving (detail), Museum Martena, Franeker, Netherlands. *174*
13. New Amsterdam, New York Public Library collection "Slavery in New York." *181*
14. Anne Hutchinson, bronze statue by Cyrus Edwin Dallin on Massachusetts State House grounds, Boston. *197*
15. Phillis Wheatley frontispiece, engraving by enslaved artist Scipio Moorhead, British Museum, London. *210*
16. Women's march, painting, *Bibliotheque Nationale de France*. *216*
17. Olympe de Gouges, attributed to Matais. *227*
18. *La Femme Libre*, first page of first issue of journal. *242*
19. Honoré Daumier lithograph from series *Les Femmes Socialistes* in *Le Charivari*, Bibliotheque Nationale de France. *251*

NOTES

INTRODUCTION: THE MYSTERY OF SENECA FALLS

[1] *Seneca County Courier*, July 14, 1848, https://www.loc.gov/rsource/rbnawsa.n7548/

[2] Stanton (1815-1902); Mott (1793-1880).

[3] Quoted from Miriam Schneir, *Feminism: The Essential Historical Writings* (NY: Random House/Vintage, 1972, 1994, 2014), pp. 77-82.

[4] *The North Star*, July 28, 1848.

[5] May 16, 1838: quoted from *Lucretia Mott Speaks,* Christopher Densmore et al., eds. (Champaign: U. of Illinois, 2017).

[6] Stanton, September 1848, Waterloo, NY; quoted from *The Selected Papers of Elizabeth Cady Stanton and Susan B. Anthony*, v. 1, Ann D. Gordon, ed. (New Brunswick, NJ: Rutgers UP, 1997), p 96.

[7] U.S. periodicals: Amelia Bloomer, *The Lily,* 1849-53; Jane Swisshelm, *Saturday Visiter,* 1848-54; Paulina Wright Davis, *Una,* 1853-55; Mathilde Anneke, *German Women's Newspaper* (*Deutsche Frauen-Zeitung*), 1852-54. European journals: Louise Otto, *Die* Frauen-Zeitung (*The Women's Newspaper*), 1849-52; Louise Dittmar, *Soziale Reform* (*Social Reform*), 1849; Eugenie Niboyet, *La Voix des femmes* (*The Women's Voice*), 1848.

[8] Rosalyn Terborg-Penn, "African-American Women and the Woman Suffrage Movement," in *One Woman, One Vote,* Marjorie Spruill Wheeler, ed. (Troutdale, OR: New Sage Press, 1995), pp. 148.

[9] *History of Woman Suffrage*, v. 1 (Rochester, NY: Charles Mann, 1881); Gage, p. 753; Stanton, p. 13.

[10] Mary R. Beard (1876-1958), *Woman as Force in History* (NY: Collier Books, 1962), "Preface," p. 168.

[11] Alden Whitman, "The Woman in History Becomes Explosive Issue in the Present," *New York Times*, November 2, 1974.

[12] Schneir, *Feminism*, p. xiv.

[13] Linda Grant de Pauw and Conover Hunt, with Miriam Schneir, *"Remember the Ladies"* (NY: Viking, 1976).

[14] Simone de Beauvoir, *The Second Sex,* Constance Borde, Sheila Malovany-Chevallier, trans. (NY: Knopf, 2009), pp. 7-8

[15] Gerda Lerner, *The Creation of Feminist Consciousness* (NY: Oxford UP, 1986), pp. 221, 4, 218.

1 WHEN WOMEN WERE GODS AND PRIESTS

[16] *The Odyssey of Homer* (first written down c. mid-8th century BCE), Robert Fagles, trans. (NY: Penguin, 1996), p. 396.

[17] Nicolas Platon, *Archaeologia Mundi Crete* (Cleveland, NY: World, 1966), p. 13.

[18] Sir Arthur Evans, *The Palace of Minos*, v. 1 (London: Macmillan, 1921), https://archive.org/stream/palaceofminoscom01evanuoft?ref=ol#page/n349/mode/2up.

[19] First palace, 1900 BCE-1700 BCE; New Palace, 1700 BCE-1450 BCE.

[20] *The Iliad of Homer,* Robert Fagles, trans. (NY: Penguin, 1990), p. 305; R. F. Willetts, *The Civilization of Ancient Crete* [1976] (NY: Barnes & Noble, 1995), p. 122.

[21] "powerful": Bonnie S. Anderson and Judith P. Zinsser, *A History of Their Own*, v. 1 (NY: Harper & Row, 1988), p. 8; "mortal": Stella Georgoudi, "Creating a Myth of Matriarchy," *A History of Women in the West*, v. 1, Pauline Schmitt Pantel, ed. (Cambridge, MA: Harvard, 1994), p. 460.

[22] Sarah B. Pomeroy, "Selected Bibliography on Women in Antiquity," *Women in the Ancient World*, John Peradotto and J. P. Sullivan, eds. (Albany: State U. of New York, 1984), p. 350.

[23] Anderson and Zinsser, p. 7.

[24] Oliver Dickinson, *The Aegean Bronze Age* (Cambridge, UK: Cambridge UP, 2014), p. 265.

[25] Gerda Lerner, *The Creation of Patriarchy* (NY: Oxford UP, 1986), p. 29.

[26] Evans, *The Palace of Minos*, v. 3, p. 406.

[27] Sinclair Hood, *The Minoans* (NY: Praeger, 1971), p. 117.

[28] Carol G. Thomas, "Matriarchy in Early Greece," *Arethusa* 6, 2 [1973]: 175-79; Marija Gimbutas, *The Language of the Goddess* (San Francisco, CA: Harper & Row, 1989).

[29] Sarah B. Pomeroy, *Goddesses, Whores, Wives, and Slaves* (NY: Schocken, 1975), p. 15; Margaret Ehrenberg, *Women in Prehistory* (London: British Museum, 1989, 1992), pp. 110-111.

[30] Joseph A. MacGillivray, *Minotaur* (NY: Hill & Wang, 2000), p. 193.

[31] Riane Eisler, *The Chalice and the Blade* (San Francisco: Harper, 1987).

[32] Willetts, p. 113, 134.

[33] Hood, p. 118.

[34] Barbara A. Olsen, "Women, Children and the Family in the Late Aegean Bronze Age," *World Archaeology* 29, 3 (1998): 389.

2 THE WEAVE OF MYCENAEAN LIFE

[35] Emily Vermeule, *Greece in the Bronze Age* (Chicago, IL: U. of Chicago, 1964), p. 257, estimates there were 180 Mycenaean (aka Helladic) settlements.

[36] Margalit Fox, *The Riddle of the Labyrinth* (NY: Ecco, 2013), p. 87.

[37] John Chadwick, *The Mycenaean World* (NY: Cambridge UP, 1980), p. ix

[38] Cynthia W. Shelmerdine, John Bennet, and Laura Preston, "Economy and Administration," in *The Cambridge Companion to the Aegean Bronze Age*, Cynthia W. Shelmerdine, ed. (Cambridge: Cambridge UP, 2008), pp. 289-309

[39] Jon-Christian Billigmeier and Judy A. Turner, "The Socio-Economic Roles of Women in Mycenaean Greece," in *Women's Studies* 8 (1981): 5-6; Shelmerdine and Bennet, pp.306-307.

⁴⁰ Chadwick, pp. 67, 78-82. Cynthia Eller, *The Myth of Matriarchal Prehistory* (Boston, MA: Beacon, 2000), p. 167.
⁴¹ *The Iliad of Homer*, Robert Fagles, trans. (NY: Penguin, 1990), p. 78.
⁴² Billigmeier and Turner, 6, 16 ftn. 33; Alexander Uchitel, "Women at Work," in *Historia* 33, 3 (1984): 257-282.
⁴³ *The Odyssey of Homer*, Robert Fagles, trans. (NY: Penguin, 1996), p. 182.
⁴⁴ Chadwick, pp. 150-151.
⁴⁵ Barbara A. Olsen, "Women, Children and the Family in the Late Aegean Bronze Age," *World Archaeology* 29, 3 (1998): 383-384.
⁴⁶ Chadwick, p. 30.
⁴⁷ Olsen, 383.
⁴⁸ Chadwick, 97; Vermeule, p. 292.
⁴⁹ Billigmeier and Turner, 8-9, 12.
⁵⁰ Thomas G. Palaima, "*Themis* in the Mycenaean Lexicon," in *Faventia*, Jan. 22/1, (2000): 9.
⁵¹ Chadwick, pp. 77, 114; Billigmeier and Turner, 9.
⁵² Chadwick, p. 74. 23. Billigmeier and Turner, 9-10.
⁵³ Billigmeier and Turner, 11.

3 THE GREAT CODE AT GORTYN
⁵⁴ *Great Dialogues of Plato*, W.H.D. Rouse, trans. (NY: New American Library, 1999), pp. 29-30; Demosthenes, "Against Neaera," quoted from Elaine Fantham *et al.*, eds., *Women in the Classical World* (NY: Oxford UP, 1994), p. 115.
⁵⁵ *Women's Life in Greece and Rome*, 2nd ed., Mary R. Lefkowitz and Maureen B. Fant, eds. (Baltimore, MD: Johns Hopkins, 1992), pp. 219-221.
⁵⁶ "priestesses": Sue Blundell, *Women in Ancient Greece* (Cambridge, MA: Harvard UP, 1995), p. 161, and Joan Breton Connelly, *Portrait of a Priestess* (Princeton, NJ: Princeton UP, 2007), p. 276. "festivals": Fantham *et al.*, p. 83.
⁵⁷ Michael Gagarin, *Early Greek Law* (Berkeley: U. of California, 1989), p. 96; Blundell, p. 158.
⁵⁸ Michael Gagarin and Paula Perlman, *The Laws of Ancient Crete* (Oxford, UK: Oxford UP, 2016), pp. 84, 101.
⁵⁹ Claudine Leduc, "Marriage in Ancient Greece," *A History of Women in the West*, v.1, Pauline Schmitt Pantel, ed. (Cambridge, MA: Harvard UP, 1992), pp. 267-268.
⁶⁰ R. F. Willetts, "Translation of the Law Code of Gortyn," in R. F. Willetts, *The Civilization of Ancient Greece* [1976] (NY: Barnes & Noble, 1995), pp. 216-223.
⁶¹ Siwan Anderson, "The Economics of Dowry and Brideprice," in *The Journal of Economic Perspectives*, 21, 4 (Fall 2007), Table 4: 157.
⁶² *The Second Sex*, Constance Borde and Sheila Malovany-Chevallier, trans. (NY: Knopf, 2009), p. 96.
⁶³ Gagarin and Perlman, p. 83.
⁶⁴ Willetts, p. 169.
⁶⁵ Putnam, *The Lady* [1910] (Chicago, IL: U. of Chicago, 1969), pp. 20-22.

4 THE HERITAGE OF CELTIC WOMEN

[66] E.g., the Hallstatt culture (800-450 BCE) and the La Tène (450-50 BCE).

[67] Myles Dillon and Nora Chadwick, *The Celtic Realms* (London: Phoenix, 2000), p. 25.

[68] Nadine Berthelier-Ajot, "The Vix Settlement and the Tomb of the Princess," in *The Celts*, Sabatino Mocati *et al.*, eds. (NY: Rizzoli, 1991), pp. 116-117; Christiane Eluère, "The Celts and Their Gold," pp. 387-388, in *The Celts*, Venceslas Kruta *et al.*, eds. (NY: Rizzoli, 1999); Peter Berresford Ellis, *Celtic Women* (Grand Rapids, MI: Eerdmans, 1995), p. 76.

[69] Jörg Biel, "The Celtic Princes of Hohenasperg," in Kruta, p. 128.

[70] Eluère, in Kruta, pp. 388-389.

[71] Pierre Roualet, "Marnian Culture of Champagne," in Kruta, pp. 165-170.

[72] "The Arras Culture," in Kruta, pp. 605-09.

[73] Tacitus (56-117 CE), *Agricola* 16 [c.98 CE], H. Mattingly, trans. (Baltimore, MD: Penguin, 1948), p. 66.

[74] *Histories* 3.45; *Annals* 12.40, Michael Grant, trans. (Baltimore, MD: Penguin, 1962).

[75] Lindsay Allason-Jones, *Women in Roman Britain* (London: British Museum, 1989), p. 17.

[76] Tacitus, *Annals* 12.31 and 14.30.

[77] Dio Cassius, *Roman History* 62, 2.3-4 [211-233 CE], Earnest Cary, trans. (Cambridge, MA: Harvard UP, 1914), p. 85.

[78] Mandy Jay *et al.*, "Chariots and Context," *Oxford Journal of Archaeology* 31:2 (2012): 161; Hans-Eckart Joachim, "The Waldalgesheim Tomb," in Moscati, p. 294.

[79] Tacitus, *Annals*, 14.31-37; Dio Cassius 42.8, says that Boudicca died a natural death.

[80] Nora Chadwick, *The Celts* (London, UK: Penguin, 1997), pp. 139-140; Dillon and Chadwick, p. 153.

[81] Chadwick, p. 158.

[82] Dillon and Chadwick, p. 144.

[83] "Sulis": Allason-Jones, p. 155; "Coventina": Chadwick, p. 153; "Sequana": Dillon and Chadwick, p. 137.

[84] Julius Caesar, *The Conquest of Gaul*, bk. 6.13,14,16, S.A. Handford, trans. (NY: Penguin, 1982).

[85] Tacitus, *Annals* 14.30, http://classics.mit.edu/Tacitus/annals.10.xiv.html.

[86] Tacitus, *Germania* 8, H. Mattingly, trans. (Baltimore, MD: Penguin, 1948), p. 107; Caesar, bk. 1.50;

[87] Tacitus: *Histories* (c.105 CE), 4.61, Clifford H. Moore, trans. (Cambridge, MA: Harvard UP, 1992), p. 65, and *Germania* 8, p. 108.

[88] William Blake, *Milton: A Poem*, v. 5, Robert N. Essick and Joseph Viscomi, eds. (Princeton, NJ: Princeton UP, 1998), p. 127.

[89] *The Collected Poems of W. B. Yeats* (NY: Macmillan, 1951), p. 143.

5 DECLINE AND FALL OF THE PATERFAMILIAS

[90] J. A. Crook, "Feminine Inadequacy and the Senatusconsultum Velleianum," in *The Family in Ancient Rome*, Beryl Rawson, ed. (Ithaca, NY: Cornell UP, 1986), p. 84; Jane F. Gardner, *Women in Roman Law and Society* (Bloomington: Indiana UP, 1986), p. 14.

[91] Susan Treggiari, *Roman Marriage* (NY: Oxford UP, 1993), pp. 361, 381; Sarah Pomeroy, *Goddesses, Whores, Wives, and Slaves* (NY: Schocken, 1976), p. 177.

[92] https://avalon.law.yale.edu/ancient/twelve_tables.asp.

[93] Treggiari, pp. 442, 467-468; Pomeroy, p. 158; Crook, "Women in Roman Succession," in Rawson, p. 59.

[94] Gardner, pp. 5-11.

[95] Justinian's *Digest* 48.5.23-24; Mary R. Lefkowitz and Maureen B. Fant, *Women's Life in Greece and Rome*, 2nd ed. (Baltimore, MD: Johns Hopkins UP, 1992), p. 108.

[96] William V. Harris, "The Roman Father's Power of Life and Death," in *Studies in Roman Law*, Roger S. Bagnall and William V. Harris, eds. (Leiden: E.J. Brill, 1986).

[97] Voconian law, 169 BCE: Garner, pp. 170-76; *The Cambridge Ancient History*, 2nd ed., v. 8 (Cambridge, UK: Cambridge UP, 1954), p. 375.

[98] Plautus: e.g., Cleostrata (in *Casina*), Matrona (in *Manaechmi*).

[99] Livy, *History of Rome*, Rev. Canon Roberts, trans., 34.1-8.

[100] Cornelius Nepos (c. 100-c. 25 BCE), quoted from Mary R. Lefkowitz and, Maureen B. Fant, eds., *Women's Life in Greece and Rome* (Baltimore, MD: Johns Hopkins UP, 1992), pp. 164-165.

[101] Josiah Osgood, *Turia* (NY: Oxford UP, 2014), pp. 157, 159.

[102] Appian, *The Civil Wars* 4.33, John Carter, trans. (NY: Penguin, 1996).

[103] Sarah B. Pomeroy, "Women in Roman Egypt," in *Reflections of Women in Antiquity*, Helene P. Foley, ed. (NY: Gordon and Breach, 1981), pp. 309-313.

[104] Pompey (106-48 BCE): *Plutarch's Lives*, v. 2, "Pompey," Arthur Hugh Clough, ed., John Dryden, trans. (NY: Random House, 1992), p. 115.

[105] Sallust, *Conspiracy of Cataline* 25; Pomeroy, *Goddesses*, p. 171.

[106] Pliny the Younger, *Letters* 1.16.6; in Fantham *et al.*, p. 349.

[107] Pomeroy, *Goddesses*, pp. 173-174.

[108] Juvenal, *Juvenal and Persius*, G. G. Ramsay, trans. (Cambridge, MA: Harvard UP, 1918), "Satire 6," pp. 117-121.

[109] Gregory S. Aldrete, *Daily Life in the Roman City* (Greenwood Press, 2004), p. 22, estimates a million between 200 BCE and 200 CE; Rawson, p. 6, estimates up to one and a half million between 100 BCE and 200 CE; re slaves: Keith R. Bradley, *Slavery and Society at Rome* (NY: Cambridge UP, 2002), pp. 29-30.

[110] Walter Burkert, *Greek Religion* (Malden, MA: Wiley-Blackwell, 1991), p. 177.

[111] R. E. Witt, *Isis in the Graeco-Roman World* (Ithaca, NY: Cornell UP, 1971), p. 85; Sharon Kelly Heyob, *The Cult of Isis Among Women in the Graeco-Roman World* (Leiden: E. J. Brill, 1975), pp. 48, 45, 52, 97-100.

[112] Juvenal, "Satire 6," pp. 127-131; Plutarch: *Moralia* 138a-146a, R. Warner, trans., quoted from Lefkowitz and Fant, p. 183.

[113] The *lex Julia* was supplemented in 9 CE by the *lex Papia Poppaea*; Fantham *et al.*, p. 303.
[114] Tacitus, *Annals* III.25.
[115] Epictetus, *Ibid.*, p. 171.
[116] Quoted from Pomeroy, *Goddesses*, p. 173 (Judith Hallett, trans.).
[117] Juvenal, "Satire 6," pp. 87, 131, 133.
[118] Soranus, *Gynecology* I.xix.61-65; John T. Noonan, Jr., *Contraception* (Cambridge, MA: Harvard UP, 1986), pp. 13-17.
[119] Tacitus, *Annals*, III.33, quoting Severus Caecina.
[120] *Suetonius* I.2, "The Deified Augustus," 171, 173, 221; Tacitus, *Annals* II.85, 49.
[121] Gaius, *Institutes* 1.190, Gordon and Robinson, trans., quoted from Lefkowitz and Fant, p. 99.
[122] *The Second Sex*, Constance Borde and Sheila Malovany-Chevallier, trans. (NY: Knopf, 2009), p. 103.
[123] Livia (58 BCE-29 CE); Agrippina the Younger (c. 15-59 CE); Faustina the Elder (d.141 CE); Julia Domna (c.170-217 CE); Julia Maesa (c. 160-c. 224 CE).

6 THE MINISTRY OF WOMEN

[124] Luke 8:1-3 mentions Susanna, Joanna, and Mary Magdalene.
[125] Mark 10:43-44; Matthew 19:24. Quotations from the New Testament, unless otherwise identified, are from the Revised Standard Version (RSV), published in 1946.
[126] "Sweeping": Luke 15:8; "sewing": Mark 2:21; "baking": Matthew 13:33; "spinning": Matthew 6:28; "childbirth": John 16:20-21.
[127] Matthew 26-28; Mark 16-19; Luke 23-24; John 19-20.
[128] Robin Lane Fox, *Pagans and Christians* (San Francisco: Harper & Row, 1986), pp. 310-311.
[129] Galatians 3:28.
[130] Corinthians 11:7-9,11; 14:34-35.
[131] Helmut Koester, *From Jesus to Christ*: Symposium: Faculty Panel, 1998, www.pbs.org/wgbh/pages/frontline/shows/religion. Ian Howard Marshall, "Brothers Embracing Sisters?" *Technical Papers for the Bible Translator* 55/3 (July 2004): 303-310.
[132] The New Revised Standard Version (1989) and the Revised English Bible (1989).
[133] Matthew 5:9; Romans 3:28.
[134] Romans 16:1. Editions: English, RSV, 1946; French, *Nouvelle Edition de Genève*, 1979; Spanish, *Biblia Reina Valera*, 1960; Italian, *Nuova Riveduta*, 1994; German, *Schlachter*, 2000.
[135] Clara Maria Henning, "Canon Law and the Battle of the Sexes," in *Religion and Sexism*, Rosemary Ruether, ed. (NY: Simon & Schuster, 1974), pp. 275-279; Aimé Georges Martimort, *Deaconesses: An Historical Study* (San Francisco: Ignatius, 1980).

[136] Romans 16:7.
[137] Acts 18.1; Corinthians 16:19, Acts 18:18, Romans 16:5.
[138] See Philemon 2, Colossians 4:15, and Acts 12:12.
[139] Eusebius, *Ecclesiastical History,* v. 5, 172, 179, https://archive.org/details/SPCKEusebius1.
[140] Peter Dronke, *Women Writers of the Middle Ages* (NY: Cambridge UP, 1984), pp. 2-4.
[141] Tertullian, *Apologeticus* 50.13.
[142] Luke 10:38-42; I Corinthians 7:8.
[143] http://www.earlychristianwritings.com/text/actspaul.html.
[144] Elaine Pagels, *The Gnostic Gospels* (NY: Vintage, 1989), p. 63.
[145] *Nicene and Post Nicene Fathers, First Series,* "On the Priesthood," 9 3, Philip Schaff, ed., W.R.W. Stephens, trans. (Buffalo, NY: Christian Literature Publishing, 1889).
[146] *Didascalia Apostolorum* XV, "How Widows Ought to Deport Themselves," http://www.earlychristianwritings.com/text/didascalia.html
[147] Councils and synods re deaconesses: Nimes (394), Orange (441), Epaeon (517), Orléans (533). Suzanne Fonay Wemple, *Women in Frankish Society* (Philadelphia: U. of Pennsylvania, 1981), pp. 127-129; Henning, p. 279.
[148] Quoted from Francine Cardman, "Women, Ministry, and Church Order in Early Christianity," in *Women in Christian Origins*, Ross Shepard Kraemer and Mary Rose d'Angelo, eds. (NY: Oxford UP, 1999), p. 301.
[149] Kevin Madigan and Carolyn Osiek, eds. and trans., *Ordained Women in the Early Church* (Baltimore, MD: Johns Hopkins UP, 2005), pp. 188-189.
[150] Letter of Atto, Bishop of Vercelli, *Points of Law,* v. 1, p. 431 (*Patres Latini* 134.114), Mary Ann Rossi, trans.
[151] Tertullian, *The Prescription against Heretics,* 41.
[152] Christine Trevett, *Montanism: Gender, Authority, and the New Prophecy* (Cambridge, UK: Cambridge UP, 1996).
[153] Epiphanius, *Panarion* IV 49.2,2, 3, p. 22.
[154] Irenaeus (c. 140-202), *Against Heresies* I.13, quoted from Pagels, *Gnostic,* pp. 59-60.
[155] *The Nag Hammadi Library*, James M. Robinson, ed. (San Francisco: Harper & Row, 1977), pp. 10-12; Pagels, *Gnostic*, pp. xiii-xxiii.
[156] Pagels, *Gnostic*, pp. 49-53, 56; Genesis 1:27 and 2:21-22.
[157] Elaine Pagels, *Beyond Belief* (NY: Random House, 2003), p. 164.
[158] Robinson, pp. 172, 411-12.
[159] *Ibid.,* p. 228.
[160] "witness": Mark 16:40, John 19:25; "seeing": Matthew 28:9-10, Mark 16:9-10, John 20:11-18.
[161] Pagels, *Gnostic*, p. 65; quoted from Robinson, p. 235.
[162] Gospel of Philip 59:9, trans. Wesley W. Isenberg.
[163] Letter, *New York Times Book Review*, Feb. 17, 1980.

[164] Jane Schaberg, *The Resurrection of Mary Magdalene* (NY: Continuum, 2002), pp. 165, 185, 357; Esther de Boer, *Mary Magdalene: Beyond the Myth* (Harrisburg, PA: Trinity Press International, 1997), p. 75.

[165] Robinson, pp. 472-474.

[166] Discovery: Schaberg, p. 357; Faith Wisdom: Pagels, *Gnostic*, p. 65.

[167] Gospel of Thomas, Marvin Meyer, trans. (San Francisco: Harper, 1992), pp. 65, 25.

[168] Luke 8:2.

[169] Pope Gregory I, Sermon 33; Luke 7:37-48, 185, 187.

[170] Brigit (c. 456-526): Barry Cunliffe, *The Celtic World* (NY: McGraw-Hill, 1979), pp 185, 187.

[171] Lisa Bitel, *Women in Early Medieval Europe* (NY: Cambridge UP, 2002), p. 35.

[172] Written c. 380 CE.

[173] Augustine sermon 186:1; written 411 CE.

[174] Augustine letter to Firmus; quoted from Peter Brown, p. 342.

7 ILLUMINATING THE DARK AGES

[175] Paul: 1 Cor. 7:1.

[176] Tertullian, *On the Apparel of Women* 1.1.

[177] Eileen Power, "The Position of Women," in *The Legacy of the Middle Ages*, G. C. Crump and E. F. Jacob, eds. (London: Oxford UP, 1926), p. 401.

[178] Augustine, *On Marriage and Concupiscence* I.5; Jerome, *Against Jovinian* I.7.

[179] Jerome: "womb": letter 22 to Eustochium; "with child" and "blush": letter 107 to Laeta, in *Select Letters of St. Jerome*, F. A. Wright, trans. (Cambridge, MA: Harvard UP, 1963); "martyrdom": Jerome, *Against Jovinian* I.26.

[180] Susanna Elm, *Virgins of God* (NY: Oxford UP, 1994), pp. 47-51.

[181] Jo Ann Kay McNamara, *Sisters in Arms* (Cambridge, MA: Harvard UP, 1996), p. 48.

[182] Bishop Ambrose of Milan, *Concerning Virgins* I.11.60.

[183] Marcella (325-410), Paula (347-404); Eustochium (368-c. 419); Jerome, letter 127 to Principia, in Wright.

[184] *Ibid.*

[185] Jerome, letter 71 to Lucinius, in *Commentary on Ephesians* 3.5.

[186] Jo Ann McNamara and John E. Halborg, with E. Gordon Whatley, *Sainted Women of the Dark Ages* (Durham, NC: Duke UP, 1992): Austreberta, pp. 310, 313; Burgundofara, pp. 158, 160; Rictrude, p. 206.

[187] *Treatise Concerning Widows*, XIII. 81.

[188] Egeria: John Wilkinson, *Egeria's Travels* (Warminster, UK: Aris and Phillips, 1999; McNamara, *Sisters*, pp. 43-52; Elm, pp. 335-337.

[189] Jerome, letter 22 to Eustochium in Wright; Cyprian, *De habitu virginum*, 5.15.

[190] Jerome, "tavern": *Against Helvidius* 23; "eunuchs": letter 22 to Eustochium, in

Wright.

[191] McNamara, *Sisters*, pp. 54-55.

[192] Clotilde (474-545): Gregory, *History* 3.18; McNamara and Halborg, pp. 48, 277. Radegund (518-587): Gregory, *History* 9.42 and *De Gloria Confessorum* 106.

[193] William E. Klingshirn, *Caesarius of Arles: Life, Testament, Letters* (Liverpool U., 1994), pp. 27, 64.

[194] Suzanne Fonay Wemple, *Women in Frankish Society* (Philadelphia: U. of Pennsylvania, 1985), p. 164.

[195] M. C. McCarthy, *The Rule for Nuns of St. Caesarius of Arles* (Washington, DC: Catholic UP, 1960), pp. 170-92;, William E. Klingshirn, *Caesarius of Arles: The Making of a Christian Community in Late Antique Gaul* (NY: Cambridge UP, 1994), pp. 119-120.

[196] Wemple, *Frankish*, pp. 159-160, 289 ftn 91.

[197] The Venerable Bede, *Ecclesiastical History of England* III.8, http://www.fordham.edu/halsall/sbook.html.

[198] *The English Correspondence of St. Boniface*, Edward Kylie, trans. (London: Chatto & Windus, 1924), pp. 61-63; Suzanne Fonay Wemple, "Women from the Fifth to the Tenth Century," in *A History of Women*, v. 2, Christiane Klapisch-Zuber, ed. (Cambridge, MA: Harvard UP, 1992), p. 191.

[199] Hilda (614-680): synod of Whitby in 664, see Bede IV. 23.

[200] Jane Tibbetts Schulenburg, "Female Sanctity," in *Women and Power in the Middle Ages*, Mary Erler and Maryanne Kowaleski, eds. (Athens: U. of Georgia, 1988), p. 111; Lina Eckenstein, *Woman Under Monasticism* [1896] (NY: Russell & Russell, 1963), pp. 85-87.

[201] Aldhelm, *De Virginite*, quoted from Christine Fell (with Cecily Clark and Elizabeth Williams), *Women in Anglo-Saxon England, and the Impact of 1066* (Bloomington: Indiana U., 1984), pp. 109-110. Eckenstein, pp. 112-116.

[202] Klingshirn, p. 39; "sisters": Wemple, *Frankish*, p. 176; Eckenstein, p. 231.

[203] C. H. Talbot, *The Anglo-Saxon Missionaries in Germany* (NY: Sheed & Ward, 1954), letter 21, Boniface to Eadburga.

[204] Wemple, *Frankish*, p. 179.

[205] *A History of Private Life*, v. 1, Paul Veyne, ed. (Cambridge, MA: Harvard UP, 1987), pp. 540-541.

[206] Rosamond McKitterick, "Nuns' Scriptoria in England and Francia in the 8th Century," in *Francia* 19 (1992), pp. 2-6, 17, 18.

[207] Meyer Schapiro, *Late Antique, Early Christian and Mediaeval Art*, "The Beatus Apocalypse of Gerona" (NY: Braziller, 1979) p. 319; Chiara Frugoni, "The Imagined Woman," in *History of Women*, v. 2, p. 415.

[208] .Bernhard Bischoff deciphered the cryptogram; "Heidenheim": Alison Beach, *Women as Scribes* (UK: Cambridge UP, 2004), p. 13.

[209] Huneberc, *Hodoeporicon*, "Prologue," in Thomas Noble and Thomas Head, eds. and trans., *Soldiers of Christ* (University Park: Pennsylvania State U., 1994), p. 153.

[210] Hroswitha, or Hrotsvit (c. 935-1002).

[211] Peter Dronke, *Women Writers of the Middle Ages* (NY: Cambridge UP, 1984), pp. 65, 68, 73, 76.

[212] Einhard, *The Life of Charlemagne*, Samuel Epes Turner, trans. (NY: Harper, 1880), http://www.fordham.edu/halsall/basis/einhard.html.

[213] Dronke, pp. 34-35.

[214] *Ibid.*, p. 82; Joan Ferrante, "Public Postures and Private Maneuvers," in Erler and Kowaleski.

[215] Penelope Johnson, *Equal in Monastic Profession* (Chicago, IL: U of Chicago, 1991), p. 234.

8 PEASANT WOMEN: THE POWER OF THE WEAK

[216] Councils of Agde (506) and Orléans (511).

[217] William E. Klingshirn, *Caesarius of Arles* (NY: Cambridge UP, 1994), pp. 222-223; Sister Mary Magdeleine Mueller, *St. Caesarius of Arles Sermons* (NY: Fathers of the Church, 1956), v. 1, p. 262.

[218] Klingshirn, p. 237.

[219] Jo Ann McNamara and John Halborg, with E. Gordon Whatley, *Sainted Women of the Dark Ages* (Durham, NC: Duke UP, 1992), p. 324.

[220] Mueller, v. 1, pp. 259, 261.

[221] Claudia Opitz, *"Life in the Late Middle Ages,"* in *A History of Women,* v. 2, Christiane Klapisch-Zuber, ed. (Cambridge, MA: Harvard UP, 1992), p. 289.

[222] Caesarius: Mueller, v. 1, p. 267; Gregory: Michel Rouche, "The Early Middle Ages in the West," in *A History of Private Life*, v. I, Paul Veyne, ed. (Cambridge, MA: Harvard UP, 1987), p. 525.

[223] "Boniface to Pope Zacharias" [742], in *The English Correspondence of St. Boniface*, Edward Kylie, trans. (London: Chatto & Windus, 1924).

[224] John T. McNeill and Helena M. Gamer, *Medieval Handbooks of Penance* [1938] (NY: Columbia UP, 1990), pp. 41-42. Also, Mueller: "venerate": v. 3, 33; "eclipse": v. 1, 260; "new year": v. 3, 27, 31. Re Church council: Berger, p. 78.

[225] McNeill and Gamer, p. 28,

[226] *Ibid.*, pp. 23-24.

[227] Rouche, p. 520

[228] McNeill and Gamer, pp. 23-24, 321, 323.

[229] Georges Duby, *Women of the Twelfth Century*, v. 3, Jean Birrell, trans. (Chicago, IL: U. of Chicago, 1998), p. 11.

[230] McNeill and Gamer: "turf," 339; "fates," 338; "penance," 343-44; "henbane," 341.

[231] Caesarius: Mueller, v.1, p. 260; Martin: David Herlihy, *Opera Muliebria* (NY: McGraw-Hill, 1990), pp. 34-35.

[232] McNeill and Gamer, pp. 330-331; 335.

[233] *Ibid.*, "The Penitential of Silos," 189; "Egbert," 246-247; Burchard: "herbs," 31; "bier," 334.

[234] *Against Jovinian* I.28.

[235] *Etymologiae* 11.2.23, cited in *Woman Defamed and Woman Defended*, Alcuin Blamires, ed., with Karen Pratt and C. W. Marx (NY: Oxford UP, 1992), p. 43.
[236] McNeill and Gamer: "monk," 90; "seventh-century," 196.
[237] Rouche, p. 523.
[238] Duby, *Twelfth Century,* v. 3, p. 13.
[239] Emmanuel Le Roy Ladurie, *Montaillou* (NY: Vintage, 1979), p. 32.
[240] McNeill and Gamer: pp. 331, 340.
[241] Duby, *Twelfth Century,* v. 3, p. 12.
[242] Georges Duby, *The Knight, the Lady and the Priest*, Barbara Bray, trans. (NY: Pantheon, 1983), p. 29.
[243] McNeill and Gamer, p. 185.
[244] *Against Jovinian* I.47.
[245] McNeill and Gamer, pp. 340-341;
[246] Abbot Regino of Prüm, "*De Ecclesiastica Disciplinis.*"
[247] Duby, *Twelfth Century* v. 3, p. 15.

9 AL-ANDALUS

[248] María J. Viguera, "On the Social Status of Andalusī Women," Gonzalo Viguera, trans., in Salma Khadra Jayyusi, *The Legacy of Muslim Spain* (Leiden: Brill, 1992), pp. 713, 715.
[249] Manuela Marín, "Marriage and Sexuality in al-Andalus," in *Marriage and Sexuality in Medieval and Early Modern Iberia*, Eukene Lacarra Lanz, ed. (NY: Routledge, 2016), p. 16; Nikki R. Keddie, "The Past and Present of Women in the Muslim World," in *Journal of World History*, 1, 1 (1990): 94; Qur'an re veiling of head and chest: 24:30, 31.
[250] Tirso de Molina, *The Trickster of Seville* [1630], Roy Campbell, trans., in "*Life is a Dream and Other Spanish Classics,*" Eric Bentley, ed. (NY: Applause, 1985), p. 143.
[251] Qur'an, 4:7.
[252] Maya Schatzmiller, "Women and Property Rights in al-Andalus and the Mahgrib," in *Islamic Law and Society* 2, 3 (1995), p. 238.
[253] Qur'an, 4:3. Mary Elizabeth Perry, *The Handless Maiden* (Princeton, NJ: Princeton UP, 2005), pp. 49-50.
[254] Ehud Toledano, *Slavery and Abolition in the Ottoman Middle East* (Seattle: U. of Washington, 1998), pp. 13-14.
[255] Viguera, in Jayyusi, p. 718.
[256] Dwight F. Reynolds, "The Qiyan of al Andalus," in *Concubines and Courtesans*, Matthew S. Gordon and Kathryn A. Hain, eds. (NY: Oxford UP, 2017), pp. 100, 118.
[257] Ibn Hayyam, *Kitab al-Muqtabis*, quoted from *Ibid.*, pp. 109-110.
[258] Louis Crompton, *Homosexuality and Civilization* (Cambridge, MA: Harvard UP, 2003), pp. 166-167. Daniel Eisenberg, "Homosexuality," in *Medieval Iberia*, E. Michael Gerli, ed. (NY: Routledge, 2003), p. 398.
[259] Subh (c. 940-c. 999): Stephen O'Shea, *Sea of Faith* (NY: Walker & Co., 2006), p. 89; Desmond Stewart, *The Alhambra* (NY: Newsweek, 1974), pp. 58-59; Fatima

Mernissi, *The Forgotten Queens of Islam* (Minneapolis: U. of Minnesota, 2006), pp. 44-49.

[260] Hroswitha (935-1002), "Pelagius," in Katharina M. Wilson, *Hrotsvit of Gandersheim* (Suffolk, UK: Brewer, 2000), pp. 29-40.

[261] Anahi Cardillo, "La Mujer en el Islam," http://www.transoxiana.org/0105/mujer.html.

[262] *The Ring of the Dove,* Anthony J. Arberry, trans., www.muslimphilosophy.com/hazm/ dove/ringdove.html.

[263] Viguera, pp. 718-719.

[264] Robert Hillenbrand, "Medieval Córdoba as a Cultural Centre," in Jayyusi,. p. 121.

[265] María Jesús Rubiera, quoted from María Luisa Avila, "Women in Andalusi Biographical Sources," in Manuela Marín and Randi Deguilem, *Writing the Feminine* (London: I.B. Tauris, 2002), p. 156.

[266] Teresa Garulo, *Diwan de la poetisas de Andalus* (Madrid: Hyperion, 1985).

[267] Wallada (d. 1091); *Classical Poems by Arab Women*, Abdullah al-Udhari, ed. and trans. (London, UK: Saqi Books, 1999), p. 184.

[268] Hafsa (d. c.1190); *Ibid.*, p. 230.

[269] Marla Segol, "Representing the Body in Poems by Medieval Muslim Women," in *Medieval Feminist Forum* 45, 1 (2009): 157.

[270] Dunash: Peter Cole, ed. and trans., *The Dream of the Poem* (Princeton, NJ: Princeton UP, 2007), p. 27; Qasmuna: al-Udharri., p. 128.

[271] Heath Dillard, *Daughters of the Reconquest* (NY: Cambridge UP, 1984), pp. 214, 216.

[272] Max and Madaline Nichols, *"Las Siete Partidas,"* in *California Law Review* 20, 3; Colin Smith, *Christians and Moors in Spain,* v. 2 (Warminster, UK.: Aris & Phillips, 1989).

[273] Ibn Rushd (also known as Averroes), quoted from Hillenbrand, in Jayyusi, p. 121.

[274] Quoted from Marcelin Defourneaux, *Daily Life in Spain in the Golden Age* (London: Allen & Unwin, 1970), p. 159.

[275] Miguel de Cervantes, *Don Quixote* [1615], Edith Grossman, trans. (NY: HarperCollins, 2003), part 2, ch. 49, pp. 779-781.

10 WOMEN OF THE NORTHLANDS

[276] *The Anglo-Saxon Chronicle,* http://www.gutenberg.org/cache/epub/657/pg657 images.html.

[277] Sigudur Nordal, "Introduction," in Snorri Sturluson , *The Prose Edda*, Jean I. Young, ed. and trans. (Berkeley: U. of California., 1966), p. 8; Jesse L. Byock, *Viking Age Iceland* (NY: Penguin, 2001), p. 23.

[278] Introduction, *The Saga of the People of Laxardal*, Keneva Kunz, trans., in *The Sagas of Icelanders*, (NY: Penguin, 2001), p. 274.

[279] Judith Jesch, *Women in the Viking Age* (Woodbridge, UK: Boydell Press, 1996), pp. 79-82.

[280] *Laxardal*, p. 278.

[281] *Ibid.* pp. 287-290.
[282] Jenny M. Jochens, "Consent in Marriage," in *Scandinavian Studies* 58, 2 (Spring 1986), pp. 142-176.
[283] *Laxardal*, p. 284.
[284] Jenny Jochens, *Women in Old Norse Society* (Ithaca, NY: Cornell UP, 1995), p. 58.
[285] Snorri Sturluson, *Egil's Saga*, Bernard Scudder, trans., in *Icelanders*, p. 154.
[286] *Njal's Saga*, M. Magnusson, trans. (NY: Penguin, 1960), pp. 14, 60.
[287] Jorunn in *Laxardal*, p. 286 in *Icelanders*; Thorbjorg in *The Saga of Grettir the Strong*, Chapt. 52; *Egil's Saga*, p. 109 in *Icelanders*.
[288] *Njal's Saga*, pp. 3, 54, 98.
[289] Jochens, *Women*, p. 61.
[290] *Laxardal*, pp. 292-296.
[291] *Gisli Sursson's Saga*, Martin S. Regal, trans., in *Icelanders*, pp. 510-511.
[292] *Laxardal*, p. 369.
[293] Jochens, *Women*, pp. 134-136.
[294] *Njal's Saga*, p. 311, Notes, Chapter 2, note 1.
[295] *Njal's Saga*, p. 177.
[296] *Prose Edda, The Deluding of Gylfi*, pp. 48, 53, 60, 61.
[297] *Njal's Saga*, p. 304.
[298] *Eirik's Saga*, Magnus Magnusson and Hermann Palsson, trans., in *The Vinland Sagas* (Baltimore, MD: Penguin, 1966), pp. 81-83.
[299] *Ibid*, pp. 93-100
[300] *Graenlendinga Saga*, in *The Vinland Sagas*, pp. 67-69.
[301] Helge Ingstad, *Westward to Vinland* (NY: St. Martin, 1969), pp. 214-216.

11 HERETICAL WOMEN

[302] Councils (1123, 1139, 1179): Norman P. Tanner, *Decrees of the Ecumenical Councils*, v. 1 (Washington, DC: Georgetown, 1990), pp. 191, 203, 217.
[303] Michel Roquebert, *Cathar Religion*, Audrey Wagner, trans. (Toulouse: Editions Loubatière, 1994), pp. 6, 8-11; Michael Lambert, *The Cathars* (Oxford, UK: Blackwell, 1998), pp. 29-32.
[304] "An Appeal from Eberwin of Steinfeld ... ," in *Heresies of the High Middle Ages*, Walter L. Wakefield and Austin Evans, eds. and trans. (NY: Columbia UP, 1969), p. 132.
[305] "A Sermon by Bernard of Clairvaux Against Heresy," in *Ibid.*, pp. 132-138.
[306] John Hine Mundy, *Men and Women at Toulouse in the Age of the Cathars* (Toronto: Pontifical Institute of Mediaeval Studies, 1990), pp. 41, 43.
[307] Jacques Le Goff, *Medieval Civilization*, Julia Barrow, trans. (NY: Basil Blackwell, 1988), p. 286.
[308] Gratian, *Corpus Iuris Canonici* [1879-1881], A. Friedberg, ed., causa 33, question 5, chapters 12, 17.
[309] De Vitry, *Sermons for All*, #66; quoted in *Woman Defamed and Woman Defended*, Alcuin Blamires, ed. (NY: Oxford UP, 1992), p. 146.

[310] Jane Tibbetts Schulenburg, "Sexism and Celestial Gynaeceum, 500-1200," in *Journal of Medieval History* 3 (1978), p. 131 ftn. 8.

[311] "La Femme au Serpent où la Luxure," from the église d'Oo in Alsace, seen at Musée des Augustins, Toulouse.

[312] Chiara Frugoni, "The Imagined Woman," in *A History of Women*, v. 2, Christiane Klapisch-Zuber, ed. (Cambridge, MA: Harvard UP, 1992), p. 351.

[313] Anne Brenon, *Les Femmes Cathares*, M. Schneir and Aimée Kron, trans. (Paris: Librairie Académique Perrin, 1992), p. 99.

[314] Lambert, p. 142.

[315] Shulamith Shahar, *The Fourth Estate* (NY: Methuen, 1983), p. 39; Brenon, pp. 127-129.

[316] Brenon, p. 240; Lambert, p. 75.

[317] Abels and Harrison, pp. 225-240.

[318] Brenon, pp. 369-370.

[319] Joseph R. Strayer, *The Albigensian Crusades* (Ann Arbor: U. of Michigan, 1992), p. 32.

[320] A fifth bishopric was created in Razés, near Limoux, in 1226.

[321] Wakefield and Evans, pp. 196, 704 ftn. 1.

[322] Tanner, p. 203.

[323] Strayer, pp. 62-63, 80, 117-118.

[324] *Ibid.*, 112; "*Défense de Toulouse contre Simon de Montfort*," Jean-Paul Laurens fresco.

[325] Lucien Bély, *The Cathars*, Angela Moyon, trans. (France: Editions Sud Ouest, 1995), pp. 54-55, 58; Lambert, pp. 125-128; Strayer, pp. 149-151.

[326] Abels and Harrison, pp. 239-240.

[327] Brenon, *Les Femmes*, pp. 239-260; Lambert, pp. 140-141, 168-169.

[328] Albi council, 1254: Ladurie, p. 239.

[329] Roquebert, p. 4; Peter Biller and Anne Hudson, eds., *Heresy and Literacy* (NY: Cambridge UP, 1994), pp. 46-47.

[330] Bruschi and Biller, p. 138.

[331] Geoffroy of Auxerre, quoted from Beverly Mayne Kienzle, "The Prostitute-Preacher," in Kienzle & Walker, pp. 101, 103.

[332] Brenda Bolton, "Daughters of Rome," in *Medieval Women*, Derek Baker, ed. (Oxford, UK: Basil Blackwell, 1978), p. 103; Grundmann, pp. 139, 154.

[333] Walter Simons, *Cities of Ladies* (Baltimore, MD: Johns Hopkins, 2000), p. 81; David Nicholas, *Medieval Flanders* (London: Longman, 1992), p. 251; Claudia Opitz, "Life in the Late Middle Ages," in Klapisch-Zuber, p. 313.

[334] Joan Kelly, *Women, History and Theory* (Chicago, IL: University of Chicago, 1984), p. 68.

[335] Jeanne (1194-1244); Margaret (1202-1280). Simons, p. 54; Ernest W. McDonnell, *The Beguines and Beghards in Medieval Culture* (New Brunswick, NJ: Rutgers UP, 1954), p. 479.

[336] David Herlihy, *Opera Muliebria* (NY: McGraw Hill, 1990), p. 6.

[337] Frankfurt, Strasbourg: Martha Howell, with Suzanne Wemple and Denise Kaiser, "A Documented Presence," in *Women in Medieval History and Historiography,* Susan Mosher Stuard, ed. (Philadelphia: U. of Pennsylvania, 1987), p. 120; Cologne: Opitz, in Klapisch-Zuber, p. 312.

[338] Michael D. Bailey, *Battling Demons* (University Park: Pennsylvania State U., 2003), pp. 65-66; Norman Cohn, *The Pursuit of the Millennium* (NY: Oxford UP, 1974), p. 164.

12 THE FREEDOM OF THE CITIES

[339] Guibert, *A Monk's Confession,* Paul J. Archambault, trans. (University Park: Pennsylvania State U., 1996), bk.3, pp. 189-90.

[340] Paris: David Herlihy, *Opera Muliebria* (NY: McGraw-Hill, 1990), p. 137; York: P.J.P. Goldberg, *Women, Work, and Life Cycle in a Medieval Economy* (NY: Oxford UP, 1992), p. 282 and table 6.1, pp. 284-287.

[341] "The Wife of Bath's Prologue," in *Chaucer,* Louis O. Coxe, ed. (NY: Dell, 1963), pp. 139-140.

[342] France: Shulamith Shahar, *The Fourth Estate,* Chaya Galai, trans. (NY: Methuen, 1983), p. 204; England: Goldberg, pp. 168-178.

[343] London: Shahar, p. 205; Ghent: David Nicholas, *The Domestic Life of a Medieval City* (Lincoln: U. of Nebraska, 1985), 104.

[344] Basel: Erika Uitz, *The Legend of Good Women* (Wakefield, RI: Moyer Bell, 1994), p. 64; Florence: Klapisch-Zuber, in Hanawalt, pp. 65-67.

[345] Goldberg, pp. 298-299, 313-322.

[346] Claudia Opitz, "Life in the Late Middle Ages," in *A History of Women,* v. II, Christiane Klapisch-Zuber, ed. (Cambridge, MA: Harvard, 1992), p. 294.

[347] "The Customs of Touraine and Anjou," in *The Etablissements de Saint Louis,* F.R.P. Akehurst, ed. (Philadelphia: U. of Pennsylvania, 1996).

[348] Uitz, p. 48.

[349] England: Eileen Power, *Medieval Women,* M. M. Postan, ed. (NY: Cambridge UP, 1975), p. 10; Ghent: Nicholas, pp. 78, 95-96.

[350] Rabbi Eliezer ben Nathan, quoted in Avraham Grossman, *Pious and Rebellious* (Lebanon, NH: University Press of New England, 2004), pp. 121-122.

[351] Herlihy, pp. 139, 141.

[352] Margery Kempe (1373–c.1438), *The Book of Margery Kempe,* Book 1, chapter 2, W. Butler-Bowden, ed. (NY: Devin-Adair, 1944).

[353] Opitz, p. 282.

[354] *The Fabliaux,* Nathaniel E. Dubin, trans. (NY: Norton, 2013).

[355] Power, pp. 56-57.

[356] Martha C. Howell, *Women, Production, and Patriarchy in Late Medieval Cities* (Chicago, IL: U. of Chicago, 1988), p. 14; Ghent: Nicholas, *Domestic Life,* p. 26.

[357] Frances and Joseph Gies, *Marriage and the Family in the Middle Ages* (NY: Harper & Row, 1987), pp. 189-190.

[358] Herlihy, pp. 128-30; Warren Hollister and Judith M. Bennett, *Medieval History*, 9th ed. (NY: Mcgraw-Hill, 2002), p. 156.

[359] Herlihy, pp. 131-150.

[360] Merry E. Wiesner, "Spinsters and Seamstresses," in *Rewriting the Renaissance*, Margaret Ferguson *et al*., eds. (Chicago, IL: U. of Chicago, 1986), p. 193.

[361] Herlihy, pp. 127-130, 136.

[362] *Ibid.*, p. 149.

[363] Jacques de Vitry, *Historia occidentalis*, cited by James A. Brundage, "Prostitution in the Medieval Canon Law," in *Signs: Journal of Women in Culture and Society* 1, 4 (1976): 841.

[364] Herlihy, pp. 157-159.

[365] Iwan Bloch, *Die Prostitution*; cited in Brundage, p. 841 ftn. 92.

[366] Ruth Mazo Karras, "The Regulation of Brothels in Late Medieval England," in *Sisters and Workers in the Middle Ages*, Judith M. Bennett *et al*., eds. (Chicago, IL: U. of Chicago, 1989), p. 103.

[367] Vern Bullough and Bonnie Bullough, *Women and Prostitution* (Buffalo, NY: Prometheus, 1987), p. 125.

[368] Mary Elizabeth Perry, *Gender and Disorder in Early Modern Seville* (Princeton, NJ: Princeton UP, 1990), p. 3; Uitz, p. 100.

[369] Bullough and Bullough, pp. 124-125.

[370] Uitz, pp. 71-72.

[371] Paris: Joan M. Ferrante, "The Education of Women in the Middle Ages in Theory, Fact, and Fantasy," in *Beyond Their Sex*, Patricia H. Labalme, ed. (NY: NYU Press, 1984), p. 11; Ghent: Nicholas, pp. 128-129; Germany: Opitz, p. 298; Florence: Shahar, p. 215.

[372] Eve Levin, "Novgorod Birchbark Documents," in *Medieval Archaeology*, Charles L. Redman, ed. (Binghamton: State U. of New York, 1989), pp. 127, 129; Valentin L. Yanin, "Archaeology of Novgorod," in *Scientific American*, February 1990, pp. 84-91.

[373] Gostyata, #199; Anna, #531; bequests, #672, #580; Maria, #53, Svetlana Chervonnaya, trans.

[374] Love letters, #752 and #377.

[375] *Chartulary of the University of Paris*, E. Chatelain and H. Denifle, eds. (Paris: Delalain, 1891).

[376] Opitz, p. 299; Power, p. 88; *The Indispensible Medieval Reader,* James Bruce Ross and Mary Martin McLaughlin, eds. and trans. (NY: Book Society, 1950), pp. 635-640; Monica H. Green, "Getting to the Source," https://ir.uiowa.edu/cgi/viewcontent.cgi?article=1057&context=mff.

[377] Katharine Park, *Doctors and Medicine in Early Renaissance Florence* (Princeton, NJ: Princeton UP, 1985), cited by Monica Green, "Women's Medical Practice and Care in Medieval Europe," in. Bennett *et al*, p. 76 ftn. 112.

[378] Shahar, pp. 190-191, 194, 196.

[379] Maryanne Kowaleski and Judith M. Bennett, "Crafts, Gilds, and Women in the Middle Ages," in. Bennett *et al*., pp. 18-20; Herlihy, p. 147; Howell, p. 124.

[380] Strasbourg: Opitz, p. 302; Exeter: Kowaleski, in Hanawalt, p. 153.
[381] Nicholas, pp. 98-99, 101-102.
[382] Goldberg, pp. 86, 93, 104-106, 133.
[383] William Langland, *Piers Plowman*, B-version, Vision 2, Passus 5.
[384] *Statutes of the Realm* i, 379; quoted from Uitz, p. 54; Shahar, p. 197.

13 CHRISTINE DE PIZAN AND HER READERS

[385] *The Women Troubadours*, Meg Bogin, trans. (NY: Norton, 1980), pp. 133, 123; Peter Dronke, *Women Writers of the Middle Ages* (NY: Cambridge UP, 1984), pp. 97-103.

[386] *Songs of the Women Trouvères*, Eglal Doss-Quinby *et al.*, trans. (New Haven, CT: Yale UP, 2001), pp. 1-6, 26.

[387] Marianne Shapiro, "The Provençal *Trobairitz* and the Limits of Courtly Love," in *Signs* 3, 3 (1978): 561.

[388] Eleanor (1122-1204); Marie (1145-98): John F. Benton, "The Court of Champagne as a Literary Center," in *Speculum* 36, 4 (October 1961): 561-562.

[389] Marie de France (fl. 1160 to 1215): quoted from Denis Piramus, *The Lais of Marie de France*, Glyn S. Burgess and Keith Busby, trans. (NY: Penguin, 1999), p. 11.

[390] Monica Green, "Women's Medical Practice and Health Care in Medieval Europe," in Bennett *et al.*, eds. (Chicago, IL: U. of Chicago, 1989), p. 67.

[391] *Vita nuova*, in *The Portable Dante*, Mark Musa, trans. (NY: Penguin, 1995), p. 627.

[392] Dante, *De vulgari eloquentia*, Stephen Botterill, ed. (NY: Cambridge UP, 1996).

[393] Dante, "The Letter to Can Grande," in *Literary Criticism of Dante Alighieri*, Robert S. Haller, ed. and trans. (Lincoln: U. of Nebraska, 1973).

[394] Boccaccio, *Concerning Famous Women*, Virginia Brown, ed. and trans. (Cambridge, MA: Harvard UP, 2001), pp. 3-5, 9, 11-13, 23.

[395] Susan Groag Bell, "Medieval Women Book Owners," in Bennett *et al.*, pp. 137-138, 143.

[396] Christine De Pizan (c. 1364-1430). Charity Cannon Willard, *Christine de Pizan: Her Life and Works* (NY: Persea, 1984), p. 45.

[397] "Christine's Vision," in *The Writings of Christine de Pizan*, Charity Cannon Willard, ed. (NY: Persea, 1993), p. 17.

[398] Letter to Jean de Montreuil [1401], quoted from *A History of Women*, v. 2, Arthur Goldhammer, trans., p. 438; Joseph L. Baird and John R. Kane, *La Querelle de la Rose* (Chapel Hill: U. of North Carolina, 1978), pp. 46-56.

[399] *The Book of the City of Ladies*, Earl Jeffrey Richards, trans. (London: Pan Books, 1983).

[400] Pizan, *City*, pp. 3-6, 10-11.
[401] *Ibid.*, p. 63.
[402] Boccaccio, p. 75; Pizan, *City*, pp. 69-70, 189-90.
[403] Pizan, *City*, pp. 184-185.

[404] *A Medieval Woman's Mirror of Honor*, Charity Cannon Willard, trans. (NY: Persea, 1989), p. 224; another edition is titled *The Treasure of the City of Ladies or The Book of the Three Virtues*, Sarah Lawson, trans. (NY: Penguin, 1985).

[405] Pizan, *Honor*, pp. 168-179, 209-223.

[406] *Ibid.*, pp. 98-99, 186.

[407] *Ibid.*, pp. 197-201.

[408] Tjitske Akkerman and Siep Stuurman, eds., *Perspectives on Feminist Political Thought in European History* (London, UK: Routledge, 1998), p. 1.

[409] Pizan, *City*, p. 85.

[410] James Laidlaw, "Christine and the Manuscript Tradition," in *Christine de Pizan*, Barbara K. Altmann and Deborah L. McGrady, eds. (NY: Routledge, 2003), pp. 231, 241.

[411] Pizan, *Honor*, p. 224.

[412] Pizan, *The Boke of the Cyte of Ladyes*, Brian Ansley, trans.

[413] Joan of Arc (c. 1412-1431): "The Tale of Joan of Arc," in *The Selected Writings of Christine de Pizan*, Renate Blumenfeld-Kosinski and Kevin Brownlee, trans. (NY: Norton, 1997).

14 THE RENAISSANCE FOR WOMEN

[414] Paul F. Grendler, *The Universities of the Italian Renaissance* (Baltimore, MD: Johns Hopkins UP, 2002), pp. 12, 20, 96, 384-385.

[415] Stanley Chojnacki, *Women and Men in Renaissance Venice* (Baltimore, MD: Johns Hopkins UP, 2000), p. 44.

[416] Francesco Barbaro, "On Wifely Duties" [1416], in *The Earthly Republic*, Benjamin G. Kohl, trans. (Philadelphia: U. of Pennsylvania, 1981); Leon Battista Alberti, "On the Family" [1434], in *The Family in Renaissance Florence*, Renee Neu Watkins, ed. and trans. (Columbia: U. of South Carolina,1969).

[417] Christiane Klapisch-Zuber, *Women, Family and Ritual in Renaissance Italy* (Chicago, IL: U. of Chicago, 1985), p. 120.

[418] Gian Giorgio Trissino, "*Epistola del Trissino de la vita, che dee tenere una donna vidova*," ("Concerning the Life That a Lady Who Is a Widow Should Live") [1524], cited in Constance Jordan, *Renaissance Feminism* (Ithaca, NY: Cornell UP, 1990), pp. 71-72.

[419] Battista da Montefeltro Malatesta (1383-1450).

[420] Leonardo Bruni, "On the Study of Literature," in *The Humanism of Leonardo Bruni*, Gordon Griffiths, James Hankins, and David Thompson, eds. (Binghamton, NY: Renaissance Society of America, 1987), pp. 240-250.

[421] Margaret L. King and Albert Rabil, Jr., *Her Immaculate Hand* (Binghamton, NY: Center for Medieval and Early Renaissance Studies, 1983), pp. 36-38.

[422] Malatesta descendants: Costanza Varano (1428-1447); Cecilia Gonzaga (1425-1451); Vittoria Colonna (1490-1547). Nogarola family: Angela (d. c. 1436); Ginevra (1417-1461/8); Isotta (1418-1466); Veronica Gambara (1485-1550). Margaret L. King, "Book-Lined Cells," in *Beyond Their Sex*, Patricia H. Labalme, ed. (New York UP, 1984), pp. 67, 83 ftn. 3.

[423] "To Antonio Borromeo," [1436/7], in Isotta Nogarola, *Complete Writings*, Margaret L. King and Diana Robin, eds. and trans. (Chicago, IL: U. of Chicago, 2004), pp. 38-39.

[424] From Lauro Quirini, in King and Rabil, pp. 112-116.

[425] Nogarola, *Writings*, pp. 38-39.

[426] King, *Cells*, p. 72; Margaret King, *Women of the Renaissance* (Chicago, IL: U. of Chicago Press, 1991), p. 197.

[427] From "Pliny," June 1439, in Nogarola, *Writings*, p. 68.

[428] King, "cells": p. 74.

[429] "Of the Equal or Unequal Sin of Adam and Eve," in King and Rabil, pp. 59-69.

[430] Nogarola, *Writings*, pp. 136, 175.

[431] Laura Cereta (1469-1499), *Collected Letters of a Renaissance Feminist*, Diana Robin, ed. and trans. (Chicago, IL: U. of Chicago, 1997): "Translator's Introduction," pp. 3-18; "loved me": 134; "politics": 161-164, 169-174; "women": 63-86; "planets": 65-66, 100-101; "religion": 27, 39; "math": 27; "sick": 62.

[432] *Ibid.*, "war": 62, "republic": 80 "sister": 23, 129, 135, 140; "we women": 79, 86, 120, 124; "freedom": 78, 81-86.

[433] *Ibid.*, pp. 65-72, 74-80.

[434] Italian Women Writers, www.lib.uchicago.edu/efts/iww; Virginia Cox, *Women's Writing in Italy, 1400 to 1650* (Baltimore, MD: Johns Hopkins UP, 2008), p. 86.

[435] Stampa (1523-1554), *Selected Poems*, Laura Anna Stortoni and Mary Prentice Lillie, eds. and trans. (NY: Italica, 1994); Copernicus, p. 191.

[436] Franco (c. 1546-1591), *Poems and Selected Letters*, Ann Rosalind Jones and Margaret F. Rosenthal, eds. and trans. (Chicago, IL: U of Chicago, 1998).

[437] Margaret T. Rosenthal, *The Honest Courtesan* (Chicago, IL: U. of Chicago, 1998).

[438] Franco, *Poems*, Letter 22, pp. 37-40; Capitolo 24, p. 245.

[439] Anthony Newcomb, *The Madrigal at Ferrara*, v. 1 (Princeton, NJ: Princeton UP, 1980), pp. 7-11, 35-46, 66-68.

[440] Tim Carter, "Finding a Voice," in *Feminism and Renaissance Studies*, Lorna Hutson, ed. (NY: Oxford UP, 1999), pp. 450-462; *Women Making Music*, Jane Bowers and Judith Tick, eds. (Urbana: U. of Illinois, 1986), pp. 95-100.

[441] Casulana (c. 1544-c. 1590): quoted from Bowers and Tick, p. 140.

[442] Carole Collier Frick *et al.*, *Italian Women Artists from Renaissance to Baroque*, National Museum of Women in the Arts, Washington, D.C., March 16-July 15, 2007; Fredrika H. Jacobs, "Woman's Capacity to Create," in *Renaissance Quarterly* 47 (Spring 1994): 74-101.

[443] Anguissola (c. 1535-c. 1625): *Italian Women Artists*, pp. 106-121; Mary D. Garrard, *Renaissance Quarterly* 47, 3 (Autumn 1994): 556.

[444] Spilimbergo (1538-1559); Fontana (1552-1614).

[445] *Italian Women Artists*, pp. 135-165; Cox, pp. 87, 306 n. 111; Anne Jacobson Schutte, "Irene Spilimbergo," *Renaissance Quarterly* 44 (Spring 1991): 42-61.

[446] Letter to Don Antonio Ruffo, 1649.

[447] *Women Artists from the State Hermitage Museum*, Jordana Pomeroy and Rosalind P. Blakesley, eds. (NY: Merrell, 2003).
[448] Anne MacNeil, *Music and Women of the Commedia dell' Arte in the Late Sixteenth Century* (NY: Oxford UP, 2003).
[449] Andreini (1562-1604). Nancy Dersofi, "Isabella Andreini," in *Italian Women Writers,* Rinaldina Russell, ed. (Westport, CT: Greenwood, 1994), pp. 18-24; Stortoni and Lillie, pp. 227-231.
[450] Andreini, *La Mirtilla: A Pastoral,* Julie D. Campbell, trans. (Tempe, AZ: Arizona Center for Medieval and Renaissance Studies, 2002), p. 70.
[451] Dava Sobel, *A More Perfect Heaven* (NY: Walker, 2011), p. 95.
[452] Jutta Giseling Sperling, *Convents and the Body Politic in Late Renaissance Venice* (Chicago, IL: U. of Chicago, 2000), p. 18.
[453] Orazio Lombardelli, "On the Duties of a Married Woman" (Florence, 1583) Pietro Belmonte's letter to his daughter (Rome, 1587); Bishop of Verona, Agostino Valerio, "Instructions for Married Women" (Venice, 1575). Merry E. Wiesner, *Women and Gender in Early Modern Europe*, 2nd ed. (NY: Cambridge UP, 2000), pp. 29-30; Margaret L. King, *Women of the Renaissance* (Chicago, IL: U. of Chicago, 1991), pp. 38-39.
[454] King, *Women*, p. 186, quoting Cardinal Silvio Antoniano.
[455] "Onofrio Filarco," *Vera narratione della operationi delle donne* [1586]; Cipriano Giambelli, *Discorso intorno alla maggioranza dell'huomo, e della donna* [1589]; Guiseppe Passi, *I donneschi difetti* [1599]: Virginia Cox.
[456] Marinella (1571-1653), *The Nobility and Excellence of Women,* Anne Dunhill, ed. and trans. (Chicago, IL: U. of Chicago, 1999).
[457] *Ibid.*, "inherit": "mercantile": 74, 118; "Aristotle": 68, 72, 79; "excellence": 39; "earth": 121.
[458] *Ibid.*, "Nogarola": 89, 91; "Cereta" : 85.
[459] Fonte, aka Modesta Pozzo Zorzi (1555-1592), *The Worth of Women*, Virginia Cox, ed. and trans. (Chicago, IL: U. of Chicago, 1997).
[460] *Ibid.*, "Dedicatory Letter," 28.
[461] *Ibid.*, "happy": 47; "tyrants": 59; "bullying": 61; "learning": 236; "sex": 89; "law": 96, 204.
[462] *Ibid.,* pp. 62, 63, 113, 71.
[463] *Ibid.,* Virginia, p. 9; Cornelia, 68-70; Corinna, 113-114; "clarion call," 237.
[464] Angelo Poliziano, 1491, in King and Rabil, p. 127.

15 DAUGHTERS OF THE WORLD
[465] Reigned: Jane Grey, 1553; Mary I, 1553-1558; Elizabeth I, 1558-1603.
[466] Mary Sidney (Herbert) (1561-1621), in "Even now that Care"; "Sowernam" in *Ester Hath Hang'd Haman* [1617], quoted from *Half Humankind*, Katherine Usher Henderson and Barbara F. McManus, eds. (Urbana: U. of Illinois, 1985), p. 231; "Diana Primrose," in *Chaine of Pearle* [1630] quoted from *The Paradise of Women*, Betty Travitsky, ed. (NY: Columbia UP, 1989), p. 110; Makin, *An Essay to Revive the Antient*

Education of Gentlewomen [1673]; Bradstreet, "In Honour of ... Queen Elizabeth, of Happy Memory" [1643], in *The Works of Anne Bradstreet in Prose and Verse*, John Harvard Ellis, ed. (Charlestown, MA: Abram E. Cutter, 1867), p. 359.

[467] Carlo Cipolla, *Before the Industrial Revolution,* 3d ed. (NY: Norton, 1994), Table A.1, p. 283.

[468] Susan Amussen, *An Ordered Society* (NY: Columbia UP, 1988), p. 122; David Underdown, "The Taming of the Scold," in *Order and Disorder in Early England*, Anthony Fletcher and David Stevenson, eds. (Cambridge, UK: Cambridge UP, 1985), pp. 116-135.

[469] "Anger" a woman: Ferguson, p. 58; Gerda Lerner, *The Creation of Feminist Consciousness* (NY: Oxford UP, 1993), pp. 150-151; Henderson and McManus, pp. 20-24; Pamela. J. Benson, *The Invention of the Renaissance Woman* (University Park: Pennsylvania State U., 1992), p. 223.

[470] Quoted from Ferguson, pp. 58-72.

[471] Keith Thomas, *Religion and the Decline of Magic* (NY: Oxford UP, 1971), pp. 440-441.

[472] Wright, pp. 486-487; Henderson and McManus, pp. 193, 196, 201, 214.

[473] Speght (1597-unknown), *A Mouzell for Melastomus*, in *The Polemics and Poems of Rachel Speght,*. Barbara Kiefer Lewalski, ed. (NY: Oxford UP, 1996), pp. 1-27.

[474] female authorship: Joan Kelly, "Early Feminist Theory and the *Querelle des Femmes*, 1400-1789," in *Women, History and Theory* (Chicago, IL: U. of Chicago, 1984), p. 76; Henderson and McManus, pp. 20-24; Travitsky, *Paradise*, pp. 107, 109. Lewalski, p. xv: "the authors may be women or (perhaps more likely) men."

[475] Quoted from Henderson and McManus, pp. 218-243.

[476] Quoted from *Women Writers Project (hereafter, WWP)*, Brown University, http://www.wwp.brown.edu.

[477] Quoted from *Ibid.*

[478] Thomas Dekker and Thomas Middleton (London: Thomas Archer, 1611).

[479] Quoted from Linda Woodbridge, *Women and the English Renaissance* (Urbana: U. of Illinois Press., 1984), p. 140.

[480] John Williams, "A Sermon of Apparell" (1619) and William Gamage, *Linsi-Woolsie* (1613), from *Ibid.*, pp. 142-143.

[481] Letters of John Chamberlain, in Edward Phillips Statham, *A Jacobean Letter-Writer* (NY: Dutton, 1920), p. 182.

[482] *"Custome Is an Idiot,"* Susan Gushee O'Malley, ed. (Urbana: U. of Illinois, 2004), pp. 263-300.

[483] Samuel Rowlands, *Heavens Glory, Seeke It. Earths Vanitie, Flye It. Hells Horror, Fere It,* quoted from Wright, p. 303 ftn. 66.

[484] Patricia Higgins, "The Reactions of Women," in *Politics, Religion and the English Civil War*, Brian Manning, ed. (NY: St. Martin's, 1973), pp. 185-186.

[485] Ellen A. McArthur, "Women Petitioners and the Long Parliament," in *English Historical Review* XXIV (1909), pp. 698-699; Higgins, p. 186 ftn. 39, 187.

[486] "Petition of Anne Stagg *et al.*," *WWP*.

[487] Quoted from McArthur, pp. 703, 707-708.
[488] Higgins, p. 197.
[489] *England's Moderate Messenger* 1 (23-30 April 1649); quoted from Sharon Achinstein, "Women on Top in the Pamphlet Literature of the English Revolution," in *Feminism and Renaissance Studies*, Lorna Hutson, ed. (NY: Oxford UP, 2000), p. 346.
[490] The reference is to the Petition of Right, enacted 1628.
[491] McArthur, p. 708. The possible author was Katherine Chidley (c.1598-c. 1650); Katharine Gillespie, *Domesticity and Dissent in the Seventeenth Century* (NY: Cambridge UP, 2004), pp. 87-91.
[492] Claire Gheeraert-Braffeuille, "Leveller Women Petitioners and the Rhetoric of Power in the English Revolution," https://journals.openedition.org/caliban/1994.

16 ENTERPRISING WOMEN IN THE DUTCH REPUBLIC

[493] James Howell, *The Familiar Letters of James Howell* [1622], Joseph Jacobs, ed. (Whitefish, MT: Kessinger, 2005), p. 128.
[494] *Of the Excellence of the Female Gender* [1639, 1643], quoted from Simon Schama, *The Embarrassment of Riches* (NY: Vintage, 1997), p. 419.
[495] Quoted from Jan De Vries and Ad van der Woude, *The First Modern Economy* (NY: Cambridge UP, 1997), pp. 627-631.
[496] Jonathan Israel, *The Dutch Republic* (NY: Oxford UP, 1998), pp. 686-688.
[497] *An Essay in Defence of the Female Sex* (London, 1696), pp. 16-17.
[498] *The Jurisprudence of Holland*, trans. Robert W. Lee (UK: Oxford UP, 1926), p. 31.
[499] Robert W. Lee, *An Introduction to Roman-Dutch Law*, 5th ed. (London, 1953), pp. 67-70, 396.
[500] Quoted from Elizabeth Alice Honig, "Desire and Domestic Economy," *Art Bulletin* 83, 2 (June 2001): 304.
[501] *Memoirs and Travels of Sir John Reresby* (London: Edward Jeffery, 1813), p. 159.
[502] Fletcher and Massinger, *The Tragedy of Sir John van Olden Barnavelt* [London, 1619], Wilhelmina P. Frijlinck, ed. (Amsterdam, 1922).
[503] Schama, pp. 455-460.
[504] Jean de Parival, *Les Delices de la Hollande* (Leiden, 1662), quoted from Adriaan Barnouw, *The Dutch* (NY: Columbia UP, 1940), p. 154.
[505] Heinrich Bentham [1694], in Israel, p. 2.
[506] "bleaching": Rudolf M. Dekker and Anne Epstein, "Getting to the Source," in *Journal of Women's History,* 10, 2 (Summer 1998); "spinning": De Vries and van der Woude, p. 597; "orphanages": Martha C. Howell, *Women, Production and Patriarchy in Late Medieval Cities* (Chicago, IL: U. of Chicago, 1986), p. 68; Charles R. Boxer, *The Dutch Seaborne Empire, 1600-1800* (NY: Knopf, 1965), p. 54.
[507] De Vries and van der Woude, pp. 627-631, 351-352.
[508] Manon van der Heijden and Ariadne Schmidt, "For the Benefit of All?" paper presented to conference on Gender and Work in the Early Modern Northern European

World, Uppsala U., December 11-13, 2007, pp. 10-11; De Vries and van der Woude, pp. 414, 596-597.

[509] Lotte van de Pol, *The Burgher and the Whore* (NY: Oxford UP, 2011), p. 2; Schama, pp. 476-477.

[510] Ruysch (1664-1750); Leyster (1609-1660). Also, Maria van Oosterwyck, Margaretha de Heer, Maria Schalcken, Ariana Spilberg, Alida Withoos, Margaretha Walsraat, Maria de Grebber, Barbara van Broeck, Anthonia de Houbraken, and Geertruid Roghman.

[511] Ann Sutherland Harris and Linda Nochlin, *Women Artists: 1550-1950* (NY: Knopf, 1977), pp. 158-160.

[512] Wayne Franits, *Dutch Seventeenth-Century Genre Painting* (New Haven, CT: Yale UP, 2004), pp. 48, 51; Harris and Nochlin, pp. 137-140.

[513] Merian (1647-1717): Kim Todd, *Chrysalis* (NY: Harcourt, 2007); Natalie Zemon Davis, *Women on the Margins* (Cambridge, MA: Harvard UP, 1995), pp. 140-203.

[514] Van Schurman (1607-1678): Joyce L. Irwin, *Anna Maria van Schurman* (Chicago, IL: U. of Chicago, 1998).

[515] Letters to Dr. Andreas Rivet, quoted from Una Pope-Hennessy, *Anna van Schurman* (London: 1909), pp. 70, 71, 73.

[516] Correspondents: English educator Bathsua Makin, Queen Christina of Sweden, Princess Elisabeth of Bohemia, Princess Anne de Rohan of France, Lady Dorothy Moore of Dublin (author of "On the Education of Girls"), and Birgitte Thott of Denmark, see Pieta van Beek, "Alpha Virginium," in *Women Writing Latin* v. 3, Laurie Churchill, Phyllis R. Brown, and Jane E. Jeffrey, eds. (NY: Routledge, 2002), pp. 271-279.

[517] Gournay (1566-1645); quoted from Irwin, p. 13, ftn. 18.

[518] Quoted from Pope-Hennessy, p. 77.

[519] Anne R. Larsen, "The French Reception of Anna Maria van Schurman's Letters on Women's Education," in *Women's Letters Across Europe*, Jane Couchman and Ann Crabb, eds. (Burlington, VT: Ashgate, 2005), p. 313.

[520] E.g., Elizabeth Elstob (1683-1756), *An English-Saxon Homily on the Birth-Day of St. Gregory* [1709], cited by Elizabeth Green, "Elizabeth Elstob," in *Female Scholars*, Jean R. Brink, ed. (Montreal: Eden Press, 1980), p. 148.

[521] Mather, *Magnalia Christi Americana* [1702], Rev. Thomas Robbins, ed. (Hartford, CT: Silas Andrus & Son, 1855), p. 135.

[522] Erxleben (1715-1762); quoted by Eileen O'Neill, "Disappearing Ink," in *Philosophy in a Feminist Voice*, Janet A. Kourany, ed. (Princeton, NJ: Princeton UP, 1998), p. 19. The later book, by Amalia Holst, was published in Berlin in 1802.

17 SHE-MERCHANTS

[523] Letter from Isaak de Rasière to the Amsterdam Chamber of the West India Company (WIC), 1626, doc. F, http://www.rootsweb.ancestry.com/~nycoloni/huntdoc.html. A skilled male worker in Holland earned about a guilder a day; 20 stivers equaled one guilder.

[524] "Charter of the Dutch WIC, 1621," in *The Federal and State Constitutions, ... and Other Organic Laws ...*, Francis Newton Thorpe, ed. (Washington, DC: Govt. Printing Office, 1909), http://www.yale.edu/lawweb/avalon/westind/htm.

[525] Evan T. Pritchard, *Native New Yorkers*, (San Francisco, CA: Council Oak, 2002), p. 70; James Axtell, *The Invasion Within* (NY: Oxford UP, 1986), p. 138.

[526] "Notification of the Purchase of Manhattan by the Dutch, 1626," in *Documents Relative to the Colonial History of the State of New York* (hereafter *DHNY*), E. B. O'Callaghan and Berthold Fernow, eds. and trans. (Albany, NY: Weed, Parsons, 1853-1887).

[527] Oliver Rink, *Holland on the Hudson* (Ithaca, NY: Cornell UP, 1986), pp. 200-201.

[528] Leslie M. Harris, *In the Shadow of Slavery* (Chicago, IL: U. of Chicago, 2003), pp. 18, 21; *The Negro in New York*, Roi Ottley and William J. Weatherby, eds. (NY: NY Public Library, 1967), pp. 2-3.

[529] "Charter of Freedoms and Exemptions to Patroons," 1629, in *Van Rensselaer Bowier Manuscripts* (hereafter *VRBM*), A.J.F. Van Laer, ed. and trans. (Albany: U. of the State of New York, 1908), pp. 137-153.

[530] *VRBM*, pp. 306-312; Russell Shorto, *Island at the Center of the World* (NY: Doubleday, 2004), p. 87.

[531] *VRBM*, pp. 209, 218, 281, 612.

[532] Johannes Megapolensis, "Account of the Mohawk Indians," in *In Mohawk Country*, Dean R. Snow, Charles T. Gehring, and William A. Starna, eds. (NY: Syracuse UP, 1996), p. 43.

[533] Jemison (c. 1743-1833); James E. Seaver, *A Narrative of the Life of Mary Jemison* [1824], June Namais, ed. (Norman: U. of Oklahoma, 1995), pp. 16, 83-84.

[534] Jemison, "Editor's Introduction," p. 22.

[535] Rink, pp. 164-168.

[536] William Pencak, *Jews and Gentiles in Early America* (Ann Arbor: U. of Michigan, 2008), p. 19.

[537] Daniel Denton, *A Brief Description of New York* [1670] (NY: William Gowans, 1845), p. 7.

[538] *Historical Statistics of the U.S., Colonial Times to 1957* (Washington, DC: U.S. Bureau of the Census, 1960), p. 756.

[539] Marriages, 1639 to 1801 (NY: Genealogical and Biographical Society, 1890).

[540] *Journal of Jasper Danckaerts*, Bartlett B. James and J. Franklin Jameson, eds. (NY: Scribner's, 1913), p. 65.

[541] "The Representation of New Netherland, 1650," in *Narratives of New Netherland*, J. Franklin Jameson, ed. (NY: Scribner's, 1909), p. 330.

[542] *DHNY*, pp. 335, 343, 425.

[543] *Calendar of Historical Manuscripts*, v. 1, E. B. O'Callaghan, ed. (Albany, 1865), pp. 258-259.

[544] "Harmensen": Michael E. Gherke, "Dutch Women in New York and New Netherland," p. 171, https://researchrepository.wvu.edu/etd/1430/; "another": Court

Minutes of New Amsterdam v. 2, pp. 203, 298, cited by Susanah Shaw, "New Light from Old Sources," in *de Halve Maen* 74, 1 (Spring 2001): 13-14.

[545] Danckaerts, pp. 215-216.

[546] Van Slijck (aka Van Olinda): "Hudson-Mohawk Genealogical and Family Memoirs," www.schenectadyhistory.org/ families/hmgfm/vanslyck.html.

[547] Maria van Cortlandt (1645-1689). *Correspondence of Jeremias van Rensselaer*, A.J.F. van Laer, ed. and trans. (Albany: U. of the State of New York, 1932), pp. 176, 377, 401. Peter R. Christoph, "'Worthy, Virtuous Juffrouw Maria van Rensselaer,'" in *de Halve Maen* 52, 2 (Summer 1997): 25-40.

[548] Danckaerts, p. 214.

[549] Hardenbroeck (c.1659-1690). Miriam Schneir, "'She Merchants' in 17th Century Holland and New Netherland," pre-print, Program in Sex Roles and Social Change, Columbia U., 1980; Jean Zimmerman, *The Women of the House* (NY: Harcourt, 2007).

[550] The Dutch regained control in 1673 but lost it again in 1674.

[551] David M. Ellis, *A Short History of New York State* (Ithaca, NY: Cornell UP, 1957), p. 67.

[552] David Narrett, "Dutch Customs of Inheritance," in William Pencak and Conrad Wright, *Authority and Resistance* (NY: New-York Historical Soc., 1988), Tables 2.1, 2.2, pp. 46-47.

[553] David E. Narrett, "Men's Wills and Women's Property Rights in Colonial NY," in *Women in the Age of the American Revolution*, Ronald Hoffman and Peter J. Albert, eds. (Charlottesville: U. Press of Virginia, 1990), p. 99.

[554] Rev. Charles Wolley, *Two Years' Journey in New York and Part of its Territories* (c. 1678), quoted from Mrs. Schuyler (Mariana G.) Van Rensselaer, *History of the City of New York*, v. 2 [1909] (NY: Cosimo, 2007), p. 225; Biemer, pp. 92, 105 note 25.

[555] Roderick Phillips, *Untying the Knot* (NY: Cambridge UP, 1991), p. 39; Matteo Spalletta, "Divorce in Colonial N.Y.," in *N.Y. Historical Society Quarterly* (Oct. 1955): 422-440.

[556] John M. Murrin, "The New York Charter of Liberties," in *Roots of the Republic*, Stephen Schechter *et al.*, eds. (Madison, WI: Madison House, 1990), pp. 72-73.

[557] Act for Quieting of Men's Estates, in *The Colonial Laws of NY ...*, Charles Z. Lincoln *et al.*, eds. (Albany, NY: J.B. Lyon, 1894), p. 155.

[558] https://web.archive.org/web/20160614121602/http://slaverebellion.org/index.php?page=new-york-slave-rev.t-1712

[559] William Smith, Jr., *The History of the Province of New-York* (Cambridge, MA: Harvard UP, 1972), p. 226.

[560] Caitlin Shuster, "Huguenot Education in Colonial America," http://www.nyu.edu/classes/keefer/waoe/shuster.htm.

[561] New York *Weekly Journal*, XII, Jan. 21, 1734 (new-style date).

[562] Colden to John Falconer, May 4, 1724, NY Historical Society Collections 50 (1917): 51-53

18 DISSENT AND DEFIANCE IN NEW ENGLAND

[563] John Winthrop sermon, "A Model of Christian Charity" (1630).

[564] *America's Families,* Donald M. Scott and Bernard Wishy, eds. (NY: Harper & Row, 1981), pp. 13-16. 594.

[565] Connecticut General Court, 1643, quoted from Mary Beth Norton, *Founding Mothers & Fathers* (NY: Knopf, 1996), p. 27.

[566] Samuel Hooker, *Righteousness Rained from Heaven* (Cambridge, MA: Samuel Green, 1677), p. 25; Thomas Cobbett, *A Fruitful and Usefull Discourse* (London, 1656), quoted from Morgan, pp. 133-134.

[567] John Trumbull, *Blue Laws of Conn.* (Hartford, 1878); Edmund S. Morgan, *The Puritan Family* (Boston: Harper & Row, 1956), p. 145; Nathaniel B. Shurtleff, *Records of the Governor and Company of the Massachusetts Bay in New England,* v. II (Boston, MA: William White, 1854), pp. 211-212.

[568] Henry Kamen, *Early Modern European Society* (NY: Routledge, 2000), p. 159.

[569] *The Works of John Robinson,* v. 1 (London: John Snow, 1851), Chapter LIX "Of Marriage," http://oll.libertyfund.org/title/855/144407/2703076.

[570] Proverbs 31.

[571] Samuel Willard, *Compleat Body of Divinity*, Quest. 64, Sermon 178, pp. 609-610. (Posthumously published, 1726; original date unknown.), http://www.puritansermons.com/willard/will0178.pdf.

[572] Cornelia Hughes Dayton, *Women before the Bar* (Chapel Hill, NC: Institute of Early American History and Culture, 1995), p. 4.

[573] Richard Morris, *Studies in the History of American Law* (NY: Columbia UP, 1930), p. 126.

[574] John Demos, *A Little Commonwealth* (NY: Oxford UP, 2000), p. 75.

[575] http://www.mass.gov/anf/docs/lib/body-of-liberties-1641.pdf, p. 51.

[576] John to Margaret (c.1591-1647), in Alice Morse Earle, *Margaret Winthrop* (NY: Scribners, 1895), p. 129.

[577] Lucy (1601-1679) to John, 1636, *Ibid.*, pp. 225-226.

[578] Letters, 1631, *Ibid.*, pp. 161-162; Wilsons: Arthur B. Ellis, *History of the First Church in Boston* (Boston, MA: Hall and Whiting, 1881), p. 53.

[579] Thomas Weld, "Preface" to John Winthrop's *A Short Story of the Rise, reign, and ruine of the Antinomians, Familists and Libertines*, 2nd ed., 1644, in *The Antinomian Controversy,* David D. Hall, ed. (Middletown, CT: Wesleyan U., 1968), pp. 209, 211.

[580] Hutchinson (1591-1643). Three children had died. Cotton arrived in Boston, 1633.

[581] Cotton, *The Way of Congregational Churches Cleared* (London, 1648), in Hall, 412.

[582] Winthrop, *Short Story,* in Hall, p. 263.

[583] Dyer (c. 1611-1660).

[584] Hall: Hutchinson, p. 268; Winthrop, p. 264.

[585] *The Journal of John Winthrop*, Richard S. Dunn, James Savage, and Laetitia Yeandle, eds. (Cambridge, MA: Harvard UP, 1996), pp. 208-209.

[586] Winthrop, *Short Story*; Cotton, *Congregational Churches*; in Hall, pp. 248, 423.

[587] *Wonder-Working Providence of Sion's Saviour in New England*, Franklin Jameson, ed. (NY: Scribner's, 1910), p. 127.
[588] Winthrop's *Journal*, pp. 210, 214-215, 232-234.
[589] Winthrop, *Short Story*, in Hall, p. 248.
[590] Earle, *Winthrop* (1637), pp. 269-270.
[591] Winthrop, *Short Story*, in Hall, p. 265.
[592] "The Examination of Mrs. Anne Hutchinson," in Hall, pp. 312-348.
[593] Winthrop, *Short Story*, in Hall, pp. 219-310.
[594] *Examination of Hutchinson*, in Hall, pp. 336-348.
[595] Shurtleff, v. 1 (Nov. 20, 1637), pp. 212-213.
[596] Winthrop's *Journal*, p. 244.
[597] John Underhill, *Newes from America* (London, 1638), p. 5, http://digitalcommons.unl.edu/etas/37.
[598] Thomas Shepard, in Hall, p. 365.
[599] Thomas Weld Preface, in Hall, pp. 205-206.
[600] Peter Bulkeley in Hall, p. 362; Cotton, in Hall, pp. 370, 372.
[601] Hall, p. 388.
[602] Wilson, in Hall, p. 384; Winthop, *Short Story* in Hall, p. 307.
[603] *Journal*, pp. 275-276.
[604] Shurtleff, v. 1 (March 12, 1638), p. 224; (June 1641), p. 329; *Journal*, p. 255.
[605] E.g., see Weld, "Preface" to *Short Story*, in Hall, p. 218.
[606] Shurtleff, v. 4 (Oct. 19, 1658), p. 345.
[607] http://www.rootsweb.ancestry.com/~nwa/mdnotes.html#wdyer.

19 REVOLUTIONARY WOMEN IN AMERICA

[608] Abigail (1744-1818) to John, Mar. 31, May 7; John to Abigail, Apr. 14; Adams Family Papers: An Electronic Archive, Massachusetts Historical Society, http://www.masshist.org/digitaladams.
[609] To Catharine Livingston, Oct. 20, 1776; quoted from Linda K. Kerber, *Women of the Republic* (Chapel Hill: U. of North Carolina, 1997), p. 35 (emphasis in original).
[610] *Pennsylvania Journal*, August 23, 1764.
[611] Daniel Dulany, *Considerations on the Propriety of Imposing Taxes in the British Colonies* (1765), p. 66, http:www.archive.org/details/ cihm_20394.
[612] *The World's Famous Orations*, v. 8, William Jennings Bryan, ed. (NY: Funk and Wagnalls, 1906), http://www.bartleby.com/268/8/10.
[613] *Documentary History of NY*, v. 1, p. 734.
[614] *Origin and Progress of the American Rebellion* [1781], Douglass Adair and John A. Schutz, eds. (Stanford, CA: Stanford UP, 1967), p. 64.
[615] Ulrich, "'Daughters of Liberty,'" in *Women in the Age of the American Revolution*, Ronald Hoffman and Peter Albert, eds. (Charlottesville: U. Press of Virginia, 1989), pp. 215-222.
[616] David Ramsay, *History of the American Revolution*, v. I (London, 1793), p. 70.

[617] Rolla M. Tryon, *Household Manufactures in the U.S.* (Chicago, IL: Chicago UP, 1917), pp. 30, 56; *Boston Gazette*, Sept. 19, 1768.

[618] William Bagnall, *The Textile Industries of the U.S.*, v. 1 (Boston, MA: Riverside Press, 1893), p. 42.

[619] *Massachusetts Gazette and Boston Weekly News Letter,* March 1, 1770, and March 8, 1770 supplement.

[620] *Pennsylvania Gazette*, August 9, 1775.

[621] *American Archives*, Series 4. v. 2 (Washington, 1837-46), pp. 142-143.

[622] The Society for the Promotion of Arts, Agriculture, and Economy: Bagnall, pp. 52-53.

[623] *Boston Evening Post*, February 1770; quoted in Mary Beth Norton, *Liberty's Daughters* (Ithaca, NY: Cornell UP, 1996), pp. 160-161.

[624] http://www.sc.edu/library/digital/collections/ tennent.html.

[625] "Association Signed by Ladies of Edenton, North Carolina," in *The North Carolina Experience*, Lindley S. Butler and Alan D. Watson, eds. (Chapel Hill: U. of North Carolina Press, 1984), pp. 136-137.

[626] February 21, 1775, quoted in Louis Morton, *Robert Carter of Nomini Hall* (Williamsburg: U. Press of Virginia, 1941), pp. 73, 105.

[627] *Virginia Gazette*: February 7, 1776; Aug 23, 1776; Feb. 14, 1777.

[628] Victor Selden Clark, *History of Manufactures in the U.S.* (Washington, D.C.: Carnegie Institution, 1916), p. 191.

[629] Also, Sybil Luddington, Prudence Wright, Nancy Hart, Catherine Moore Berry, and Lydia Darragh.

[630] Deborah Sampson [Gannett] (c.1760-1827). Alfred F. Young, *Masquerade* (NY: Random House, 2004).

[631] Linda Grant DePauw, "Women in Combat," in *Armed Forces and Society* 7, no. 2 (Winter 1981), p. 211.

[632] *The Writings of George Washington ...,* John C. Fitzpatrick, ed.: "a clog": August 4, 1777, General Orders, v. 8, p. 181; "oldest and best": Jan. 29, 1783, letter to Supt. of Finance, v. 26, pp. 78-79; Nancy K. Loane, *Following the Drum* (Washington, DC: Potomac Books, 2009), pp. 3-4, 137; John U. Rees, "proportion": http://www.revwar75.com/library/rees/proportion.htm#9.

[633] Dunmore Proclamation, 1775; Philipsburg Proclamation, 1779.

[634] Benjamin Quarles, *The Negro in the American Revolution* (Chapel Hill: U. of North Carolina, 1996), pp. 171-172; Bernard Bailyn, "The Idea of Atlantic History," in *Itinerario*, 20 (1996): 26.

[635] http://www.blackloyalist.com/canadiandigitalcollection/documents/ official/black_loyalist_ directory.htm.

[636] Jacqueline Jones, in Hoffman and Albert, p. 306.

[637] Joanne Pope Melish, *Disowning Slavery* (Ithaca, NY: Cornell UP, 1998).

[638] Elizabeth Freeman, aka "Mum Bett" (1742-1829); Catherine Adams and Elizabeth Pleck, *Love of Freedom* (NY: Oxford UP, 2010), pp. 139-142.

[639] Petition, probably drafted by Black abolitionist Prince Hall, http://www.medfordhistorical society.org/belinda.php.

[640] Wheatley (c. 1754-1784). David Grimsted, "Anglo-American Racism and Phillis Wheatley's `Sable Veil'..." in Hoffman and Albert, pp. 338-444.

[641] *Poems on Various Subjects, Religious and Moral* (London, 1773), p. 34.

[642] Wheatley to Rev. Samson Occom, Feb. 11, 1774, http://www.pbs.org/wgbh/aia/part2/2h19t/html.

[643] Letter, Abigail to John, 17 June, 1782.

[644] Caroline Gilman, *Letters of Eliza Wilkinson* ... (London: Forgotten Books, 2012), p. 61.

[645] Susan Branson, *These Fiery Frenchified Dames* (Philadelphia: U. of Pennsylvania, 2001) pp. 69, 72-73, 78.

[646] Anne Willing Bingham (1764-1801). Jefferson Papers XIII 151, 393, ed. Julian P. Boyd *et al.*

[647] J. S. Murray (1751-1820), *Massachusetts Magazine*, v. 2, March and April 1790, https://digital.library.upenn.edu/women/murray/equality/equality.html.

[648] Frank Luther Mott, *A History of American Magazines* [1938] (Cambridge, MA: Harvard UP, 1958), pp. 65-66; Kerber, p. 223.

[649] *Vindication* (London: Joseph Johnson, 1792), quoted from Dover unabridged edition, 1996, p. 25.

[650] to Julia Stockton Rush, March 1793, quoted from *Only for the Eye of a Friend*, Carla Mulford, ed. (Charlottesville: U. of Virginia, 1995), pp. 304-305.

[651] *Diary of Elizabeth Drinker* (Philadelphia: U. of Pennsylvania., 2010), p. 163.

[652] Letter to Moses Porter, June 1, 1801, published in *A Girl's Life Eighty Years Ago*, Clarence Cook, ed. (NY: Scribner's, 1887), pp. 58-62.

[653] To James Morris, Jan. 25, 1794, in *The Diary of Elihu Hubbard Smith*, James Cronin, ed. (Philadelphia, PA: American Philosophical Society, 1973), pp. 109-111.

[654] Marion B. Savin and Harold J. Abrahams, "The Young Ladies' Academy of Philadelphia," in *History of Education Journal* 8, 2 (winter 1957): 58-67.

[655] Priscilla Mason, "Oration," May 15, 1793, *Rise and Progress of the Young Ladies' Academy*, pp. 90-95.

[656] E.g., Emma Willard's Troy Female Seminary, NY, 1821; Catharine Beecher's school for girls, Hartford, CT, 1823; Van Doren's Collegiate Institute for Young Ladies, Lexington, KY, 1831, Prudence Crandall's school for African-American girls, Canterbury, CT, 1833.

[657] *The Gleaner*, v. 3.

20 *CITOYENNES*

[658] Olwen Hufton, "Women in Revolution 1789-1796," in *Past and Present* 53 (Nov. 1971): 90-108.

[659] Testimony of Stanislas Maillard, in *Women in Revolutionary Paris*, Darline Gay Levy, Harriet Branson Applewhite, and Mary Durham Johnson, eds. and trans. (Urbana: U. of Illinois, 1979), pp. 37-38.

[660] *Rêquete des dames l'Assemblée Nationale* (1789), Karen Offen, trans., http://chnm.gmu.edu/revolution/d/629/.
[661] Dominique Godineau, *The Women of Paris and Their French Revolution*, Katherine Streip, trans. (Berkeley: U. of California, 1998), pp. 101-103.
[662] Beaune: *Le Moniteur*, July 28, 1790, quoted from Jane Rendall, *The Origins of Modern Feminism* (NY: Schocken, 1984), pp. 47-48; Bordeaux:, quoted from Suzanne Desan, *The Family on Trial in Revolutionary France* (Berkeley: U. of California, 2004), p. 87.
[663] "*Sur l'admission des femmes aux droits de Cité*," quoted from *The French Revolution and Human Rights*, Lynn Hunt, ed. (NY: St. Martin's, 1996), pp. 119–121.
[664] Godineau, p. 100, http://www.historywiz.com/primarysources/const1791text.html.
[665] "Appeal to the Nation," quoted from R. B. Rose, *The Making of the Sans-culottes* (Dover, NH: Manchester UP, 1983).
[666] Gouges, born Marie Gouze (1748-1793); quoted from Levy, Applewhite, and Johnson, pp. 87-96.
[667] "journalist": Louise Robert (1758-1822). Rose, p. 112.
[668] Méricourt, born Anne-Josèphe Terwagne (1762-1817). Elisabeth Roudinesco, *Madness and Revolution*, Martin Thom, trans. (NY: Verso, 1991), pp. 7, 84, 226.
[669] Palm (1743-1799). Desan, p. 105, Rose, pp. 97-98, 112; Léon (1768-1838): Godineau, pp. 393-394.
[670] *Lettre ... de la vérité*, Mar. 23, 1791, in Levy, Applewhite, and Johnson, pp. 68-71.
[671] Godineau, pp. 103-104, 369.
[672] Olwen Hufton, *Women and the Limits of Citizenship in the French Revolution* (U. of Toronto, 1999), p. 23; Godineau, p. 108; petition: Levy *et al.*, pp. 72-74.
[673] Speech before the Fraternal Society of Minims, Mar. 26, 1792, quoted from Godineau, p.109.
[674] Wollstonecraft (1759-1797. *Emile*, François Richard and Pierre Richard, eds. (Paris: Garnier, 1964), p. 446.
[675] Godineau, p. 111.
[676] *Ibid.*, pp. 39-41; Desan, pp. 93-100 and Appendix II, p. 326.
[677] Godineau, pp. 243-247.
[678] Hufton, pp. 27-28; Levy, Applewhite, and Johnson, pp. 131-132.
[679] Godineau, pp. 114-118.
[680] *Ibid.*, pp. 173-174, 135-137.
[681] Abray, p. 48; Godineau, p. 137.
[682] Corday (1768-1793).
[683] Levy, Applewhite, and Johnson, pp. 186-196.
[684] Godineau, pp. 158-161.
[685] Levy, Applewhite, and Johnson, pp. 213-217.
[686] *Feuille de Salut Public*, quoted from *Women, the Family, and Freedom*, v. 1, Susan Groag Bell and Karen M. Offen, eds. (Stanford, CA: Stanford UP, 1983), p. 22.

[687] *"Voix,"* quoted from Laura S. Strumingher, "Looking Back," in Harriet Applewhite and Darline Levy, eds., *Women and Politics in the Age of the Democratic Revolution* (Ann Arbor: U. of Michigan, 1990), p. 289.

[688] Gay L. Gullickson, *Unruly Women of Paris* (Ithaca, NY: Cornell UP, 1996), p. 97.

[689] D. H. Barry, "Community, Tradition, and Memory among Rebel Working-Class Women of Paris," in *European Review of History* 7, 2 (2000): 270-271; *The* [London] *Times*, May 6, 1871, "The French Siege of Paris."

21 FIRESIDE TO FACTORY

[690] Graeme Milne, *Trade and Traders in Mid-Victorian Liverpool* (Liverpool, UK: Liverpool UP, 2000), p. 53.

[691] Ivy Pinchbeck, *Women Workers and the Industrial Revolution* [1930] (London, UK: Virago, 1969), pp. 111, 137, 143.

[692] Henry Fishwick, *A History of Lancashire* (London, UK: E. Stock, 1894), p. 266.

[693] Quoted from Alfred P. Wadsworth and Julia De Lacy Mann, *The Cotton Trade and Industrial Lancashire* (Manchester, UK: Manchester UP, 1965), pp. 375, 499; Pinchbeck, p. 151.

[694] Jan Rendall, *Women in an Industrializing Society* (Oxford, UK: Basil Blackwell, 1990), pp. 83-84.

[695] *The Examiner*, Jan. 29, 1832; quoted from Pinchbeck, p. 199.

[696] Quoted from E. P. Thompson, *The Making of the English Working Class* (NY: Vintage, 1966), pp. 717-718.

[697] M. L. Bush, "The Women at Peterloo," in *History* 89, 294 (April 2004): 209-232.

[698] Owen, *The Book of the New Moral World*, v. 6.

[699] Frances Morrison (1807-1898).

[700] Quoted from *Women and Radicalism in the Nineteenth Century*, Mike Sanders, ed. (London, UK: Routledge, 2001), "letter": Feb. 2, 1834, p. 178; "ladies": Mar. 8, 1834, p. 179; "aristocratic": Apr. 26, 1834, p. 206.

[701] *The Pioneer*, Apr. 5, 1834; Barbara Taylor, "The Men Are as Bad as Their Masters…," in *Feminist Studies* 5, 1 (Spring 1979): 7-40.

[702] Jutta Schwarzkopf, *Women in the Chartist Movement* (London: Mcmillan, 1991), pp. 202, 59.

[703] James Chastain, *Encyclopedia of 1848 Revolutions*, http://www.ohiou.edu/~chastain/rz/womchart.htm.

[704] Malcolm Chase, *Chartism* (Manchester, UK: Manchester UP, 2007), p. 267.

[705] Hamilton, U.S. Dept. of Treasury (Boston, MA: Home Market Club, 1892), p. 41.

[706] Alice Kessler-Harris, *Out to Work* (NY: Oxford UP, 2003), p. 28; Philip S. Foner, *Women and the American Labor Movement* (NY: Free Press, 1979), p. 21, refers to 40 mills in RI and 30 in MA.

[707] Foner, p. 23.

[708] Robinson, *Loom and Spindle* (NY: Crowell, 1898), p. 4.

[709] Quoted from William Moran, *The Belles of New England* (NY: St. Martin's, 2002), pp. 4, 27.

[710] Larcom, *A New England Girlhood*, http://www.gutenberg.org/ebooks/2293, pp. 178-179.

[711] Robinson, pp. 81-82; re Grimkés: Kathryn Kish Sklar, *Women's Rights Emerges within the Antislavery Movement* (NY: Bedford/St. Martin's, 2000), p. 122.

[712] Helen L. Sumner, "The Historical Development of Women's Work in the United States," in *Proceedings of the Academy of Political Science in the City of NY* (NY: The Academy of Political Science, 1910), pp. 11-26.

[713] Thomas Dublin, *Women at Work* (NY: Columbia UP, 1979), p. 39.

[714] John R. Commons *et al.*, *History of Labour in the U.S.*, v. 1 (NY: Macmillan, 1918), p. 156; Kessler-Harris, p. 40.

[715] Jan. 7, 1829, quoted from John B. Andrews, *History of Women in Trade Unions* (Washington, DC: Govt. Printing Office, 1911), pp. 23-24.

[716] Foner, p. 42.

[717] *Ibid.*, p. 26; Helen L. Sumner, *History of Women in Industry in the U.S.*, v. 9 (Washington, DC: Govt. Printing Office, 1911).

[718] Feb. 17 and 18, 1834, quoted from Commons, p. 423.

[719] Andrews, p. 29; Dublin, p. 92.

[720] Commons, p. 432; Andrews, pp. 36-45.

[721] Andrews, p. 47; Commons, pp. 291-293.

[722] Robinson, p. 84.

[723] Dublin, pp. 98-101.

[724] *Voice of Industry*, Feb. 27, 1846; Bagley (1806-1889).

[725] https://iiif.lib.harvard.edu/manifests/view/drs:2577568$5i.

[726] *Voice of Industry* letters, "Manchester": Jan 9, 1846; "Munroe": Mar 13, 1846; "an operative": Apr 16, 1847.

[727] *Ibid*, Feb. 13, 1846; Foner, p. 80.

[728] https://www.newenglandhistoricalsociety.com.sarahbagley

[729] Lily Martin Spencer (1822-1902).

[730] historymatters.gmu.edu/mse/sia/murphyletter3.htm.

22 FREE WOMEN

[731] Enfantin: Claire G. Moses, *French Feminism in the Nineteenth Century* (State U. of NY Press, 1985); Claire G. Moses, "Saint-Simonian Men/Saint-Simonian Women," in *Journal of Modern History* 54 (June 1982): 240-267; "spokesman": Leslie F. Goldstein, "Early Feminist Themes in French Utopian Socialism," *Journal of the History of Ideas* 43, 1 (1982): 231.

[732] Marie-Reine Guindorf (1812-1837), Desirée Véret [Gay] (1810-c. 1891).

[733] Contributors included the two founders as well as Suzanne Voilquin, later the chief editor (1801-c. 1877), Claire Démar (1799-1833), Jeanne Deroin (1805-1894), Anna Wheeler (1785-1848), Pauline Roland (1805-1852), and Eugènie Niboyet (1796-1889).

[734] Nov. 4, 1832; quoted from Moses, "Saint-Simonian Men."

[735] Quoted from Bonnie Anderson, *Joyous Greetings* (NY: Oxford UP, 2000), p. 8.

[736] The probable author was Jeanne Deroin; quoted from Susan Groag Bell and Karen M. Offen, eds., *Women, the Family and Freedom* (Palo Alto, CA: Stanford UP, 1983), pp. 146-147.

[737] Anne Knight (1786-1862): Anderson, p. 88; *Crisis* 2, 23 (June 25, 1833): 182. (The translator added passages of her own.)

[738] Dolores Dooley, *Equality in Community* (Cork: Cork UP, 1996), pp. 71-72.

[739] "visited London": Desirée Véret [Gay] and Flora Tristan (1803-1844); Bell and Offen, p. 120; Anderson, pp. 68, 142.

[740] William Thompson, *Appeal of One Half of the Human Race, Women, Against the Pretensions of the Other Half, Men, to Retain them in Political, and Hence in Civil and Domestic, Slavery* (London: Richard Taylor, 1825). Thompson credited Wheeler with supplying the principal ideas of the work, although her name was not on the title page.

[741] Michèle Riot-Sarcey, "Desirée Gay," in *Encyclopedia of 1848 Revolutions*, https://www.ohio.edu/chastain.htm.

[742] S. Joan Moon, "Jeanne Deroin," in *Ibid.*

[743] Malcolm Chase, *Chartism* (Manchester, UK: Manchester UP, 2007), p. 59; Charles McPhee, "Pauline Roland," in *Encyclopedia of 1848 Revolutions*.

[744] Lyon: *Le Conseiller des femmes* (*The Women's Advisor*), 1833-1834; Paris: *La Gazette des femmes*; Joan B. Landes, *Women and the Public Sphere* (Ithaca, NY: Cornell UP, 1988), p. 190.

[745] Apr. 29, 1848, in *Pest Fashion Magazine*, cited by Robert Nemes, "Women in the 1848-1849 Hungarian Revolution," in *Journal of Women's History* 13, 3 (2001): 193-207.

[746] Gabriella Hausch, "Did Women Have a Revolution?" in *1848—A European Revolution?* Axel Körner, ed. (NY: St. Martin's, 2000), pp. 65-66.

[747] Stanley Zucker, "German Women and the Revolution of 1848," in *Central European History*, 13, 3 (Sept. 1980): 237; Adolf Wolff, *Berliner Revolutionschornik im Jahre 1848*.

[748] Louise Dittmar (1807-1884); Louise Otto [Peters] (1819-1895); quoted from Anderson, pp. 9, 99.

[749] Marie-Reine Guindorf, Anna Wheeler, and Flora Tristan had died.

[750] Pauline Roland tried to vote in Boussac; Anderson, p. 157.

[751] S. Joan Moon, "Women's Rights in France," in *Encyclopedia of 1848 Revolutions*.

[752] Petition dated March 16, 1848: Anderson, p. 109.

[753] Published 6 times a week, March to June, 1848.

[754] S. Joan Moon, "Women's Rights," in *Encyclopedia of 1848 Reolutions*.

[755] Riot-Sarcey, "Desirée Gay," in *Ibid.*

[756] Judith DeGroat, "Ateliers nationaux des femmes," in *Ibid.*; Claire G. Moses, *French Feminism in the Nineteenth Century* (State U. of NY Press, 1985), pp. 143-144.

[757] Riot-Sarcey, "Eugénie Niboyet," in *Encyclopedia of 1848 Revolutions*; quoted from *La Liberté*, June 12, 1848.

[758] Joan Wallach Scott, in *Only Paradoxes to Offer* (Cambridge, MA: Harvard UP, 1997), p. 81 ftn.

[759] Riot-Sarcey, *La Démocratie à l'épreuve des femmes* (Paris: A. Michel, 1994), p. 216.
[760] Sand, born Amantine Lucile Aurore Dupin (1804-1876).
[761] *Voix*, Apr. 10, 1848, p. 2; quoted from Anderson, p. 163.
[762] Naomi Schor, *George Sand and Idealism* (NY: Columbia UP, 1993), p. 80.
[763] Elizabeth Harlan, *George Sand* (New Haven, CT: Yale UP, 2004), p. 249.
[764] Bell & Offen, p. 249.
[765] *L'Opinion*, Aug. 21, 1848, and 6 issues in 1849; S. Joan Moon, "The Feminist Press in France," in *Encyclopedia of 1848 Revolutions;* Scott, p. 58.
[766] Proudhon, in *La Liberté,* quoted from Harlan, p. 247.
[767] Slavery had been abolished in France and the French colonies in 1848.
[768] Quoted from Miriam Schneir, *Feminism: The Essential Historical Writings* (NY: Random House, 1994), pp. 91-92.
[769] Most notably, Sojourner Truth, who was African American, and Ernestine Rose, a Jewish immigrant from Poland.

CODA
[770] *Report of the International Council of Women*, Assembled by the National Woman Suffrage Association, Mar 25-Apr 1, 1888, "education": May Wright Sewall, 56; "employment": Mary A. Livermore, 134; "law": Lillie Deveraux Blake, 226.
[771] *Ibid.,* pp. 34, 330, 343, 101.
[772] Finland, Norway, Denmark, and Iceland.
[773] https://awpc.cattcenter.iastate.edu/2017/03/21/on-marriage-and-divorce-aug-18-1871/.
[774] *Report of the International Council of Women*, pp. 33, 35, 36.

INDEX

abbesses, 69, 71, 73, 74, 76
abolitionism. *See* anti-slavery movement
abortion, 51, 52-53, 79
Act for Regulating Slaves, 185
Adams, Abigail, and John, 201-202, 211
adultery, 33, 46, 53, 56, 70, 84, 95, 220
African-American women, 2-4, 181-182, 184-185, 205, 207-210, 234-235, 253-254
Albigensian Crusade, 113-116
Albigensians. *See* Cathars
Algonquian-speaking peoples, 176, 179-180, 196
Ambrose, Bishop, 68, 69
Andreini, Isabella, 150, 151
androgyny, 63, 68-69
Anguissola, Sofonisba, 149, 150
Anthony, Susan B., 3, 4, 254, 255
anti-slavery, 1-4, 5, 236, 238-239, 244, 250,, 253-254
Antoinette, Queen Marie, 215, 222
Aristotle, 145, 149, 152
Audu, Louise-Reine, 221
Augustine of Hippo, 65-67
Austin, Ann, 196
Bagley, Sarah G., 238-240
Beard, Mary Ritter, 5, 6
Beauvoir, Simone de, 6-8, 32, 53
Beguines, 117-118, 121, 123
"Belinda," 209
Benedictine Rule, 71-73
bequeath, right to, 31, 46, 90, 122, 126, 184
Bingham, Anne Willing, 211
Blandina, 58
Bloomer, Amelia, 236
Boccaccio, Giovanni, 7, 135, 138, 189
Body of Liberties, 188-189
Boniface, Saint, 73, 74, 80
Book of Legends. See Hroswitha
Book of the City of Ladies, The. See Pizan, Christine de
Boudicca, Queen, 37-39
Bradstreet, Anne, 6, 157
bridegift, 107
Brigit (also Brig), 39-40, 65

Burchard, Bishop, 81-86
Caesar, Julius, 37, 41, 48, 51
Caesaria, 70-71
Caesarius, Bishop, 70-71, 77, 79-80, 83
Canterbury Tales, The. See Chaucer
Cartimandua, Queen, 37
Casulana, 148-149
Caterpillars' Marvelous Transformation ..., The. See Merian, Maria Sibylla
Cathars, 109-116
Cattle-Raid of Cooley, The, 43
celibacy, 67-70, 112, 117, 243
Cereta. Laura, 146-147, 152
Cervantes, Miguel de, 96. 97, 230
Chadwick, John, 22
Charter of Libertyes and Priviledges, 184, 185
Chartist movement, 233-234, 244, 249
Chaucer, Geoffrey, 7, 120, 135
childbirth, 14, 24, 29, 51, 52, 69, 95, 153
childcare, 22, 23, 24, 48, 52, 79-80, 95, 102, 120, 147, 154, 211, 218, 230, 248
citizenship, 1, 29, 164-168, 211, 217-220, 223-226. *See* suffrage
Cleopatra, 51
Clotilde, 70, 137
Colonna, 144
Committee of the Rights of Woman (*Comité des droits de la femme*), 246
conception, contraception, 52, 79, 196, 244
Concerning Famous Women. See Boccaccio, Giovanni
concubinage, 56, 90, 100, 109
Condorcet, Nicolas de, 218, 220
convents, 7, 68-76, 141, 151. *See* double monasteries
Corday, Charlotte, 224, 225
Cornelia, wife of Pompey, 49
Cortlandt, Maria van, 183
Countesses Jeanne and Marguerite of Flanders, 117
Crisis, The, 244
cross-dressing, 70, 79, 161-164, 206
Danckaerts, Jasper, 182, 183
Dante Alighieri, 134, 135
Daumier, Honoré, 248, 251
deaconesses, 57, 59
Decameron. See Boccaccio, Giovanni
Declaration of the Rights of Man and of the Citizen, 215, 217, 220
Declaration of the Rights of Woman and of the Female Citizen, 218-219
Demonology, 158

Demosthenes, 29
Deroin, Jeanne, 243, 244, 245, 247- 250
Diana, 51, 80, 87
Divine Comedy, The. See Dante, Alighieri
divorce, 1, 41, 139, 172, 184, 232, 254; in *France*, 218, 220, 221, 227, 246; *Gortyn*, 32, 33; *Rome*, 45,46; *Scandinavia,* 101, 102, 103
Don Quixote. See Cervantes, Miguel de
double monasteries, 72-73, 74, 76, 99
Douglass, Frederick, 2, 4, 253
Downing, Lucy Winthrop, 189
dowry, 32, 45, 101, 103, 143
Drake, Judith, 169
Drinker, Elizabeth Sandwith, 212
Dronke, Peter, 76-77
Druids, 41, 42
Dunash Ben Labrat, wife of, 94
Dyer, Mary Barrett, 191, 195, 196-198
education, 1, 49, 71, 117, 125, 126-127, 136, 236, 253; in *al-Andalus,* 92-93*; Dutch Republic*, 169, 173-175; *Italy (renaissance)*, 143-147, 160; *Rome (ancient)*, 49; *U.S.,* 211-214
Egeria, 69-70
Eileithyia, 14, 24
Eleanor of Aquitaine, 134
Eleusinian mysteries, 30-31
Elizabeth I, Queen, 157, 158
Emile, or On Education. See Rousseau, Jean-Jacques
Erxleben, Dorothea, 175
Ester Hath Hang'd Haman. See "Sowernam, Ester"
Eustochium, 68
Evans, Sir Arthur, 13, 14 17, 18
exposure of newborns, 32, 46
Factory Tracts, 238
Fadl, 91
feme covert. See inheritance
Fisher, Ann, 196
Fontana, Lavinia, 149
Fonte, Moderata (Modesta Pozzo Zorzi), 152-154
Fourier, Charles, 232, 236, 240, 244
Franco, Veronica, 148
Fraternal Society of Patriots of Both Sexes, 218, 219, 220
Free Woman, The (Femme libre, La), 241, 242
Freeman, Elizabeth, 208
Freydis, 105-106

Friends of Truth, 220
Gage, Matilda Joslyn, 4
Gambara, Veronica, 145
Gay, Desirée Véret, 241, 243, 244, 246, 247, 248. 250
Gentileschi, Artemisia, 149
Gleaner, The. See Murray, Judith Sargent
Gnostics, 60-63
Gods, female: *Celtic,* 39-40; *Greek,* 24-25, 33, 51; *Roman,* 31, 50, 51, 83; Scandinavian, 104. *See* Diana
Good Women, 111-113, 115
Gortyn, Great Code of, 31-33, 45
Gournay, Marie de, 173-174
Grey, Jane, 157
Griffitts, Hannah, 204
guardianship, 45, 47, 52, 53
Gudrid, 105-106
guilds, 123, 127-129, 149, 172
Guindorf, Marie-Reine, 241
gynaeceum, 7, 29, 83
Gynecology. See Soranus
Haec Vir; or The Womanish-Man, 163-164
Hafsa bint al-Hajj Arrakuniyya, 93-94
Halbherr, Federico, 31
Hardenbroeck, Margaret, 183-184
Harper, Frances Ellen Watkins, 253
Hatshepsut, 17
Haudenosaunee. *See* Iroquois Confederacy
Hawkins, Jane, 191, 196
healers, 92, 102, 117, 123-124, 126-127, 182, 188, 206
herbalists, 51, 79, 80, 83-85, 124, 128
Hic Mulier; or The Man-Woman, 163
History of Woman Suffrage, 4
Homer, 13, 14, 23, 50, 229
homosexuality, 84-85, 91-92, 124-125
Hortensia, 48-49
Hroswitha, 75, 77, 92
Huneberc (or Hugeberc), 75, 76
Hutchinson, Anne Maybury, 190-198
Ibn Rushd (Averroes), 95-96, 145
Impartial Representation ... Spinners in Lancashire, An, 230
Index of Forbidden Books, 151, 152
Ingstad, Anne Stine, 106
inheritance, 123, 126, 184; in *al-Andalus,* 90, 91, 93; *France,* 218, 219, 220, 226; *Dutch*

Republic, 170; *Greece,* 31, 32; *Italy,* 152, 154; *Rome,* 46; *Scandinavia,* 102, 106, 107
Inquisitions: Counter-Reformation, 151; medieval, 90, 116-118, 120, 122; Spanish and Portuguese, 96
International Council of Women, 253-255
Iroquois Confederacy, 179-180, 183
Jane Anger, Her Protection for Women, 158
Jemison, Mary, 180
Jerome, Saint, 65, 67-70, 85
Jewish women, 51, 55, 90, 94, 122
Joan of Arc, 141, 162
Junia (or Junias), 57
Juvenal, 49-50, 51, 52
Kempe, Margery, 122
Knight, Anne, 244
Knossos, 14, 16-18, 21, 25
Kober, Alice, 22
Koester, Helmut, 56
Lacombe, Claire, 221, 223, 225, 227
Lady, The. See Putnam, Emily James
Lancelot. See Troyes, Chrétien de
Larcom, Lucy, 236
Leduc, Claudine, 32
Léon, Pauline, 219, 220, 225, 227
Lerner, Gerda, 6, 7-8, 16
Leveller movement, 166-167
lex Julia, 52
Leyster, Judith, 172, 174
Linear A and B, 21-26
literacy, 71, 116, 125, 152, 169, 231
literary salons, 49, 93, 147, 212
Livingston, Margaret, 202
Loom and Spindle. See Robinson, Harriet Hanson
Lowell Female Labor Reform Association (LFLRA), 238-239
Luddites, 230
Makin, Bathsua, 157
Malatesta, Battista, 144
Malleus Maleficarum, 158
Marcella, 68
Marie de France ("Dame Marie"), 134
Marie of France, Countess of Champagne, 134
Marinella, Lucrezia, 152-153
marriage, arranged, 45, 56, 72, 101, 123, 219
marriage, customs and laws: in *Athens,* 45, 46, 47, 53; *Dutch Republic,* 170-171; *France,*

220, 226-227; *Greece (ancient)*, 29, 31; *Italy (renaissance)*, 151-152, 154; *New England*, 187-189; *Scandinavia*, 102. *See* inheritance; African-American women; Jewish women; Muslim women; Native-American women; remarriage
martyrs, 58, 65
Mason, Priscilla, 213
Mary I, Queen, 157
Mary Magdalene, 55, 62, 63
masturbation, 84, 85
McClintock, Mary Ann, 2
McKettrick, Rosalind, 74
McNamara, Jo Ann, 68
Medea, 34, 138
Merian, Maria Sibylla, 172-173
Méricourt, Théroigne de, 219-221, 223-224, 226
midwives, 70, 80, 124, 126, 171, 182, 190-191, 196, 246
"Moll Cutpurse," (Mary Frith) 162-163
"Molly Pitcher" (Mary Ludwig Hays), 206
Montanism, 60-
Montségur, 115-116
Morrison, Frances and James, 232, 233
motherhood. *See* childcare.
Mott, Lucretia, 1, 2
"Munda, Constantia", 159-161
Murray, Judith Sargent, 211-212, 214
musicians, 92, 219, 148-149
Muslim women, 89-90, 92-97
Muzel for Melastomus, A. See Speght, Rachel
Nag Hammadi, 61-63
National American Woman Suffrage Association (NAWSA), 4, 254
National Association of Colored Women, 254
National Trades Union, 238
National Workshops (*Ateliers Nationaux*), 245, 246, 247
Native-American women, 179, 180, 253-254
Nazhun al-Garnatiya bint al-Quali'iya, 94
Niboyet, Eugénie, 244, 245-247, 250
Nogarola, Angela, 145
Nogarola, Ginevra and Isotta, 145-146, 152
North Star, The. See Douglass, Frederick
nuns, 68-77
Oliver, Mary, 195-196
Olsen, Barbara A., 19
"On the Equality of the Sexes." *See* Murray, Judith Sargent
On the Perpetual Virginity of the Blessed Mary. See Jerome, Saint

Opinion of Women (*L'Opinion des femmes*), 248
Oppian law, 47-48
Otto, Louise, 245
Owen, Robert, 232, 244
Pagels, Elaine, 62
Palm, Etta, d'Aelders, 219, 220, 226
Panathenaea, 30
Paul, Saint, 56-59, 65, 67, 69
Paula, 68
pay inequity, 127, 135, 177, 188, 238, 239, 240, 241, 245
penitentials, 81-87
perfects. *See* Good Women
Perpetua, 58
petitions, 2, 164-168, 233-234, 239
Petrarch, Francisco, 135
Philadelphia Female Anti-Slavery Society, 2
Phoebe (*diakonos*), 57, 58
physicians. *See* healers; herbalists; midwives
Pinchbeck, Ivy, 229-230
Pioneer, The, 232, 233
Pizan, Christine de, 5, 135-141
Plato, 29, 52, 95
Poems on Various Subjects.... See Wheatley, Phillis
polygyny, 90
Pomeroy, Sarah, 18, 49
Power, Eileen, 67
pregnancy. *See* childbirth
priests, female, 13-16, 25, 59-60. *See* Good Women
"Primrose, Diana," 157
Priscilla (missionary), 57, 58
prophets, sibyls, and "wise women," 39, 41, 60, 79-80, 104-105, 137
prostitutes and courtesans, 63, 121, 124-125, 139, 148, 154, 160, 171-172, 206
Purvis, Robert, 253
Putnam, Emily James, 33-34
Qasmuna bint Isma'il ibn Bagdalah, 94
qiyan, 91, 94
Quaker women, 1, 196, 206, 212
querelle des femmes, 136-137, 160
Qur'an, 90, 92
Radegund, 70, 71
rape, 33, 38, 94, 99, 125
remarriage, 46, 102, 123, 139, 188

Roaring Girle, The, 162-163
Robinson, Harriet Hanson, 235, 236, 238
Roland, Pauline, 244, 245, 249-250
Ruysch, Rachel, 172
Sampson, Deborah, 206
Saint-Simonism, 241, 243, 244
Sand, George, 247
Santorini, 13, 17
Sappho, 138
Schliemann, Heinrich, 21
Schurman, Anna Maria van, 173-175
scribes, female, 73-74
seclusion in the home in: *al-Andalus,* 89-90, 96-97; *Athens,* 29, 31
Sempronia, 49, 138
Seneca Falls convention, 1, 2, 240, 253
Seneca Falls Declaration ... and Resolutions, 1, 2
Sequana, 41, 64-65
sexual freedom, 39, 46, 52-53, 102-103
sexuality, female, 83, 84
Sidney, Mary, 157
slave revolt, 1712, NY, 185
slavery, female: in: *al-Andalus,* 90-92; *France,* 245, 249; *Greece,* 23, 29, 32; *North America,* 178, 180-182, 184-185, 205, 207-210, 236, 238-239; *Rome,* 45, 46, 48, 49, 51; *Scandinavia,* 100- 10
"snake goddess," 14-16
Society for the Emancipation of Women (*Société pour l"émancipation des femmes*), 246
Society of Revolutionary Republican Women (SRRW), 223-226
Society of the Voice of Women (*Société de la Voix des femmes*), 246
Soranus, 52-53
Southgate, Eliza, 213
"Sowernam, Ester," 157, 159-160
Sparta, 33, 34
Speght, Rachel, 159-160
Spencer, Lily Martin (aka Angelique Martin), 240
Spilimbergo, Irene di, 149
Stampa, Gaspara, 148
Stanton, Elizabeth Cady, 1-5, 253-255
suffrage, female: *Athens,* 29; *England,* 233-234; *France,* 218, 223-224, 245; *Rome,* 48; U.S., 1-4, 253, 254;
Subh, 92
Sulpicia, 49, 52
Swetnam, Joseph, 158-161
Swetnam the Woman-Hater Arraigned by Women, 161

Tacitus, 37-38, 41, 52
Terrell, Mary Church, 4, 254
Tertullian, 58, 60, 67
Thecla, 59
Thesmophoria, 31
Thompson, William, 244
Tracy, Susan Bull, 213
transgender. *See* cross-dressing
Tristan, Flora, 244
trobairitz, 133, 135
Trotula (or Trota), 134
trouvères, 133-134
Troyes, Chrétien de, 134
Twelve Tables, 45, 53
Ulrich, Laurel Thatcher, 203
veiling, 68, 89-90, 92, 93, 96
Ventris, Michael, 22
Véret, Desirée. *See* Gay, Desirée Véret
Versailles, women's march to, 215-217, 221, 228
Viguera, Maria, 89
Vindication of the Rights of Woman, A. See Wollstonecraft, Mary
Virgin Mary, 17, 55, 65
virginity. *See* celibacy
vita, 69, 80
Vix, princess of, 36, 42
Voice of Industry, The, 239-240
Voice of Women, The (La Voix des femmes), 227-228, 246-247
Voilquin, Suzanne, 246, 250
vote. *See* suffrage
wages. *See* pay inequity
Waldensians, 116-117
Wallada bint al-Mustakfi, 93
warriors, women, 37-39, 205-206, 222
Wells, Ida B., 4
Wemple, Suzanne, 74
Wheatley, Phillis, 209-210
Wheeler, Anna Doyle, 244
Widows. *See* inheritance; remarriage
Wiesner, Merry E., 124
Wilkinson, Eliza, 211
Wilson, Elizabeth Mansfield, 189-190, 192
Winthrop, Margaret Tyndal, 189-190, 192-193
"witches," 87, 196

Wives. *See* marriage, customs and laws
Wollstonecraft, Mary, 212- 213, 221, 237
Women Workers and the Industrial Revolution. See Pinchbeck, Ivy
Women's Gazette (Gazette des femmes), 245, 246
Women's News (Frauen-Zeitung). See Otto, Louise
Women's Tribune (Tribune des femmes), 243-246
work, remunerative: *brewers*, 117, 122, 129, 130, 137, 183; *factory operatives,* 229-239; *food preparers*, 129, 137, 171; *laundresses*, 121, 129, 171, 182, 222; *needle trades,* 123, 171, 182, 233, 235, 246; *servants*, 120-121, 123, 128, 139, 171, 182, 230, 235, 246; *teachers*, 92, 100, 117, 171, 213, 235, 244; *textile trades,* 92, 100, 121, 129, 136; *vendors*, 92, 100, 123, 129, 136, 137, 171, 182, 225. *See* healers; midwives; prostitutes
Young Ladies' Academy of Philadelphia, 213